Fourth edition

New Headway

Elementary Student's Book

Liz and John Soars

OXFORD
UNIVERSITY PRESS

CONTENTS   LANGUAGE INPUT

UNIT	GRAMMAR	VOCABULARY	EVERYDAY ENGLISH
1 You and me p6	**Verb *to be*** am/is/are I'm from Bristol. p6 **Possessive adjectives** my/your p6 his/her p7 **Verbs *have/go/live/like*** I have a brother. I live with my parents. p8 **Possessive *'s*** My sister's name … p8	**Personal information** email address, surname p7 **Adjectives** small, beautiful, easy p10 **Opposite adjectives** good/bad, hot/cold p11 **The family** husband, aunt, cousin p12	**Everyday conversations** Hi, Pete! Hello, Mrs Brown. See you later! Can I have a coffee, please? Nice to meet you. p13
2 A good job! p14	**Present Simple (1)** he/she/it He comes from … She teaches … p14 **Questions and negatives** What does he do? He doesn't live … p15	**Verbs** come, work, earn, go, play p15 **Jobs** nurse, hairdresser, lawyer He designs buildings. p20	**What time is it?** It's five o'clock. It's half past five. It's twenty-five past five. It's nearly three o'clock. p21
3 Work hard, play hard! p22	**Present Simple (2)** I/you/we/they I love singing. p22 Do you relax at weekends? I don't work. p23 **Adverbs of frequency** always, usually, often, never p23	**Verbs** cook, eat, finish, sing, stay p22 **In my free time** play golf, dance, go to the gym p24 **My perfect weekend** watch TV, go shopping p26	**Social expressions (1)** I'm sorry I'm late. What's the matter? Can I/you …? What does … mean? Excuse me! Pardon? p29
4 Somewhere to live p30	**There is/are** There's a big living room. p30 **some/any/a lot of** She has some plates. There aren't any glasses. She has a lot of clothes. p32 **this/that/these/those** I like that picture. How much are these? p32	**Things in the house** sofa, cooker p30 **Things in the street** post office, bench p31 **Rooms and household goods** living room, bathroom p30 towels, kettle, mugs p32 **Adjectives for *good* and *bad*** wonderful, great, awful p36 **Adverb + adjective** very big, really big p36	**Numbers** 45, 250 1½, 6.8 07861 56678 p37 **Prices** £1.50 $19.99 €12 p37
5 Super me! p38	**can/can't** She can ski. I can't speak French. p39 **Adverbs** quite well, not at all I can draw very well. p39 **was/were/could** Where were you yesterday? I could ski when I was five. p40 **was born** He was born in 1990. p41	**Words that go together** Noun + noun: bookshop, post office Verb + noun: play the guitar p44 **Prepositions** listen to music, come with me p44	**Polite requests** Can I have …? Can you open …? Could I ask you …? Could you tell me …? Sure. Sorry. p45
6 Life's ups and downs p46	**Past Simple (1)** Regular worked, lived, studied p46 Irregular began, came, had, met p48 **Time expressions** last night, yesterday morning p49	**Regular verbs** clean, look after, open p47 **Irregular verbs** caught, lost, left, won p48 **Describing feelings** bored, excited, worried p52 **Describing things** interesting, exciting p52	**What's the date?** first, second, third the third of April April the third 2001 – two thousand and one 2015 – twenty fifteen p53

SKILLS DEVELOPMENT

READING	SPEAKING	LISTENING	WRITING
A student's blog *Annalisa's blog* A student's experiences of school and family in London, England p10	**Introducing yourself** *My surname is …* *I'm 18 years old.* p7	**Personal information** *Where's he from?* p7 **Annalisa's blog** p10 Five conversations in Annalisa's day p11	**You and your life** *I'm from …* *I go to …* p9 **A blog** Keeping an online journal **Writing a blog** p104
A really good job *Babur Ali – He's 16 years old and a head teacher!* A boy from India teaches younger children p18	**The dancer and the DJ** *She's a ballet dancer.* *She lives in …* *She speaks …* p16 **Roleplay** A student and a journalist p18	**Jobs** People and their jobs *He's a pilot.* *She teaches French and Spanish.* p20 Conversations about jobs *What does he do?* *That's a good job!* p20	**Improving style** Using pronouns *I like him.* *She doesn't like it.* **Rewriting a text** p105
Town and country weekends *My perfect weekend* Jamie Cullum and Shilpa Shetty describe what they like doing p26	**Roleplay** Interviewing Lisa Parsons p23 **Questionnaire** Your work–life balance p28	**In my free time** Free time activities People talk about what they like doing in their free time p25	**Form filling** An application form – giving personal information *Date of birth* *Please tick (✓)* p106
America's most famous address *Inside the White House* A description of the building and what happens there p34	**Information gap** Describing a flat p31 **What's in your bag?** *There's a wallet.* *Are there any photos?* p33 **Discussion** Famous buildings p35	**What's in your bag?** *She has a phone.* p33 **Five conversations** What or who is it? How do they describe it? p36	**Describing your home** Linking words *and, so, but, because* **Writing a description of your home** p107
A talented family *A passion for success* The violinist Nicola Benedetti and her father p42	**What can you do?** *I can cook quite well.* p39 **Talking about you** *I was born in …* *I could walk when I was …* p41 **Discussion** Who are you close to in your family? p42	**Super kids!** A pianist and a singer Pablo Picasso p41 **Conversations** *You send a lot of text messages.* *The post office is near the traffic lights.* p44	**A formal email** Applying for a job *I am interested in the job of …* **Writing an email** p108
The meaning of life *The businessman and the fisherman* How to find happiness p50	**Talking about a student** *His mother was born in …* *He started school …* p48 **Talking about you** *I watched TV last night.* *When did you last …?* p49	**Interview** Ben Way, dotcom millionaire p48 **Conversations** *Did you enjoy the film?* *No, it was boring.* p52	**A biography** Combining sentences *However, when, until* **Writing a biography** p109

LANGUAGE INPUT

UNIT	GRAMMAR	VOCABULARY	EVERYDAY ENGLISH
7 Dates to remember p54	**Past Simple (2)** *He sold the first car in 1908.* p54 **Questions** *How many/When/Why …* p55 **Negatives** *We didn't have computers.* p55 **Time expressions** *in 1903/50 years ago/at 9.00/on Monday* p56	**Adverbs** *quickly, carefully, badly fast, hard, well fortunately, immediately* p60	**Special occasions** *birthday, Mother's Day Happy New Year! Merry Christmas!* p61
8 Eat in or out? p62	**Count and uncount nouns** *tea/cheese/apples/eggs* p62 *some tomatoes/some fruit* p63 **I like … and I'd like …** *I like pasta. I'd like some wine.* p63 **some/any** *There are some onions. We don't have many potatoes.* p65 **How much…?/How many…?** *How many onions? How much butter?* p65	**Food and drink** *yoghurt, chocolate, peas, juice, wine, milk* p62 *red wine, dry wine, sparkling water, still water* p63 *minced beef, oil* p64 **Verbs** *chop, fry, boil, mix* p65 **Daily needs** *plasters, shampoo, batteries, notebook* p68	**Shopping in the High Street** *What sort do you want? Six is too many. Four is enough. Small or large? £25 is too much.* p69 **Sounding polite** *I'd like a coffee, please. I want a latte.* p69
9 City living p70	**Comparative adjectives** *bigger, more romantic, better, worse* p70 **have got** *I've got a good job. Have you got a car?* p72 **Superlative adjectives** *busiest, most popular, best* p72	**Adjectives** *tall, wet, warm, polite* p70 *safe, dangerous* p71 **Markets** *artists, fashion, jewellery* p73 **Town and country** *square, office block, cottage, farm, path* p76	**Directions** **Prepositions** – *over, along, round, through* p77 *Can you tell me how to get to …? Is there a … near here? Go over the roundabout. Follow the signs to …* p77
10 Where on earth are you? p78	**in/at/on for places** *in bed/on holiday/at work* p78 **Present Continuous** *I'm cooking. What are you doing?* p78 **Present Simple or Continuous?** *He works … He's working …* p80 **something/nothing … somebody/nobody everywhere/anything** p81	**Describing people** *pretty, good-looking, handsome blond/fair hair brown/blue eyes* p84 **Clothes** *a dress, a suit, a skirt* p84	**Social expressions (2)** *Can I help you?/No, I'm just looking. I'm afraid I can't … Never mind.* p85
11 Going far p86	**going to future** *I'm going to be a racing driver.* p86 **Infinitive of purpose** *We're going to Egypt to see the pyramids.* p89	**Verbs** *drop, sneeze, kiss, fall* p88 **What's the weather like?** *sunny, rainy, cloudy warm, cool, dry* p92	**Making suggestions** *What shall we do? Let's … Why don't we …? I'll get my coat.* p93
12 Never ever! p94	**Present Perfect** *I've been to Rome. I haven't travelled much.* p94 **ever and never** *Have you ever met/lived …?* p95 **yet and just** *They haven't finished yet. She's just emailed.* p96 **Tense revision** *Present/past/future tenses* p97	**Past participles** *flown, given, eaten* p95 **take and get** *take place/take off/take an exam get married/get on with/ get to work* p100 **Transport and travel** *flight, return ticket, platform* p101	**Transport and travel** *bus/train/plane A day return ticket to Oxford, please. Where can I get the 360? How many pieces of hand luggage?* p101

Tapescripts p118   Grammar Reference p134   Word list p143   Pairwork Student A p149   Pairwork Student B p152

SKILLS DEVELOPMENT

READING	SPEAKING	LISTENING	WRITING
Sixty years of flight *Planes to rockets in sixty years* Just 60 years separate the first flight from landing on the moon p58	**Information gap** Bill's life p56 **Talking about my life** Life stories p57 **Telling a story** Retelling a story p60	**Talking about my life** Alisa's life p57 **Telling a story** Noises in the night p60	**Telling a story** Using time expressions *during, before, between, after* **Researching and writing about a historical character** p110
Everybody likes a sandwich! *The history of the sandwich* Who were the first to make sandwiches? p66	**Your favourite recipe** What ingredients do you need? p65 Your favourite sandwich p67	**What's your favourite sandwich?** Five people talk about their favourites p67	**Two emails** Informal and more formal *Lots of love* *Best wishes* **Writing an informal email** p112
Megacities *High-speed Tokyo, Mumbai – a city of extremes,* and *Multicultural Mexico City* Three huge cities – facts and attractions p74	**Comparing places** Two capital cities p71 I've got a bigger house than you! p72 A megacity p74	**People talk about where they live** Rob talks about living in Paris. p71 Makiko talks about Tokyo. Vimahl talks about Mumbai. Lourdes talks about Mexico City. p74	**Describing a place** Relative pronouns *which, who, where* *the book which …* *the girl who …* **Writing about your capital city** p114
The International Space Station *Living in space* The ISS is orbiting the Earth right now p82	**Project** Who is on the ISS? p82 Describing someone in the room/ in the news p84	**Who's who?** Who's who at the party? p80 **Interview** Interview with an astronaut p82 **Describing people** Descriptions of people p84	**Comparing and contrasting** Linking words *but, however, although* *For a start …* **Comparing people you know** p115
Meet Ed, Will, and Ginger *Singing for their supper* Three men walking and singing in Britain p90	**Talking about places** Why did you go there? p89 **Roleplay** Interviewing a singer p90	**We're off to see the world!** Two people talk about their travel plans p89 **What's the weather like?** A weather forecast p92	**Describing a holiday** Writing a postcard *We're having a wonderful time* **Writing a holiday postcard** p116
The Glastonbury festival *I've been to Glastonbury!* The greatest music festival in the world p98	**Talking about you** Have you ever …? p96 Music festivals p99	**The Glastonbury festival** People's experiences of a music festival p99	**A poem** Choosing the right word *Why did you leave?* **Writing poetry** p117

Extra materials p155   Irregular verbs/Verb patterns p158   Phonetic symbols p159

1 You and me

am/is/are • my/your/his/her • Verbs – have/go/live/like • Possessive 's
Word groups • Everyday conversations

STARTER

1 **T 1.1** Say the alphabet round the class.
A, B, C, D, E, F ...

2 Stand up in alphabetical order. Introduce yourself to the class.

Hello. I'm Alicia. | Hi. I'm Carla. | Hello. I'm Jerry. | My name's Steve.

HELLO!
am/is/are – my/your

1 **T 1.2** Read and listen. Practise the conversation.

A Hello. What's your first name?
B My name's Bill.
A And what's your surname?
B Frasier.
A How do you spell that?
B F – R – A – S – I – E – R.
A And where are you from, Bill?
B I'm from Chicago. I'm American.
A Thank you very much.

2 Complete the conversation.
T 1.3 Listen and check.

C Hello. My _name's_ Carla. What's _____ name?
D David.
C _____ are you from, David?
D _____ from Bristol. Where _____ you from?
C _____ _____ Bristol, too!
D Oh! Nice to meet you!

3 Stand up! Say hello to the other students.

Hello! My name's .... What's your name?
Freddy.
Where are you from, Freddy?
I'm from ....

GRAMMAR SPOT

What's = What is   name's = name is   I'm = I am

6 Unit 1 • You and me

PERSONAL INFORMATION
he/she – his/her

1 Look at the information about Bill and Sabine.

name	Bill Frasier	Sabine Ganz
city	Chicago	Zurich
age	30	22
phone number	312-555-0749	43 44 900 4754
email address	bfrasier@gmail.com	sabinegz@swissmail.ch
married?	No	No

email addresses: @ = at   . = dot

2 **T 1.4** Listen and complete the questions about Bill.
1. What's __his__ surname?   *Frasier*
2. _____ his first name?   *Bill*
3. Where _____ he from?   *Chicago*
4. How old _____ he?   *30*
5. What's _____ phone number?   *312-555-0749*
6. _____ _____ email address?   *bfrasier@gmail.com*
7. Is _____ married?   *No, he isn't.*

Practise the questions and answers with a partner.

3 **T 1.5** Listen and complete the questions about Sabine.
1. What's __her__ surname?
2. What's _____ first name?
3. Where _____ she from?
4. How old _____ _____ ?
5. What's _____ phone number?
6. _____ _____ email address?
7. _____ _____ married?

Ask and answer the questions with a partner.

GRAMMAR SPOT

1. Complete the chart of the verb *to be*.

Positive	Negative
I am = I'm	I _'m not_
you are = you're	you _aren't_
he is = he's	he _____
she is = she's	she _____

2. Write the possessive adjectives.

Pronouns	Possessive adjectives
I	_my_
you	_____
he	_____
she	_her_

▶▶ Grammar Reference 1.1 – 1.2 p134

Talking about you

4 Ask and answer questions with a partner.
- What's your surname?
- What's your first name?
- How do you spell your surname?
- How old are you?
- What's your phone number?
- What's your email address?
- Are you married?   *Yes, I am. / No, I'm not.*

Yes, I am.   NOT ~~Yes, I'm.~~

Unit 1 • You and me   7

RICK'S FAMILY
Verbs – *have/go/live/like*

1. **T 1.6** Listen to and read about Rick Wilson's life and family.

2. Complete the sentences about Rick.
   1. I _____ to Kingston University.
   2. I _____ a brother and a sister.
   3. I _____ with my parents in a house in West London.
   4. My family really _____ Lily!

   T 1.7 Listen and check.

3. Complete the sentences about you.

   I go to ...   I have ...
   I live with ...   I really like ...

   Tell a partner.

Possessive *'s*

4. Read the Grammar Spot. Find more examples of *'s* in the text. Are they *is* or possession?

> **GRAMMAR SPOT**
>
> Look at the sentences.
>
> My name**'s** Rick.   *'s = is*
> My brother**'s** name is Edward.   *'s = possession*
>   *= his name*
>
> ▶▶ Grammar Reference 1.3 p134

5. Answer the questions.
   1. Who's Edward? *He's Rick's brother.*
   2. Who's Rosie? Peter? Helen? Lily?
   3. What's his father's job? *He's a ...*
   4. What's his mother's job?

My name's Rick Wilson, and I'm from London.

I'm 19 years old, and I'm a student. I go to Kingston University. I have a brother and a sister. My brother's name is Edward. He's 16 and he's at school. My sister's name is Rosie. She's 23, and she's married. I live with my parents and my brother in a house in West London. My father, Peter, is a salesman, and my mother, Helen, is a teacher. I'm not married, but I have a girlfriend. Her name's Lily. She's lovely! My family really like her!

Me with Mum and Dad

Me and Lily

Edward

Rosie

8 Unit 1 • You and me

PRACTICE

be – am, is, are

1 Complete the sentences with the verb *to be*.

1 Where _____ you from?
2 '_____ you from London?' 'Yes, I _____.'
3 'How old _____ you?' 'I _____ 15.'
4 '_____ your sisters married?' 'No, they _____.'
5 I like you. You _____ my friend.

6 Hans _____ from Germany, he's from Switzerland.

7 '_____ your mother a doctor?' 'No, she _____.'
8 I _____ Italian. I'm French.

T 1.8 Listen and check.

2 What is 's, *is* or possession?

1 My name's Juan.   's = is
2 My sister's friend isn't married.   's = possession
3 Sonia's Italian.
4 She's a teacher.
5 Her brother's wife isn't English.
6 My brother's children are beautiful.

Pronunciation

3 **T 1.9** Listen and tick (✓) the sentence you hear.

1 a ☐ He's from Italy.
  b ☐ She's from Italy.
2 a ☐ What's his name?
  b ☐ What's her name?
3 a ☐ Your English is good.
  b ☐ You're English. Good.
4 a ☐ Where's she from?
  b ☐ Where's he from?
5 a ☐ His teacher is from England.
  b ☐ He's a teacher in England.
6 a ☐ You aren't English.
  b ☐ We aren't English.

Spelling

4 **T 1.10** Listen and complete the names and email addresses.

Names
1 V __ __ E __ __ __ A
2 J __ S __ __ __ __ B __ __ E __
3 K __ T __ __ __ M __ __ __ __ __ __ __ __ S

Email addresses
4 g._____8@yahoo_____
5 zac_____@gmail.co_____

Talking about you

5 Make true sentences about you with the verb *to be*.

1 I *'m not* at home.
2 We _____ in class.
3 We _____ in a café.
4 It _____ Monday today.
5 My teacher's name _____ Richard.
6 My mother and father _____ at work.
7 I _____ married.
8 My grandmother _____ seventy-five years old.

Read your sentences to your partner.

Writing

6 Write about you and your life.
Read it aloud to the rest of the class.

My name's...
I'm from...
I'm a...
I go to...
I have...
My sister's name is...
I live...
My father's a...

Unit 1 • You and me 9

READING AND LISTENING
A student's blog

1 Look at the photos of London. What can you see? What other famous places do you know in London?

2 Work with a partner. Complete the sentences with suitable adjectives from the box.

big	small	nice	beautiful
expensive	interesting	difficult	easy
friendly	cold	sunny	

1 London is/isn't a/an _____ city.
2 The people are/aren't _____ .
3 The weather is/isn't _____ .
4 English is/isn't a/an _____ language.

Discuss your ideas with the class.

3 **T 1.11** Annalisa is a student in London. Read and listen to her blog. Are the sentences true (✓) or false (✗)? Correct the false sentences.

1 Annalisa is from Italy. ✓
2 She's in Rome. ✗ *She isn't in Rome. She's in London.*
3 Peter and Helen have two sons.
4 She's in a small school.
5 Her school is in the centre.
6 The students in her class are all from Europe.
7 Rosie is Annalisa's teacher.
8 The National Gallery is expensive.
9 The Underground is difficult to use.
10 The coffee is good.

MY LONDON FAMILY

4 Complete the questions about Annalisa. Ask and answer them with your partner.
1 *Where's* Annalisa from? *Italy.*
2 _____ her school? *In the centre of London.*
3 What's _____ name? *Charlotte.*
4 _____ name? *Wilson.*
5 _____ their _____ ?
 In Notting Hill, in West London.
6 How _____ the two brothers?
 Edward's 16 and Rick's 19.
7 _____ OK?
 Yes, it is. It's cold and sunny.

T 1.12 Listen, check, and practise.

MY SCHOOL

5 Look at the photos in Annalisa's blog. What/Who can you see?

LONDON

ANNALISA'S BLOG

DAY 1: Welcome to my blog! It's in English!!
POSTED ON APRIL 6TH BY ANNALISA

Hello! I'm an Italian student. I'm in Notting Hill, London, England! I'm here to learn English.
My English family are the Wilsons. Peter (the husband) and Helen (the wife) have three children: Edward, 16, Rick, 19, and Rosie, 23. Rosie's married. They're very friendly, but they speak very fast! It's difficult to understand them.

DAY 3: My first day at school!
POSTED ON APRIL 8TH BY ANNALISA

Today is my first English class at St Martin's College. It's a big school in the centre – in Covent Garden. It's near a lot of shops, cafés, and theatres. It's great! My class is very international! The students are from Mexico, Japan, Egypt, Spain, Hungary, and Switzerland. Our teacher's name is Charlotte. She's very young and she's very nice. I really like her. She's a good teacher.

DAY 10: I love London!!
POSTED ON APRIL 15TH BY ANNALISA

Hello again! It's great here. I love London! It's big, but interesting. I like shopping, but it's very expensive. I go to the parks. They are really beautiful. And I go to museums and galleries. The National Gallery is free! I go by bus or by Underground – it's very easy. The weather's OK, cold but sunny. The food is OK, too! And the coffee is great! There are a lot of Italian coffee bars in London! Check out my photos!

Listening

6 **T 1.13** Listen to five conversations. Complete the chart.

	Where's Annalisa?	Who is she with?
1		
2		
3		
4		
5		

Vocabulary work

7 What is the opposite adjective?

1 a *good* student — a **bad** teacher
2 a *big* city — a _____ town
3 a *hot* day — _____ weather
4 *horrible* coffee — a _____ meal
5 a *cheap* café — an _____ restaurant
6 an *old* man — a _____ girl
7 a *slow* bus — a _____ car
8 an *easy* exercise — _____ homework

GRAMMAR SPOT

1 Complete the verb *to be*.

I	am
you	___
he	___
she	___
it	___
we	are
they	___

2 Complete the possessive adjectives.

I	my
you	___
he	___
she	___
we	___
they	their

▶▶ Grammar Reference 1.1 – 1.2 p134

▶▶ WRITING A blog p104

Unit 1 • You and me   11

VOCABULARY AND SPEAKING
The family

1 Complete the diagram with words from the box.

| ~~mother~~ | boyfriend | wife | son |
| niece | brother | aunt | grandmother |

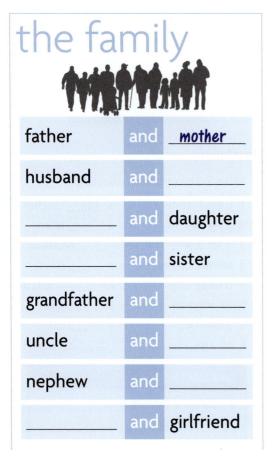

the family

father	and	_mother_
husband	and	_____
_____	and	daughter
_____	and	sister
grandfather	and	_____
uncle	and	_____
nephew	and	_____
_____	and	girlfriend

2 Complete the sentences.
1 My mother's father is my _grandfather_ .
2 My father's mother is my _____ .
3 My mother's sister is my _____ .
4 My aunt's husband is my _____ .
5 My sister's son is my _____ .
6 My brother's daughter is my _____ .

Use these words to complete sentences 7, 8, and 9.

| cousins | children | parents |

7 Your mother and father are your _____ .
8 Your son and your daughter are your _____ .
9 Your aunt's children are your _____ .

3 **T 1.14** Listen and write the names.

| Richard | Andrea | Nancy | Tom | John | Odile | Marie | Isabel |

4 Write the names of some people in your family. Ask and answer questions with a partner.

| Alberto | Marta and Raquel | Louis |

Who's Alberto?
He's my father.

Who are Marta and Raquel?
They're my cousins.

Who's Louis?
He's …

5 Talk to your partner about your family.

My grandmother is 72. My grandfather is …
They live …
I like my aunt … and …
I have … cousins …

12 Unit 1 • You and me

EVERYDAY ENGLISH
Everyday conversations

1 Work with a partner. Make different conversations.

Student A			Student B		Student A	
Hi, Hello, Good morning,	Pete. Sally. Mr Simpson. Mrs Brown.	How are you?	Fine, Very well, All right, OK, Not bad,	thank you. thanks.	And you?	Fine, Very well, All right, OK, Not bad,	thanks. thank you.

2 **T 1.15** Listen and compare. Practise again.

3 Look at the pictures. Complete the conversations.

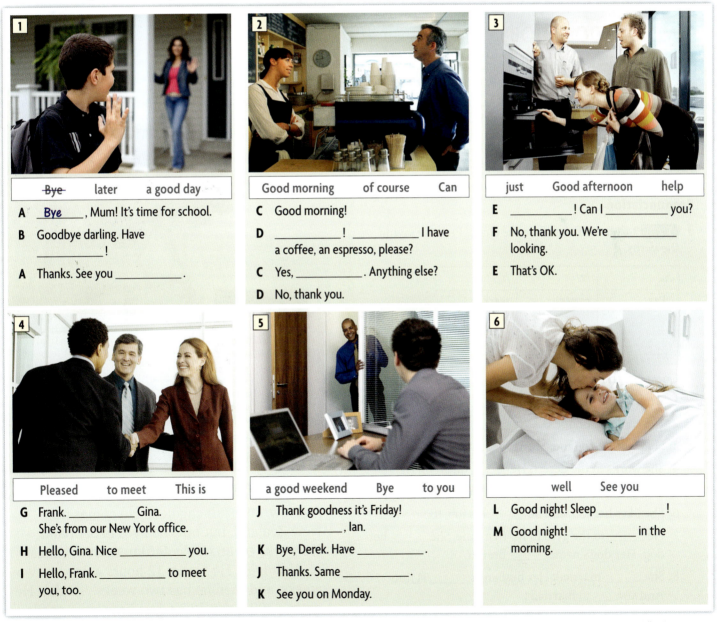

1
Bye   later   a good day
A ~~Bye~~ Bye____, Mum! It's time for school.
B Goodbye darling. Have _____!
A Thanks. See you _____.

2
Good morning   of course   Can
C Good morning!
D _____! _____ I have a coffee, an espresso, please?
C Yes, _____. Anything else?
D No, thank you.

3
just   Good afternoon   help
E _____! Can I _____ you?
F No, thank you. We're _____ looking.
E That's OK.

4
Pleased   to meet   This is
G Frank. _____ Gina. She's from our New York office.
H Hello, Gina. Nice _____ you.
I Hello, Frank. _____ to meet you, too.

5
a good weekend   Bye   to you
J Thank goodness it's Friday! _____, Ian.
K Bye, Derek. Have _____.
J Thanks. Same _____.
K See you on Monday.

6
well   See you
L Good night! Sleep _____!
M Good night! _____ in the morning.

T 1.16 Listen and check.

4 Work with a partner. Learn the conversations. Stand up! Act out the conversations.

2 A good job!

Present Simple (1) – *he/she/it* • Questions and negatives
Jobs • What time is it?

> **STARTER**
>
> What are the jobs of the people in your family? Tell the class.
>
> My father is a doctor.   My mother's a …   My brother …

TWO OUTDOOR JOBS
Present Simple – *he/she/it*

1 **T 2.1** Listen to and read about Andrew Johnson and Claudia Luke. What are their jobs? Where do they work?

2 <u>Underline</u> all the verbs in the text: *is*, *comes*, … What is the last letter of these verbs?

Pronunciation

3 **T 2.2** Listen and complete the chart. Practise saying the verbs.

/s/	/z/	/ɪz/
likes	comes	teaches

4 Complete the sentences.
1 Andrew is an engineer. Claudia _____ a zoologist.
2 She comes from the US. He _____ from New Zealand.
3 He lives in Scotland. She _____ in California.
4 She works in the desert. He _____ on an oil rig.
5 He earns £200 a day. She _____ $60,000 a year.
6 She likes her job, and he _____ his job, too.
7 He _____ to the gym in his free time. She _____ her dog. Her dog's name _____ Brewer.
8 She _____ married. Her husband's _____ is Jim. Andrew _____ married.

T 2.3 Listen and check. Read the sentences aloud.

ENGINEER
Andrew Johnson

Andrew, 30, <u>is</u> an engineer. He <u>comes</u> from New Zealand, but now he lives in Scotland. He works on an oil rig 440 km from the coast of Aberdeen. He works 12 hours a day for two weeks, and then he has two weeks' holiday. He earns £200 a day. In his free time he goes to the gym and plays snooker. He isn't married.

5 Complete the chart about Andrew and Claudia.

	Andrew	Claudia
surname		
age		
country		
job		
salary		
free time		
married?		

6 Close your books. What do you remember about Andrew and Claudia? Talk about them with a partner.

Andrew's surname is Johnson. He's 30 and he comes from New Zealand. ...

Claudia's surname is ...

ZOOLOGIST
Claudia Luke

Claudia, 41, is American. She's a zoologist and she teaches at a university. She lives in California and works with her husband, Jim, at the Research Centre in the Mojave Desert where she studies snakes and other animals. She likes working in the desert. In her free time she writes songs and walks her dog, Brewer. She earns about $60,000 a year.

WHAT DOES HE DO?
Questions and negatives

1 **T 2.4** Read and listen. Complete the lines about Andrew. Practise them with a partner.

1 What does Andrew do? (= What's his job?)   He's an _____.
2 Where does he come from?   New _____.
3 Does he live in Scotland?   _____, he does.
4 Does he live in New Zealand?   _____, he doesn't.
5 He _____ married. He doesn't have any children.

GRAMMAR AND PRONUNCIATION

1 Complete these sentences with the correct form of *live*.
   Positive
   He _____ in Scotland.
   Negative
   He _____ _____ in New Zealand.
   Question
   Where _____ he _____ ? In Scotland.

2 **T 2.5** Listen. Practise the pronunciation of *does* and *doesn't*.
   /dəz/   /dʌz/   /dʌznt/
   Does he play football?   Yes, he **does**./No, he **doesn't**.

▶▶ Grammar Reference 2.1 – 2.2 p135

---

2 Complete the questions and answers about Andrew.

1 'Where _does_ Andrew _work_ ?'
   'On an oil rig.'
2 '_____ he work hard?'
   'Yes, he _____.'
3 'How much _____ he earn?'
   '£ _____ a day.'
4 'What _____ he do in his free time?'
   'He _____ and he _____ ?'
5 '_____ he like his job?'
   'Yes, he _____.'
6 '_____ he have a dog?'
   'No, he _____.'

T 2.6 Listen and check. Ask and answer questions about Andrew with a partner.

3 Ask and answer questions about Claudia.

What does Claudia do?   She's a zoologist and a ...

Unit 2 • A good job! 15

PRACTICE

The dancer and the DJ

1 Look at the photos of Darcey /ˈdɑːsɪ/ Bussell and David Guetta /ˈgetə/. Do you know them?

2 Read the information about them. Talk to a partner.   *Darcey's a ballet dancer and David's a DJ. She comes from …*

Darcey Bussell *Ballet dancer*

Job	ballet dancer and model
Country	London, England
Home now	Sydney, Australia
Place of work	mainly London and Sydney
Languages	English, and a little French
Family	married to an Australian banker, Adam Forbes two daughters, Phoebe and Zoë
Free time	writes stories about ballet for children

David Guetta DJ SUPERSTAR

Job	DJ (disc jockey)
Country	France
Home now	Paris
Place of work	all over the world: Ibiza, Miami, Mauritius
Languages	French and English
Family	married to Cathy from Senegal a son, Tim-Elvis, and a daughter, Angie
Free time	writes songs and likes playing music for his friends

Asking questions

3 Complete the questions about Darcey or David. Ask and answer them with your partner.

> *What does Darcey do?*   *She's a ballet dancer.*

- What … do?
- Where … live now?
- … speak French?
- What … her/his children's names?
- Where … come from?
- Where … work?
- How many children …?
- What … in her/his free time?

Stress and intonation

4 **T 2.7** Listen and respond to eight sentences about Darcey and David. Correct the wrong sentences.

> *Darcey comes from London.*   *Yes, that's right.*
>
> *She lives in England.*   *No, she doesn't. She lives …*

T 2.8 Listen and check. Practise again.

16 Unit 2 • A good job!

Talking about family and friends

5 Complete the sentences with the verbs in the correct form.
1. My husband _comes_ (come) from Belgium.
2. My grandmother _____ (live) in the next town.
3. My mother _____ (love) reading.
4. My father _____ (travel) a lot in his job.
5. My sister _____ (speak) Spanish very well. She _____ (want) to learn French, too.
6. My little brother _____ (watch) TV a lot.
7. My friend Tom _____ (write) a blog on the Internet.

6 Match the questions to the sentences in exercise 5 to continue the conversations.
a ☐ Does she want to be an interpreter?
b ☑ Where exactly in Belgium?
c ☐ Does she visit you often?
d ☐ What does he write about?
e ☐ What does she read?
f ☐ Where does he go?
g ☐ What does he like watching?

7 **T 2.9** Listen and check. What extra information do you hear?

Listening

8 **T 2.10** Listen to five conversations. What are they about?

9 **T 2.10** Listen again. For each conversation, write some of the verbs you hear.
1 _do,_____   4 _____
2 _____   5 _____
3 _____

10 Write the name of a friend or relative. Ask and answer questions with your partner.

Charlotte — Who is she? — A friend.
What does she do? — She's a …
Where does she live? — In …
What does she like doing? — She likes …

11 **T 2.11** Listen and tick (✓) the sentence you hear.
1 a ☐ He likes his job.
  b ☐ She likes her job.
2 a ☐ She loves walking.
  b ☐ She loves working.
3 a ☐ He's married.
  b ☐ He isn't married.
4 a ☐ Does she have three children?
  b ☐ Does he have three children?
5 a ☐ What does he do?
  b ☐ Where does he go?

▶▶ **WRITING** **T 2.12** Improving style *p105*

Unit 2 • A good job! 17

READING AND SPEAKING
A really good job

1 Look at the pictures. Read these sentences about Babur Ali. <u>Underline</u> what you think is true.
   1 Babur gets up at *5 a.m. / 8 a.m.*
   2 He helps his *mother in the house / father at work*.
   3 He goes to school by *bus / car*.
   4 He studies hard until *1 p.m. / 4 p.m.*
   5 He begins *his homework / the classes* at 5 p.m.
   6 He *likes / doesn't like* his work.
   7 He *speaks / doesn't speak* English.
   8 He *wants / doesn't want* to go to university.

2 Read the first paragraph about Babur. Ask and answer the questions with a partner.
   1 Where does Babur come from?
   2 Where does he live?
   3 Does his village have a school?
   4 Why is he lucky?   Because …
   5 How much does his school cost?
   6 What does he teach the children?
   7 Are all the classes outdoors?
   8 What's his school's name? Is it free?

3 Read about Babur's *Busy days*. Ask and answer questions about the times in Babur's day.

   > What time does he get up?   At 5 o'clock.

4 Read about *Babur's ambitions*. Correct the sentences.
   1 The school has 60 students.
      It doesn't have 60 students. It has …
   2 It has five teachers.
   3 Babur wants to stop teaching.
   4 He wants to be a doctor.

5 Look back at exercise 1. Were your answers correct?

Roleplay – An interview

5 Work with a partner. Complete the questions.
   1 How many students …?   5 … your teacher's name?
   2 How many teachers …?   6 … a good teacher?
   3 What time … start/finish?   7 What … teach?
   4 How much … cost?   8 … he work hard?

Student A
You are a journalist. Ask the questions.

Student B
You are one of Babur's students. Answer the questions.

T 2.13 Listen and compare.

18 Unit 2 • A good job!

AROUND THE WORLD

BANGLADESH
West Bengal
Kolkata
INDIA

Babur Ali teaching his class

Babur Ali

'I love teaching. I am never tired.'

He's 16 years old and a head teacher!

Babur Ali comes from West Bengal in India. He is 16 years old and lives in the small village of Bhabta. His village doesn't have a school, but Babur is lucky because he goes to a private school in the next village. His school costs 1,000 rupees, £12 a year. This is too expensive for many children in Babur's village, but they want to learn, so Babur teaches them everything that he learns. More and more children want to learn, so Babur's friends help him teach. The classes are in bamboo huts, but sometimes they sit outdoors. The school is free and now has a name, the Anand Shiksha Niketan School, and Babur is the head teacher.

Busy days

Babur's days are very busy. He has no free time. He gets up at 5 o'clock in the morning and helps his mother with the housework. At 8 o'clock he goes by bus to his school three miles away. He studies hard all day until 4.00 in the afternoon. Then he travels back to his village and at 5.00 he begins the classes. He teaches English, Bengali, history, and maths until 8.00 in the evening. He says, 'I love teaching. I am never tired.'

Babur's ambitions

Now the school has 650 students and ten teachers. Babur wants to study at university, but he doesn't want to stop teaching. He says,

'I always want to teach poor children.'

VOCABULARY AND LISTENING
Jobs

1 Match a picture with a job.
- [ ] architect
- [ ] dentist
- [ ] taxi driver
- [ ] nurse
- [ ] receptionist
- [ ] hairdresser
- [ ] pilot
- [ ] lawyer
- [ ] journalist
- [ ] accountant

2 Complete the sentences with a job.
1. She's a _____. She cuts hair.
2. He's a _____. He flies from Heathrow airport.
3. She's a _____. She works in a hotel.
4. He's an _____. He designs buildings.
5. She's a _____. She works for a family law firm.
6. He's a _____. He knows all the streets of London.
7. She's a _____. She writes news stories.
8. He's a _____. He looks after people's teeth.
9. She's a _____. She works in the City Hospital.
10. He's an _____. He likes working with money.

T 2.14 Listen and check.

3 **T 2.15** Listen. Complete the conversations with the jobs.

1. **A** What does your brother do?
   B He's a _____. He writes for *The Times* newspaper.
   A Oh, that's a good job.

2. **C** What does your father do?
   D He's an _____. He works for a big firm in the city.
   C And your mother? What does she do?
   D She's a _____. She teaches French and Spanish.

3. **E** Does your sister work in the centre of town?
   F Yes, she does. She's a _____. She works in the Ritz Hotel.
   E Oh, that's near where I work.

4. **G** Are you a _____?
   H No, I'm not. I'm a _____.
   G Oh, but I want to see a _____.

5. **I** I want to be a _____ when I'm big.
   J I want to be a _____. They earn lots of money.
   I _____ earn a lot too, *and* they travel the world.

Practise the conversations with a partner.

Speaking

4 Work with a partner. Have similar conversations about your friends and family.

What does your sister do? *She's a student.* *Oh, what does she study?* *Physics.*

20 Unit 2 • A good job!

EVERYDAY ENGLISH
What time is it?

1 Look at the clocks. Write the times.

It's five o'clock.

It's half past five.

It's quarter past five.

It's quarter to six.

It's five past five.

It's twenty past five.

It's twenty-five to six.

It's ten to six.

T 2.16 Listen and check. Practise saying the times. What time does your lesson end?

2 **T 2.17** Listen. Look at the times.

It's nearly three o'clock.

It's just after five o'clock.

It's about half past two.

3 With a partner, draw clocks on a piece of paper. Ask and answer about the time.

What time is it? It's twenty past seven.

Can you tell me the time, please? It's just after three.

4 **T 2.18** Listen and complete the conversations. Practise them with a partner.

1   A Excuse me. Can you tell me the _____, please?
     B Yes, of course. It's _____ after _____ o'clock.
     A Thank you _____ much.

2   C _____ me. Can you _____ me the time, please?
     D I'm _____. I don't have a watch.
     C Never mind.

3   E Excuse me. What time does the bus leave?
     F At _____ _____ ten.
     E Thank you. What time is it now?
     F It's _____ five past.
     E Five past ten?!
     F No, no, five past _____. You're OK. No need to hurry.

4   G When does this lesson _____?
     H At four o'clock.
     G Oh dear! It's only _____ past three!

3 Work hard, play hard!

Present Simple (2) – I/you/we/they • In my free time • Social expressions (1)

STARTER

1 What day is it today? Say the days of the week.   Monday   Tuesday   Wednesday   Thursday   Friday   Saturday   Sunday

2 Which days are the weekend? Which days are you busy?

I LIVE AND WORK IN NEW YORK
Present Simple – I/you/we/they

1 **T 3.1** Look at the pictures of Lisa Parsons. Close your books and listen to Lisa. Where does she live? Is she 24, 32, or 42? What are her two jobs?

2 Read and complete the text with the correct verbs from the box.

| cook | eat | have | finish | ~~live~~ | love |
| sing | stay | work | don't do | don't go | |

T 3.1 Listen again and check. Read the text aloud.

Lisa's two jobs

'Hi, I'm Lisa Parsons. I'm 24 years old and I ¹_live_ in New York City. I'm always very busy, but I'm very happy.

From Monday to Friday I ²____ in a bookstore, the Strand Bookstore in Manhattan. Then on Saturdays I ³____ another job – I'm a singer with a band. It's great because I love books and I ⁴____ singing.

On weekdays I usually ⁵____ work at 6 o'clock, but sometimes I ⁶____ late, until 9 or 10 o'clock at night. On Saturday evenings, I ⁷____ in nightclubs in all parts of the city. I ⁸____ to bed until 3 or 4 o'clock in the morning.

On Sundays, I ⁹____ much at all. I often ¹⁰____ in a little restaurant near my apartment. I never ¹¹____ on a Sunday. I'm too tired.'

22 Unit 3 • Work hard, play hard!

Questions and negatives

3 **T 3.2** Listen and complete Lisa's answers. Practise the questions and answers with a partner.

1 Where do you live?   _____ New York.
2 Do you like your job?   Yes, I _____.
3 Do you relax at weekends? No, I _____.
4 Why don't you relax at weekends? Because I _____ in nightclubs.

Roleplay

4 Work with your partner. One of you is Lisa Parsons. Ask and answer questions.

How old … ?

… you live in New York?

Where … you work?

What time … you finish work?

How many jobs … you have?

… you like your jobs?

Why … you like them?

What … you do on Sundays?

… you cook on Sundays?

> How old are you, Lisa?
>
> I'm 24.

T 3.3 Listen and compare.

GRAMMAR SPOT

1 Complete the chart.

Present Simple	Positive	Negative
I/you	work	don't work
he/she/it	_____	_____
we/they	_____	_____

2 Complete the questions and answers.

   Where _____ you work?
   Where _____ she work?
   _____ you work in London?   Yes, I _____.
   _____ he work in London?   No, he _____.

3 Find the adverbs in the text.

   always   usually   often   sometimes   never

▶▶ Grammar Reference 3.1 – 3.2 p135–136

Listening and pronunciation

5 **T 3.4** Listen and tick (✓) the sentence you hear.

1 a ☐ Lisa, why do you like your job?
   b ☐ Lisa, why don't you like your job?

2 a ☐ When do you leave New York?
   b ☐ Where do you live in New York?

3 a ☐ What do you do on Tuesday evenings?
   b ☐ What do you do on Thursday evenings?

4 a ☐ She really loves singing.
   b ☐ He really loves singing.

5 a ☐ She reads a lot.
   b ☐ She eats a lot.

6 a ☐ Where does she go on Sundays?
   b ☐ What does she do on Sundays?

Unit 3 • Work hard, play hard! 23

PRACTICE

Talking about you

1 Use the words in the box to complete the questions. Match the questions and answers.

| Who | How | ~~What time~~ | Do | Where | When | Why | What |

Questions	Answers
1 _What time_ do you get up?	a My mother and brothers.
2 _____ do you go on holiday?	b To Turkey or Egypt.
3 _____ do you do on Sundays?	c When I get home.
4 _____ do you do your homework?	d At about 7 o'clock on weekdays.
5 _____ do you live with?	e I always relax.
6 _____ do you like your job?	f Usually by bus.
7 _____ do you travel to school?	g Yes, I do sometimes.
8 _____ you go out on Friday evenings?	h Because it's interesting.

T 3.5 Listen and check.

2 Ask and answer the questions with a partner. Give true answers.

3 Tell the class about you and your partner.

> I live with my parents and my grandmother.
> Mario lives with his parents, too.

Positives and negatives

4 Make the sentences opposite.
  1 She's French. _She isn't French._
  2 I don't like cooking. _I like cooking._
  3 She doesn't speak Spanish.
  4 They want to learn English.
  5 We're tired and we want to go to bed.
  6 Roberto likes watching football on TV, but he doesn't like playing it.
  7 I work at home because I have a computer.
  8 Amelia isn't happy because she doesn't have a new car.
  9 I smoke, I drink, and I don't go to bed early.
  10 He doesn't smoke, he doesn't drink, and he goes to bed early.

5 Write two false sentences. Get the other students to correct them.

> I'm English.
>> You aren't English! You're Croatian!

> Ana Mari goes to university.
>> She doesn't go to university! She works in a bank!

VOCABULARY AND LISTENING
In my free time

1 Answer the questions.
  • What season is it now? Name the other seasons.
  • What month is it now? Say all the months.
  • Which months are the different seasons?

2 Look at the pictures. Match the words and pictures.

Which season(s) do the activities go with?

> You play golf in summer.
>> But I play golf in all seasons!

☐ playing golf
☐ going to the cinema
☐ listening to music
☐ swimming
☐ watching TV
☐ going to the gym
☐ windsurfing
☐ playing computer games
☐ cooking
☐ playing tennis
☐ playing cards
☐ skiing
☐ dancing
☐ sailing
☐ running
☐ reading
☐ cycling

j

n

o

Listening

3 **T 3.6** Listen to five people. What do they like doing in their free time? When exactly? Complete the chart.

	What?	When?
Andy		
Roger		
Linda		
Ben & Josh		
Sandra & Brian		

like + -ing
I **like** play**ing** golf.
I **don't like** runn**ing**.

▶▶ Grammar Reference 3.3 p136

4 What do you think your teacher likes doing? Discuss in your groups and make a list.

> I think he/she likes going to the cinema.

> No, I think he/she prefers watching TV.

Ask your teacher questions to find out who is correct.

> Do you like ... -ing?

Talking about you

5 Tell each other what you like doing and what you don't like doing in your free time. Ask questions to find out details.

> I don't like watching TV, but I like reading very much.

> Oh, really? What do you read?

> Why don't you like watching TV?

▶▶ **WRITING** Form filling *p106*

Unit 3 • Work hard, play hard! 25

READING AND SPEAKING
Town and country weekends

1 Match a verb in **A** with the words in **B**.

watch TV

A	B
watch	cards
listen to	shopping
play	dancing
go	music
get up	the piano TV late
cook	French films dinner

T 3.7 Listen and check. Can you remember the sentences?

2 Look at the pictures and read the introductions about Jamie Cullum and Shilpa Shetty. What do they do? What do they like doing at weekends?

3 Work in two groups.
Group A   Read about **Jamie Cullum**.
Group B   Read about **Shilpa Shetty**.

4 Answer the questions about your person.
1 Does he/she stay in the town or country at weekends?
2 Who does she/he like to be with?
3 What does he/she do on Friday evening?
4 What does she/he like doing on Saturday morning?
5 Where does he/she go shopping?
6 What does she/he do on Sunday?
7 Does he/she like playing cards?
8 Does she/he like cooking?

5 Work with a partner from the other group. Compare Jamie and Shilpa.
- What things do they both like doing?
- What things are different?

Speaking

6 On a piece of paper write down two things you like doing at weekends.

going to clubs and cycling

Give the paper to another student.
Read aloud the activities. Who is it?

It's Pierre!   No, it's Marcus!

7 **T 3.8** Listen to part of a song by Jamie Cullum. Do you like his music?

26 Unit 3 • Work hard, play hard!

MY PERFECT

Jamie Cullum

Song-writer and jazz pianist Jamie Cullum lives in London with his wife Sophie Dahl, the model and cookery writer. He enjoys going to markets, French films, and playing cards at weekends.

JAMIE SAYS, 'In my work I travel a lot and I stay in different hotels, so my perfect weekend is at home with my family and friends. I live in a flat in north-west London next to my brother, Ben, and at weekends I like being with him and my wife, Sophie. On Friday nights, we often go to a club – we all love dancing.

On Saturdays, we get up late and I make breakfast; that's important to me. Then I sit at my piano – it's in my kitchen – and I play for a couple of hours. I don't write songs, I just play. My cat, Luna, listens. Sometimes in the afternoon we go shopping in Portobello Market. I love old things. I have black leather cowboy boots from there. Also, I look for old postcards – I like reading about people from the past. In the evening, we often watch a French or Japanese film – I enjoy foreign films.

After that I like playing cards – poker – with friends, sometimes until early Sunday morning. We sleep late on Sundays, but then I like cooking Sunday dinner, usually roast chicken. I really enjoy cooking. In the evening I call my parents and my nan – they like hearing about my week.'

WEEKEND

Shilpa Shetty

Indian film actress and model Shilpa Shetty has homes in Mumbai and England. She enjoys takeaway pizza, going to garden centres, and playing cards at weekends.

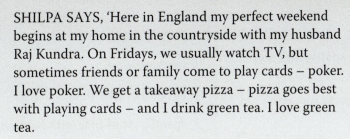

SHILPA SAYS, 'Here in England my perfect weekend begins at my home in the countryside with my husband Raj Kundra. On Fridays, we usually watch TV, but sometimes friends or family come to play cards – poker. I love poker. We get a takeaway pizza – pizza goes best with playing cards – and I drink green tea. I love green tea.

On Saturdays, I get up late, at about 10.45, and then I have a long bath. Sometimes I watch TV in the bath or listen to music. I like staying in the country at weekends – I love walking barefoot on the grass. We go to a pub for lunch – I like the puddings, especially sticky toffee pudding. I prefer to have Saturday evening at home. We like watching cookery programmes; Jamie Oliver is my favourite. I like cooking Indian food, but not at weekends.

On Sundays, I love shopping and gardening. I always buy my clothes from small boutiques, and I love visiting garden centres. I love flowers. My homes in Mumbai and England are always full of beautiful white lilies. I don't cook on Sunday, we prefer eating out and sometimes, if we have time, we go to a spa hotel for a swim and a massage. It's a great way to end a perfect weekend.'

SPEAKING AND LISTENING
Your work–life balance

1 Read and complete the questionnaire about you. Write ✓ or ✗. Then look at the answer key. Do you have a good work–life balance?

2 Ask your teacher the questions, then ask two students. Complete the questionnaire about them.

3 Discuss in small groups. Who has a good work–life balance? Who lives to work?

4 **T 3.9** Listen to Dr Susan Hall, an expert on the work–life balance. Answer the questions.
   1 Why does she say that work is important?
   2 Why is 'play' important?
   3 What is the problem with taking work home?
   4 What's her final advice?

What do you think?
- How many people do you know who love their work?
- Do you know people who don't love their work?
- 'If you like your job, you never have to work again.' Do you agree?

Writing
5 Write about your partner. Use the information from the questionnaire.

Maria is a student. She likes her classes very much. She doesn't have many free-time activities. She ...

Questionnaire
Your work–life balance

Do you live to work ... or work to live?

DO YOU ...?	Me	T	S1	S2
1 like your work				
2 have many free-time activities				
3 spend a lot of time with family and friends				
4 relax at weekends				
5 have breakfast before you go to work				
6 travel far to work				
7 sometimes stay late at work				
8 often bring work home				
9 have trouble sleeping				
10 think about work when you are at home				

KEY:

Scoring points
Answers 1 – 3   2 points for YES
Answers 4 – 5   1 point for YES
Answers 6 – 10 0 points for YES

How do you score?
0 – 2 points = You live to work.
3 – 5 points = Your work–life balance is OK.
6 – 8 points = Your work–life balance is excellent.

EVERYDAY ENGLISH
Social expressions (1)

1 Look at the pictures of Hakan, a student of English in Oxford. Where is he? Who are the other people?

2 Look at the first lines of conversations in **A**. They are all conversations in Hakan's day. Who says the lines? Is it …?
- Hakan
- another student
- his host family
- the woman who works in the coffee bar
- his teacher

A
1 Bye! Have a nice day!
2 I'm sorry I'm late. The traffic's very bad this morning.
3 What's the matter, Hakan? Do you have a problem?
4 Can I open the window? It's really warm in here.
5 Can you help me? What does *bilingual* mean?
6 Do you want a macchiato?
7 Excuse me! Is this seat free?
8 *Parlez-vous français?*
9 Hi, Hakan! How was your day?

3 Match a line in **A** with a line in **B**.
T 3.10 Listen and check.

B
___ Never mind. Come and sit down.
_1_ Thanks. Same to you. See you later.
___ Good, thanks. Really interesting. How about you?
___ Yes, it is. Do sit down if you want.
___ Yes. I don't understand this exercise.
___ It means *in two languages*.
___ I'm sorry. I don't speak French.
___ Sure. Good idea. It is hot in here, isn't it?
___ Pardon? Can you say that again?

4 Work with a partner. Practise some of the conversations. Try to continue them.

> A Bye! Have a nice day!
> B Thanks. Same to you. See you later.
> A Right! At about four o'clock?
> B Well, er … school doesn't finish till four.
> A Oh, OK! See you about 4.30, then!

T 3.11 Listen and compare your conversations.

Unit 3 • Work hard, play hard! 29

4 Somewhere to live

There is/are • some/any/a lot of • this/that/these/those
Adjectives • Numbers and prices

STARTER

1 Write the words in the correct column.

sofa	cooker	bus stop	fridge
DVD player	table	post office	oven
café	armchair	pavement	washing machine
chemist's	bookshelves	traffic lights	mirror

living room	kitchen	street

2 **T 4.1** Listen and check. Practise the words.

A FLAT TO RENT
There is/are – prepositions

1 **T 4.2** Josie wants to rent a flat. Listen and complete her conversation with her friend Emily.

J Here's a flat in Queen's Road!
E Is it nice?
J <u>There's</u> a big living room.
E Mmm!
J And <u>there are</u> two bedrooms.
E Great! What about the kitchen?
J _____ a new kitchen.
E Wow! How many bathrooms _____ ?
J Er … _____ just one bathroom.
E _____ a garden?
J No, _____ a garden.
E It doesn't matter. It sounds great!

Practise the conversation with a partner.

30 Unit 4 • Somewhere to live

GRAMMAR SPOT

Complete the chart.

Positive	There _is_ a shower.
	There _____ two bedrooms.
Negative	There _____ a garden.
	There _aren't_ any carpets.
Question	_____ _____ a dining room?
	How many bathrooms _____ _____ ?

▶▶ Grammar Reference 4.1 – 4.2 p136

2 Look at the photos of the flat. Describe the living room.

There's a sofa.   There are two armchairs.

3 Ask and answer questions about the flat.

Is there … ?
- a shower
- a fridge
- a dining room

Is there a shower?
Yes, there is.

How many … are there?
- bedrooms
- bathrooms
- armchairs

Are there any … ?
- pictures
- bookshelves
- carpets

T 4.3 Listen and check.

Signature LETTINGS

Queen's Road
£250 per week

big living room
two bedrooms
new kitchen
bathroom and shower

Prepositions

4 Complete the sentences with the correct preposition.

on ~~in~~ under next to opposite above near outside

1 The flat's _in_ Queen's Road.
2 It's _____ the first floor.
3 It's _____ a chemist's.
4 The chemist's is _____ a clothes shop.
5 There's a mobile phone shop _____ the clothes shop.
6 There's a post office _____ the flat.
7 The bus stop is _____ the café.
8 There's a bench _____ a tree.

T 4.4 Listen and check.

PRACTICE

Location, location, location

1 Work with a partner. Ask and answer questions.

Student A Look at the advert for a flat on p149.
Student B Look at the advert for a different flat on p152.

2 **T 4.5** Look at the advert on p149. Listen to the description. There are nine mistakes. Shout *Stop!* when you hear a mistake.

Stop! There aren't four bedrooms! There are only three!

3 Work with a partner. Draw a plan of your home. Show the plan and describe your home to your partner.

In my living room there's a . . .

Unit 4 • Somewhere to live 31

A NEW FLAT
some/any/a lot of

1 Josie is in her new flat. What does she have? What doesn't she have? Tell a partner.

plates ✓✓
clothes ✓✓✓✓
glasses ✗
pictures ✓✓
CDs ✓✓✓✓
mugs ✗
shoes ✓✓✓✓
towels ✗
cups ✓✓

> She has some plates.
> She has a lot of clothes.
> She doesn't have any glasses.

T 4.6 Listen and check.

GRAMMAR SPOT

1 What's the difference between the sentences?
   She has **five** plates.
   She has **some** plates.
   She has **a lot of** plates.

2 When do we use *some*? When do we use *any*?
   There are **some** cups.
   There aren't **any** glasses.
   Does she have **any** clothes?

▶▶ Grammar Reference 4.3 – 4.4 p136

32 Unit 4 • Somewhere to live

this/that/these/those

2 Look at Josie's shopping list. What does she need?

Things to buy
glasses   towels   a lamp
kettle   mugs

3 Look at Josie and Emily shopping. Complete the conversations.

1

J How much is this _____, please?
A It's £45.

2

J I like that _____.
E Yes, it's lovely!

3
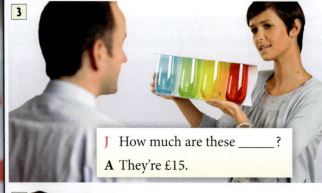
J How much are these _____?
A They're £15.

4

J I love those _____!
E They're fabulous!

5
J Look at _____ _____!
E They're beautiful!

6
E Do you like _____ _____?
J Yeah! It's a great colour!

7
J How much are _____ _____?
A £5 each.

8
J Look at _____ _____!
E You don't need any more clothes!

T 4.7 Listen and check. Practise the conversations.

Singular	this	that
Plural	these	those

▶▶ Grammar Reference 4.5 p136

PRACTICE

In our classroom

1 Complete the sentences with *some*, *any*, or *a*.

1 I have **a** dictionary and **some** books on my table.
2 There aren't _____ Chinese students in our class.
3 Do we have _____ homework tonight?
4 I need _____ help with this exercise.
5 Is there _____ test this week?
6 There are _____ difficult exercises in this book, but we have _____ very good teacher.

2 Write sentences, then talk about things in your classroom.

There's a big window.   *There are some chairs.*
These are my books.   *That's the teacher's bag.*

What's in your bag?

3 **T 4.8** Listen to Christina. Tick (✓) the things she has in her handbag.

☐ a phone   ☐ a diary   ☐ a lipstick   ☐ an address book   ☐ pens
☐ photos   ☐ an iPod   ☐ stamps   ☐ keys   ☐ a purse

4 What does she have? What doesn't she have?

She has a phone and some pens. She doesn't have an iPod, and she doesn't have any stamps.

5 Work with a partner. Ask and answer questions about what's in your bag.

Do you have a wallet?   *Yes, I do.*
Is there a pen?   *Yes, of course!*

Check it

6 Tick (✓) the correct sentence.

1 ☐ Do you have some dictionary?
  ☐ Do you have a dictionary?
2 ☐ Here are some photos of my children.
  ☐ Here are any photos of my children.
3 ☐ I have a lot of books.
  ☐ I have a lot books.
4 ☐ Pete, this is Dave. Dave, this is Pete.
  ☐ Pete, that is Dave. Dave, that is Pete.
5 ☐ I don't have some money.
  ☐ I don't have any money.
6 ☐ Look at these people over there.
  ☐ Look at those people over there.

Unit 4 • Somewhere to live 33

READING AND SPEAKING
America's most famous address

1 Look at the pictures of the White House. What can you see?

2 What do you know about the White House? Do you think these sentences are true (✓) or false (✗)?
1. The White House is more than 200 years old. ✓
2. No one lives in the White House.
3. All the rooms are government offices.
4. The Oval Office is where the President works.
5. The White House is open to the public.
6. There are a lot of things for a president to do in his free time.

3 Read the text and check your answers.

4 Answer the questions.
1. The White House has two uses. What are they?
2. Where exactly in the White House does the President live?
3. Where does he work?
4. Where do special guests stay?
5. What is in the Oval Office?
6. What does each new president change?
7. How much does it cost to visit the White House?
8. How many people work in the White House?
9. What can the President do to relax?

5 Find the numbers in the text. What do they refer to?
50 – *There are fifty states.*

| 50 | 304 million | 6,000 | 132 | 35 | five | six | 140 |

INSIDE THE

The White House, 1600 Pennsylvania Avenue, Washington DC, is the most famous address in America. It is where the United States President works, but it is also his private home where he lives with his family. He has children's birthday parties, holiday dinners, and weddings in this world-famous building.

THE BUILDING

First built in 1800, the White House is where the President of the United States governs a country of 50 states and 304 million people.

He lives with his family on the second and third floors. There are 16 bedrooms, a living room, a kitchen, and a dining room. Special guests stay in the Queen's Bedroom or the Lincoln Bedroom.

In the West Wing are the staff offices. The President's own office, the Oval Office, is also there. It has three large windows behind the President's desk, and there is a fireplace at the other end.

Each new president chooses new curtains, new furniture, and a special new carpet. There are pictures of old presidents on the wall, and there is the famous desk, a gift from the British Queen Victoria in 1880.

34 Unit 4 • Somewhere to live

WHITE HOUSE

THE WHITE HOUSE DAY BY DAY

The White House is open to visitors. It is free. About 6,000 people a day visit. The President meets special guests in the East Room, and he talks to journalists in the Press Room.

About 150 people work for the President in the West Wing and for the First Lady in the East Wing. Another 100 people look after the building day and night.

There are 132 rooms, 35 bathrooms, and five kitchens, all on six floors. There are three elevators*. The State Dining Room is big enough for 140 guests.

Outside, gardeners grow fruit and vegetables. There is also a tennis court, a jogging track, and a swimming pool. Inside there is a movie theater*, a billiard room, a bowling alley, and a library. As former President Reagan said,

'The White House is like an eight-star hotel!'

---
* elevator (US) = lift   * movie theater (US) = cinema

Language work

6 Ask and answer questions about things in the White House.
- a cinema
- many offices
- many bathrooms
- a swimming pool
- a library
- any elevators
- a tennis court
- a vegetable garden

Is there a cinema?
Yes, there is.

Are there many offices?
Yes, there are a lot.

7 Match a **verb** with a **place**. Make sentences.
You can cook in the kitchen.

Verb	Place
cook	bedroom
sleep	office
have a shower	dining room
relax	living room
eat	garden
work	kitchen
read	bathroom
grow vegetables	library

Project

Research a famous building in your country. Where is it? Is it a government building? A cathedral? A museum?

Tell the other students about it.

▶▶ WRITING **T 4.9** Describing your home *p107*

Unit 4 • Somewhere to live 35

VOCABULARY AND LISTENING
Adjectives for *good* and *bad*

1 There are a lot of different words for *good* and *bad*. Write the words in the chart.

2 **T 4.10** Listen to the intonation.

It's wonderful! They're awful! She's fantastic!

Listen again and repeat. Practise the other adjectives.

3 **T 4.11** Listen to the conversations. Match the nouns with the adjectives.

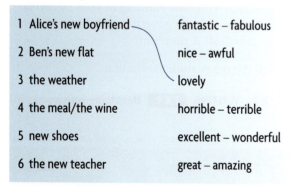

Look at **T 4.11** on p122, and practise the conversations.

4 Work with a partner. Continue these conversations.
1 'The weather's lovely, isn't it?'
2 'It's a great party, isn't it?'
3 'Do you like Thomas?'
4 'How's your meal?'
5 'What do you think of your boss?'
6 'Do you like my new flat?'

Adverb + adjective

5 Look how we use adverbs to make an adjective stronger or not so strong.

6 **T 4.12** Listen to five conversations. Who/What are they talking about? What adverb + adjective do they use?

1	Angela's car	really expensive, ...
2		
3		
4		
5		

T 4.12 Listen again. Practise the conversations.

7 Work with a partner. Have conversations. Start:
1 'Is your town old?'
2 'Is your school nice?'
3 'Is your flat big?'

Is your town old?

Well, there are some parts that are old, but there are a lot of very new buildings as well ...

No, it isn't very old. There are ...

EVERYDAY ENGLISH
Numbers

1 Look at the pictures. Say the numbers.

2 Say these numbers.

8	10	12	15
20	32	45	60
76	99	187	250
300	1,000	1,000,000	

T 4.13 Listen and check. Practise again.

3 How do we say these numbers in English?

1½   2¼   6.8   17.5   020 7481 6490   07861 56678

T 4.14 Listen and check. Practise the numbers.

4 **T 4.15** Write the numbers you hear.

1 _30,..._   3 _____
2 _____   4 _____

Prices

5 Say these prices.

6 **T 4.16** Listen and write the numbers and prices you hear.

1 ____ 3 ____ 5 ____ 7 ____
2 ____ 4 ____ 6 ____ 8 ____

7 Work with a partner. One of you works in a shop, the other is a customer. Have conversations.

8 Write numbers and prices from your everyday life. Tell your partner about them.

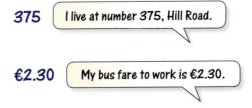

5 Super me!

can/can't • was/were/could • Words that go together • Polite requests

> **STARTER**
>
> Do you know the comic hero, Superman? Where does he come from? What can he do?
>
> **T 5.1** Listen and compare your ideas.

SUPERMAN IS FANTASTIC!
can/can't

1 Alfie and his cousin Ivy are talking about Superman.
   Complete what Alfie says using *can* and the verbs in the box.

Alfie	Superman's fantastic!
Ivy	Hmm! What **can** he **do**?
Alfie	He **can do** everything!
Ivy	No, he **can't**!
Alfie	Yes, he **can**. He ____ ____ at the speed of light, he ____ ____ through buildings, *and* he ____ ____ every language in the world!

   speak   see   fly

   T 5.2 Listen and check.

2 **T 5.3** Listen to the rest of the conversation. Answer the questions.
   • Which languages do they talk about?
   • Which sports do they talk about?

3 Complete the lines from the conversation with *can* or *can't* + verb.
   1 '_Can_ you ____ any languages?'
     'Yes, I can. I ____ ____ French and Spanish.'
   2 'You ____ ____ French at all!'
   3 'I ____ skateboard! You ____ !'
   4 '____ you ____ ?'
     'I ____ ____ a bit, but my mum and dad ____ ____ brilliantly.'
   5 'Superman ____ ____ *every*thing. There's nothing Superman ____ ____ !'

   T 5.4 Listen and check. Practise the sentences with a partner.

38 Unit 5 • Super me!

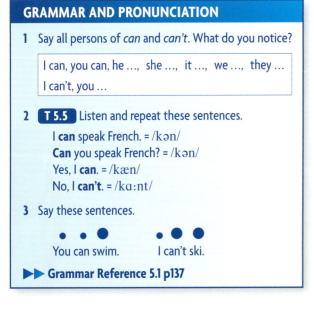

GRAMMAR AND PRONUNCIATION

1 Say all persons of *can* and *can't*. What do you notice?

> I can, you can, he …, she …, it …, we …, they …
> I can't, you …

2 **T 5.5** Listen and repeat these sentences.

> I **can** speak French. = /kən/
> **Can** you speak French? = /kən/
> Yes, I **can**. = /kæn/
> No, I **can't**. = /kɑːnt/

3 Say these sentences.

• • ●   • • ●
You can swim.   I can't ski.

▶▶ Grammar Reference 5.1 p137

PRACTICE

Ivy can't cook. Can you?

1 **T 5.6** Listen and complete the chart for Ivy. Put (✓) or (✗).

Can …?	Ivy	Your partner
speak a foreign language	✓	
cook	✗	
skateboard		
swim		
play tennis		
ski		
play any musical instruments		

2 Work with a partner. Ask and answer questions about Ivy.

> Can Ivy … ?   Yes, she can. / No, she can't.

3 Complete the sentences about Ivy with adverbs from the box.

(not) at all (x2)	a (little) bit (x2)	quite well
very well	really well	brilliantly

1 She can speak Spanish <u>a little bit</u> .
2 She can't cook _____.
3 She can swim _____.
4 She can play tennis _____.
5 She can ski _____.
6 Her dad can play the guitar _____.
7 Her mum can play the piano _____.
8 She can't play anything _____.

T 5.7 Listen and compare the sentences.

4 Ask questions to complete the chart in exercise 1 about your partner.

> Can you speak Spanish?   Yes, but not very well.

5 Tell the class about you and your partner.

> José can speak Spanish really well, but I can't.

6 **T 5.8** Listen and <u>underline</u> what you hear.
1 She *can* / *can't* cook.
2 I *can* / *can't* hear you.
3 They *can* / *can't* come to the party.
4 *Can* / *Can't* you see my glasses anywhere?
5 You *can* / *can't* always get what you want.
6 *Can* / *Can't* you do the homework?

7 With a partner, take turns saying the sentences. Say if you hear *can* or *can't*.

TODAY AND YESTERDAY
Past – *was/were/could*

1 **T 5.9** Read and listen to the questions about the present and the past. Complete the answers.

	Present	Past
1	What day is it today? It's _____ .	What day was it yesterday? It was _____ .
2	What month is it now? It's _____ .	What month was it last month? It was _____ .
3	Is it sunny today? _____ , it is. / _____ , it isn't.	Was it sunny yesterday? _____ , it was. / _____ , it wasn't.
4	Where are you now? I'm in/at _____ .	Where were you yesterday? I was in/at _____ .
5	Where are your parents now? They're in/at _____ .	Where were they yesterday? They were in/at _____ .
6	Are you in England now? _____ , I am. / _____ , I'm not.	Were you in England last year? _____ , I was. / _____ , I wasn't.
7	Can you ski? _____ , I can. / _____ , I can't.	Could you ski when you were five? _____ , I could. / _____ , I couldn't.
8	Can your teacher speak a lot of languages? Yes, _____ can./ No, _____ can't.	Could your teacher speak English when he/she was seven? Yes, _____ could. / No, _____ couldn't.

GRAMMAR AND PRONUNCIATION

1 Complete the Past Simple of *to be*.

	Positive	Negative
I	was	wasn't
you	were	weren't
he/she/it	___	___
we	were	___
they	___	___

2 What is the past of *can*?   **Positive Negative**
I/you/he/she/it/we/they   _____   _____

3 **T 5.10** Listen and repeat the sentences.

▶▶ Grammar Reference 5.2 – 5.3 p137

2 Ask and answer the questions about the past in exercise 1 with a partner.

> What day was it yesterday?
>
> It was …

3 Complete the sentences with the past of the verb *to be* and *can*.

1 I <u>wasn't</u> at school yesterday because I _____ ill.
2 My parents _____ at work last week. They _____ on holiday in Spain.
3 Where _____ you last night? I phoned, but you _____ at home.
4 I _____ read and write when I _____ just five.
5 My sister _____ read until she _____ seven.

Talking about you

4 Work with a partner. Ask and answer questions about you.
- at 8.00 this morning
- at 10.00 last night
- at this time yesterday
- last Saturday evening
- last Sunday morning

> Where were you at 8.00 this morning?
>
> I was at home/in bed/ at work/in town …

PRACTICE

Child prodigies

1 Look at the photos. Who are the children? What can they do? Why are they 'child prodigies'?

Marc Yu

Cleopatra Stratan

2 **T 5.11** Listen and complete the sentences about Marc Yu. Read them aloud.

Marc Yu – Pianist

1 He _was_ born on January _____, 19_____, in California, USA.
2 He _____ _____ the piano and the cello.
3 He _____ _____ the piano when he _____ _____.
4 He _____ _____ the cello when he _____ _____.
Last year, he played with Lang Lang, the famous Chinese pianist, in New York. They _____ a big success.

3 Work with a partner. Look at the information and make sentences about Cleopatra.

Cleopatra Stratan – Singer

1 She/born/October 7th, 2002/Moldova, near Romania.
2 She/sing beautifully when/just two years old.
3 When/three, she made an album, *La vârsta de trei ani*.
4 Her album/a big success. 150,000/sold round the world.

T 5.12 Listen and check.

4 Ask and answer questions about Marc and Cleopatra.
- When / born?
- Where / born?
- How old / when / could …?

Listening

5 Pablo Picasso was also a child prodigy. Read and complete the conversation about him.

Pablo Picasso
25 October 1881–8 April 1973

A Hey, look at that painting! It's a Picasso!
B Oh yes! Fantastic!
A Where [1] _was_ Picasso _born_ ?
B In Málaga.
A Ah! So he [2] _____ Spanish?
B Yes, he [3] _____ .
A [4] _____ his parents rich?
B Well, they [5] _____ rich and they [6] _____ poor. His father, Don José, [7] _____ a painter and a professor of art. His mother, Doña Maria, [8] _____ a housewife.
A So, [9] _____ Picasso good at drawing when he [10] _____ young?
B Oh, yes. He [11] _____ a child prodigy. He [12] _____ draw before he [13] _____ speak. His first word [14] _____ *lápiz*, which is Spanish for *pencil*.
A Wow! What a story!

T 5.13 Listen and check. Practise the conversation.

Talking about you

Work in groups. Ask and answer the questions about you.
1 When/born?
2 Where/born?
3 Where/parents born?
4 How old were you when you could …?
- walk • talk • read • swim • ride a bike
- use a computer • speak a foreign language

▶▶ **WRITING** A formal email *p108*

Unit 5 • Super me! 41

READING AND SPEAKING
A talented family

1. Do you have any talented people in your family? What can they do?

2. Look at the pictures of Nicola Benedetti and her father, Gio. Read the introduction to the article. Answer the questions.
   1. What does Nicola do?
   2. Why was 2004 special for her?
   3. Where does she live?
   4. What does her sister do?
   5. What does her father do?

3. Work in two groups.

   Group A Read about **Nicola**. Answer these questions.
   1. Was music important in her family?
   2. How old was Nicola when she could play the violin?
   3. Did her father work hard?
   4. Were her grandparents rich or poor?
   5. Is money important to Nicola and her father?
   6. Does her father like classical music?
   7. What does she teach her father? What does he teach her?
   8. When does she play the violin with her sister?

   Group B Read about **Gio**. Answer these questions.
   1. Where was Gio born?
   2. Why couldn't he buy the Jaguar car?
   3. What was Gio's business?
   4. How old was Nicola when she could play the violin?
   5. Can Gio play a musical instrument?
   6. What music does he like? What doesn't he like?
   7. Does Nicola work hard?
   8. Why does he cry?

4. Work with a partner from the other group. Tell your partner about your person.

Language work

5. Who or what do these adjectives from the text refer to?

busy	important	difficult	proud
hard-working	classical	expensive	passionate
poor	close	independent	sentimental

   Nicola's father was always busy.

What do you think?

Work as a class. Discuss the questions.
- Do Nicola and Gio have a good relationship?
- How are they similar? How are they different?
- Does Nicola have a good relationship with her sister?
- What about *your* family? Who are you close to? Why?

A PASSION FOR SUCCESS

Nicola Benedetti is a world-famous violinist. She was the BBC Young Musician of the Year in 2004 when she was 16. She lives in Chiswick, west London, near her sister, Stephanie, who is also a violinist. Their father, Gio Benedetti, is a businessman. He lives with his wife, Francesca, in Scotland.

Nicola Benedetti

A PASSION FOR *Music*

'When I was young, music wasn't very important in our house. Then, when I was four, I started playing the violin. In my first lesson, I was so happy, I couldn't stop crying.

My dad, Gio, was always busy. He was very hard-working. His parents were poor, so he wanted to give me and my sister everything. I like hard work too, and I know what I want – if someone says to me "You can't do that", I think "Oh yes I can!" That's very like my dad.

But my dad's a businessman, and I'm an artist. Money is very important to him, but for me, success isn't the same as earning lots of money. He likes the music I play, but he doesn't like classical music very much. I teach him about music, and he tells me about business.

My sister and I are very close. We sometimes play together – not professionally, but at family occasions like weddings and at Christmas.

I live for my work. I never want to stop. Music is my life.'

Gio Benedetti

A PASSION FOR Business

'I was born in a small village near Lucca in Italy. We were poor but happy. When I was ten, I came to Scotland to live with my uncle. It was very difficult.

When I was 16, there was a beautiful car – a Jaguar – in the shops but I couldn't afford it. It was too expensive. So I started a business to make money – a dry-cleaning business. Soon there were 15 shops. By the time I was 19, I could afford the Jaguar. That was a very good day!

Nicola was always independent, like me. She could play the violin when she was four. Now she plays concerts all over the world. I am so proud of her. She practises for seven hours a day. Scotland is so proud of her. Everybody knows her now.

I can't play any musical instruments. I like country and western music, but not classical. Nicola knows what she wants. She has a passion to succeed, like me, and she works very hard to get it. When she plays the violin, she's passionate – that's the Italian in her. When I see her play, I often cry. I can't help it. I'm very sentimental.'

VOCABULARY AND LISTENING
Words that go together

Noun + noun

1 Match a noun in **A** with a noun in **B**. Do we write one word or two?

post office   businessman

A	B
book	room
motor (x2)	shop/store
sun	station (x2)
living	park
bus	way
hand	bike
railway	lights
car	stop
traffic	glasses
petrol	bag

2 Test the other students on the nouns that go together.

This is where we buy books.
A book shop.

3 **T 5.14** Listen to three conversations. Write all the noun + noun combinations you hear.

1 _post office_ , _____ , _____
2 _____ , _____ , _____
3 _____ , _____ , _____ , _____

4 With a partner, write a short conversation. Include some noun + noun combinations. Act your conversation to the class.

Verb + noun

5 Match a **verb** with a **noun**.

verb	noun
send	a car
drive	children
ride	a lot of text messages
speak	a suit and tie
earn	TV a lot
live	three languages
play	a motorbike
wear	on the third floor
look after	a lot of money
watch	the guitar

6 Ask and answer questions.

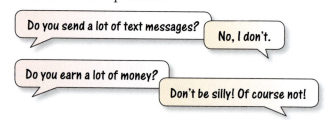

Do you send a lot of text messages?
No, I don't.
Do you earn a lot of money?
Don't be silly! Of course not!

7 **T 5.15** Listen to the short conversations. After each one say which verb + noun combinations you hear.

8 Work with a partner. Look at **T 5.15** on p123. Choose two of the conversations and learn them by heart.

Prepositions

9 Complete the sentences with a preposition from the box.

| of | to | from | on | at | with | for |

1 Do you like listening _to_ music?
2 What sort _____ music do you like?
3 Where's your girlfriend _____ ? Is she Mexican?
4 Is Paula married _____ Mike?
5 Do you want to come shopping _____ me?
6 Were there any good programmes _____ television last night?
7 What do you want _____ your birthday?
8 Can I speak _____ Dave? Is he _____ work today?

T 5.16 Listen and check. What are the replies? Practise the conversations.

44 Unit 5 • Super me!

EVERYDAY ENGLISH
Polite requests

1 **T 5.17** Listen and complete the conversations. Where are the people?

A Can I have a _____, please?
B Yes, of course.

A Can you open the _____ for me, please?
C Sure. No _____.
A Thanks.

A Could I have the _____, please?
D Certainly, Madam.

A Could you _____ me the _____, please?
E It's 10.30.
A Thanks a lot.

2 What differences are there in **A**'s requests in exercise 1?

> 1 *Can/Could I …?* and *Can/Could you …?* express a request.
> **Can/Could I** ask you a question?
> **Can/Could you** do something for me?
>
> 2 *Can/Could* express an ability.
> I **can** swim./I **could** swim when I was four.

3 **T 5.18** Listen and repeat the requests.
Notice how the intonation falls and rises.

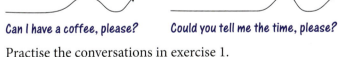

Can I have a coffee, please?   Could you tell me the time, please?

Practise the conversations in exercise 1.

4 Complete the requests with *Can/Could I …?* or *Can/Could you …?*

1 _Can I_____ have a cheese sandwich, please?
2 _____ post this letter for me, please?
3 _____ give me your email address?
4 _____ speak to you for a moment?
5 _____ lend me £20 till tomorrow?
6 _____ give me a hand with this box?

T 5.19 Listen and compare. Can you remember the replies?
Practise with a partner.

5 Have more conversations with some of these prompts.

a cola   pay by credit card
   the bill   a vanilla ice-cream
a glass of water   a return ticket
   borrow your dictionary   do me a favour
   try on these jeans   sit next to you
   give me a lift   open the window

Can I have a cola, please?
Sure. Here you are.
Of course. Diet or regular?
Sorry. We don't have any cola.

Life's ups and downs

Past Simple (1) – regular and irregular • Describing feelings • What's the date?

STARTER

When were your grandparents and great-grandparents born? Where were they born? What were their jobs? Were they rich or poor?

If you know, tell the class.

> I think my great-grandfather was a farmer.
>
> He was born in about 1920 in ....

AMERICA'S RICHEST WOMAN
Past Simple – regular verbs

1 Look at the photos. Do you know anything about the American TV star Oprah Winfrey?

2 **T 6.1** Read and listen to text **A**. Complete it with the verbs you hear. Answer the questions.
- Is Oprah Winfrey rich?
- Where does she live and work?
- How much does she earn?

3 **T 6.2** Read and listen to text **B** about her childhood. Answer the questions.
- Where and when was she born?
- Were her parents rich?
- Was she clever? What could she do?

GRAMMAR SPOT

1 Complete the sentences about Oprah with the verb *live*.

Now she _____ in California.

When she was a child, she _____ with her grandmother.

2 Read text B. Find the Past Simple of *work*, *clean*, *receive*, *study*, and *start*. How is the Past Simple formed?

▶▶ Grammar Reference 6.1 p138

Oprah
TV Star and Billionaire

A THE WOMAN

Oprah Winfrey ¹ _is_ a famous American TV star. She ² _____ in California, but she also ³ _____ an apartment in Chicago, where she ⁴ _____. Oprah is one of the richest women in America. She ⁵ _____ millions of dollars every year. She ⁶ _____ a lot of money to charity.

B HER CHILDHOOD

Oprah was born on January 29, 1954, in Kosciusko, Mississippi. Her parents were very poor. Her father, Vernon, worked in a coal mine and her mother, Vernita, cleaned houses. They couldn't look after Oprah, so she lived with her grandmother, Hattie Mae. Oprah was clever. She could read before she was three. When she was 17, she received a scholarship to Tennessee State University, where she studied drama. She also started reading the news at the local radio station.

4 What is the Past Simple of these verbs?

watch	interview	study	talk
move	start	earn	open

T 6.3 Listen and check.

5 **T 6.4** Listen to text **C**. Complete it with the Past Simple form of the verbs in exercise 4.

> **GRAMMAR SPOT**
>
> 1 Find a question with *did* and a negative with *didn't* in text **C**.
>
> 2 Look at these questions.
> Where **does** Oprah **work**?
> Where **did** her father **work**?
> *Did* is the past of *do* and *does*.
>
> 3 We use *didn't* (= *did not*) to form the negative.
> We **didn't have** much money.
>
> ▶▶ Grammar Reference 6.2 p138

C HER SUCCESS

In 1984, Oprah ¹ _moved_ to Chicago to work on a TV talk show called *A.M. Chicago*. She ² _____ to lots of interesting people about their problems. Oprah says,

> 'People's problems are my problems.'

The show was very successful, so in 1985, it was renamed *The Oprah Winfrey Show*. 49 million people in 134 countries ³ _____ it every week. In 1993, she ⁴ _____ Michael Jackson and 100 million people ⁵ _____ the programme. Last year, she ⁶ _____ $260,000,000.

Her charity work

In 1998, Oprah ⁷ _____ the charity *Oprah's Angel Network* to help poor children all over the world. In 2007, she ⁸ _____ a special school in Johannesburg, the *Oprah Winfrey Academy for Girls*. She says,

> 'When I was a kid, we were poor and we didn't have much money. So what did I do? I ⁹ _____ hard.'

There are 152 girls at the school, Oprah calls them her daughters – the children she didn't have in real life.

6 Complete the questions about Oprah.

1 Where _did_ her father work?
 In a coal mine.
2 What _____ her mother do?
 She cleaned houses.
3 Who _____ Oprah _____ with?
 Her grandmother.
4 What _____ she _____ ?
 Drama.
5 When _____ she _____ Michael Jackson?
 In 1993.

6 How much _____ she _____ last year?
 $260 million.
7 When _____ she _____ the girls' school?
 In 2007.
8 _____ her parents _____ much money?
 No, they didn't.

T 6.5 Listen and check. Practise the questions and answers with a partner.

Unit 6 • Life's ups and downs 47

PRACTICE

Talking about you

1 Complete the questions with *did*, *was*, or *were*.
   1 Where __were__ your parents born?
   2 Where _____ you live when you _____ a child?
   3 _____ you live in a house or a flat?
   4 When _____ you start school?
   5 Who _____ your first teacher?
   6 Who _____ your best friend?
   7 When _____ you learn to read and write?
   8 When _____ you get your first mobile phone?

2 Work in groups of two or three. Ask and answer the questions in exercise 1.

3 Tell the class some of the information you learned.

> Enrico's mother was born in ...
> His father ...
> He lived in ...

Pronunciation

4 **T 6.6** Listen to three different pronunciations of *-ed*.

   /t/ work**ed**
   /d/ liv**ed**
   /ɪd/ start**ed**

5 **T 6.7** Listen and write the Past Simple verbs in the chart. Then practise saying them.

/t/	/d/	/ɪd/

BEN'S UPS AND DOWNS
Irregular verbs

1 Write the Past Simple of these verbs. (There is a list of irregular verbs on p158.) Test your partner.

be	was/were	leave	_____
begin	_____	lose	_____
can	_____	make	_____
catch	_____	meet	_____
come	_____	send	_____
get	_____	take	_____
give	_____	win	_____
go	_____	write	_____
have	_____		

▶▶ **Grammar Reference 6.3 p138**

2 Read about Ben Way. What were his ups and downs?

Ben Way

He made his first million at 17. He was one of the first dotcom millionaires. Then he lost it all ... And now he's a millionaire again! How did he do it?

3 Read and complete the PROFILE of Ben with the verbs in the Past Simple. Compare your answers with a partner.

Listening

4 **T 6.8** Listen to an interview with Ben. What else do you learn about him?

5 Make the questions. Ask and answer them with a partner.
   1 What/Ben's parents do?
   2 Where/he go to school?
   3 Why/he have problems at school?
   4 What/his dad give him in 1989?
   5 Who/he help with their computers?
   6 Why/he leave school at 16?
   7 When/he win 'Young Entrepreneur of the Year'?
   8 Why/he lose his money?

> What did Ben's parents do?
> His father was a ...

48 Unit 6 • Life's ups and downs

PROFILE
Ben Way
dotcom millionaire

Year	Ben's Life
1980	He ¹ _was_ (be) born on 28, September 1980.
	He ² _____ (go) to school in a small Devon village. He was dyslexic, he ³ _____ (can not) read and write.
1989	When he was nine, his father ⁴ _____ (give) him a computer. He ⁵ _____ (take) his computer everywhere with him.
1991	At 11, he ⁶ _____ (write) his first software program.
1995	When he was 15, he ⁷ _____ (begin) his own computer company.
1996	He ⁸ _____ (leave) school at 16.
1997	At 17, he ⁹ _____ (make) his first £1 million.
1999	At 19, he ¹⁰ _____ (have) £18.5 million.
2000	At 20, he ¹¹ _____ (win) 'Young Entrepreneur of the Year.'
2001	When he was 21, he ¹² _____ (lose) everything.
2002 –NOW	BUT THEN – at 22, he started a new company called 'Rainmakers' and he became a millionaire all over again!

PRACTICE

Regular and irregular verbs

1 Complete the sentences with the verbs in the Past Simple.

1. My granddad _was_ (be) born in 1932. He _____ (die) in 2009.
2. My parents _____ (meet) in London in 1983. They _____ (get) married in 1985.
3. I _____ (arrive) late for the lesson. It _____ (begin) at 2 o'clock.
4. I _____ (catch) the bus to school today. It _____ (take) just 40 minutes.
5. I _____ (have) a very busy morning. I _____ (send) 30 emails before 10 o'clock.
6. Our football team _____ (win) the match 3–0. Your team _____ (lose) again.
7. My brother _____ (earn) a lot of money in his last job, but he _____ (leave) because he _____ (not like) it.
8. I _____ (study) Chinese for four years, but when I _____ (go) to Shanghai, I _____ (can not) understand a word.

T 6.9 Listen and check.

Talking about you

2 Make true sentences about you using a positive or negative.

1. watch TV yesterday
2. get up early this morning
3. have coffee and toast for breakfast
4. come to school by car yesterday
5. play computer games on Friday evening
6. send a text just before this lesson
7. meet some friends last night
8. go shopping yesterday

> I watched/didn't watch TV yesterday.

Compare answers with a partner.

3 Work with your partner. Ask and answer questions with *When did you last ...?* and the time expressions. Ask another question to get more information.

- have a holiday
- watch a DVD
- go to the cinema
- talk on your mobile
- send an email
- catch a bus
- give a present
- have dinner in a restaurant

yesterday ...
morning   afternoon   evening
last ...
night   week   weekend
Monday   month   year
✗ last afternoon   ✗ last evening
▶▶ Grammar Reference 6.4 p138

4 Tell the class some things you learned about your partner.

Nina had a holiday last August and she went to Italy.

▶▶ WRITING   **T 6.10**   A biography p109

Unit 6 • Life's ups and downs   49

LISTENING AND READING
The meaning of life

1. Look at the pictures and read the introduction to the story of *The Businessman and the Fisherman*. Answer the questions.
   - Where was the businessman?
   - Who did he meet?
   - Did he like the fish?
   - What did he say?
   - What nationality were the two men?

2. **T 6.11** Close your books and listen to the conversation. Who do you think has the best life?

3. Are these sentences true (✓) or false (✗)? Correct the false sentences.
   1. The businessman and the fisherman met in the morning.
   2. It took the fisherman an hour to catch the tuna.
   3. He stopped fishing because he had enough fish for his family.
   4. The fisherman is often bored because he has nothing to do.
   5. The businessman went to Harvard University.
   6. He gave the fisherman a lot of advice.
   7. The fisherman gave the businessman some fish.
   8. He went to a bar with the businessman.

4. Read and complete the story of *The Businessman and the Fisherman*.

   T 6.11 Listen again and check.

5. Retell the story round the class.

What do you think?
- Do you think the fisherman follows the businessman's advice? Why/Why not?
- What is the moral of this story:

  'Money makes the world go round.'

  'Understand what really matters in life.'

  'Don't listen to other people's advice.'

  'Work more, earn more!'

50 Unit 6 • Life's ups and downs

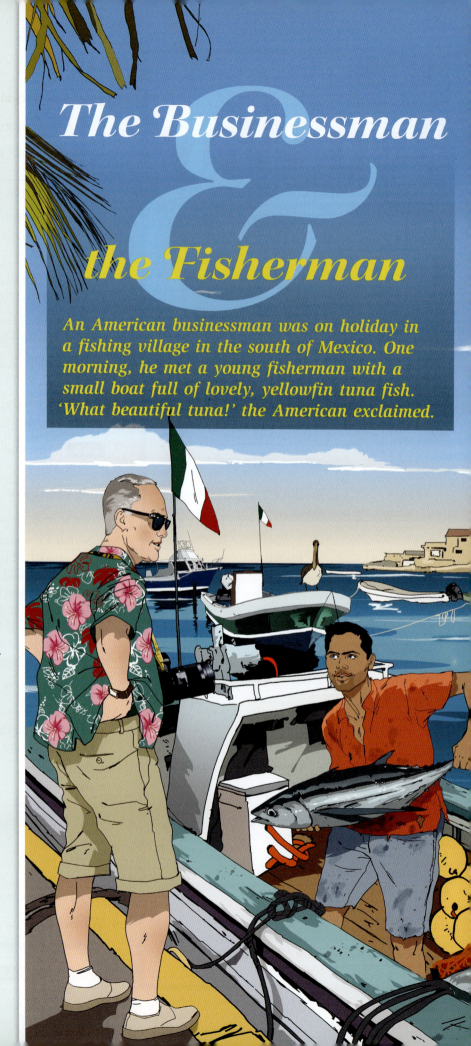

The Businessman & the Fisherman

An American businessman was on holiday in a fishing village in the south of Mexico. One morning, he met a young fisherman with a small boat full of lovely, yellowfin tuna fish. 'What beautiful tuna!' the American exclaimed.

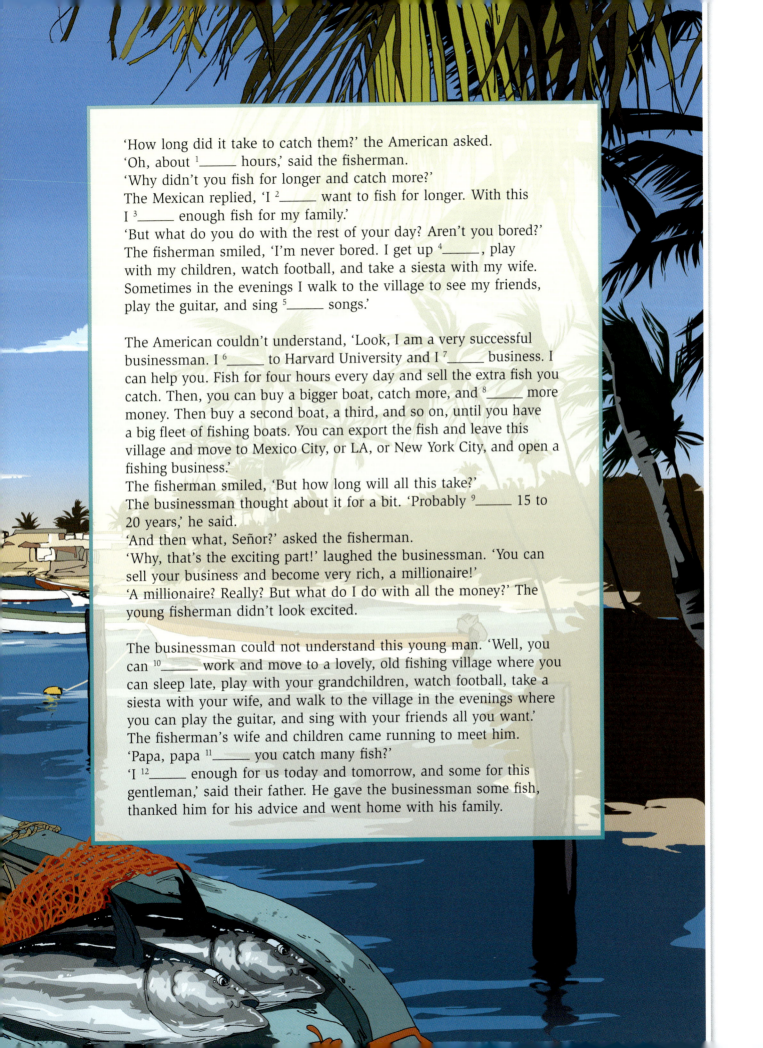

'How long did it take to catch them?' the American asked.
'Oh, about ¹_____ hours,' said the fisherman.
'Why didn't you fish for longer and catch more?'
The Mexican replied, 'I ²_____ want to fish for longer. With this I ³_____ enough fish for my family.'
'But what do you do with the rest of your day? Aren't you bored?'
The fisherman smiled, 'I'm never bored. I get up ⁴_____, play with my children, watch football, and take a siesta with my wife. Sometimes in the evenings I walk to the village to see my friends, play the guitar, and sing ⁵_____ songs.'

The American couldn't understand, 'Look, I am a very successful businessman. I ⁶_____ to Harvard University and I ⁷_____ business. I can help you. Fish for four hours every day and sell the extra fish you catch. Then, you can buy a bigger boat, catch more, and ⁸_____ more money. Then buy a second boat, a third, and so on, until you have a big fleet of fishing boats. You can export the fish and leave this village and move to Mexico City, or LA, or New York City, and open a fishing business.'
The fisherman smiled, 'But how long will all this take?'
The businessman thought about it for a bit. 'Probably ⁹_____ 15 to 20 years,' he said.
'And then what, Señor?' asked the fisherman.
'Why, that's the exciting part!' laughed the businessman. 'You can sell your business and become very rich, a millionaire!'
'A millionaire? Really? But what do I do with all the money?' The young fisherman didn't look excited.

The businessman could not understand this young man. 'Well, you can ¹⁰_____ work and move to a lovely, old fishing village where you can sleep late, play with your grandchildren, watch football, take a siesta with your wife, and walk to the village in the evenings where you can play the guitar, and sing with your friends all you want.'
The fisherman's wife and children came running to meet him.
'Papa, papa ¹¹_____ you catch many fish?'
'I ¹²_____ enough for us today and tomorrow, and some for this gentleman,' said their father. He gave the businessman some fish, thanked him for his advice and went home with his family.

VOCABULARY AND LISTENING
Describing feelings

1 Match these feelings to the pictures.

☐ annoyed ☐ excited ☐ tired
☐ bored ☐ interested ☐ worried

a b c d e f

2 Use the words from exercise 1 to complete the sentences.
1 I went to bed late last night, so I'm very _____ today.
2 My football team lost again. I'm really _____!
3 I won £20,000 in the lottery. I'm so _____!
4 I can't find my house keys. I'm really _____.
5 I have nothing to do and nowhere to go. I am so _____!
6 The professor gave a great lecture. I was really _____.

T 6.12 Listen and check.

-ed and -ing adjectives

> Some adjectives can end in both *-ed* and *-ing*.
>
> The book was **interesting**.   The lesson was **boring**.
> I was **interested** in the book.   The students were **bored**.

3 Complete each sentence with the correct adjective.
1 **excited   exciting**
   Life in New York is very _____.
   It's my birthday tomorrow. I'm really _____.
2 **tired   tiring**
   The marathon runners were very _____.
   That game of tennis was very _____.
3 **annoyed   annoying**
   The child's behaviour was really _____.
   The teacher was _____ because nobody did the homework.
4 **worried   worrying**
   We were very _____ when we heard the news.
   The news is very _____.

4 Work with a partner. Complete the conversations with *-ed* and *-ing* adjectives from exercise 3.

1 A Did you enjoy the film?
  B No, I didn't. It was _____.
  A Oh, I loved it. It was really _____, and very funny.
  B I didn't laugh once!

2 C How was your exam?
  D Awful. I'm very _____.
  C But you worked really hard.
  D I know, I studied until two in the morning, but then I was so _____ today, I couldn't read the questions.
  C Don't worry. I'm sure you'll be OK.

3 E That was a great match! Really _____!
  F Only because your team won. I was _____.
  E But it wasn't _____ at all! It was a fantastic game!
  F Well, I didn't enjoy it, and now I'm _____ because I paid £45 for my ticket.

4 G When's Nina's birthday?
  H You mean 'When *was* her birthday?' It was last Friday, March 24th.
  G Oh no! Was she _____ that I forgot?
  H No, no, she was just _____ that you didn't like her any more.

T 6.13 Listen and check. Practise the conversations.

5 Look again at the text on p51. Find examples of *-ed* and *-ing* adjectives.

EVERYDAY ENGLISH
What's the date?

1 Write the correct word next to the ordinal numbers.

fourth	twelfth	twentieth	twenty-second
second	thirtieth	thirteenth	seventeenth
fifth	tenth	sixteenth	~~first~~
third	sixth	thirty-first	

1st [first]
2nd [ ]
3rd [ ]
4th [ ]
5th [ ]
6th [ ]
10th [ ]
12th [ ]
13th [ ]
16th [ ]
17th [ ]
20th [ ]
22nd [ ]
30th [ ]
31st [ ]

T 6.14 Listen and practise saying the ordinals.

2 Say the months of the year round the class.

3 Work with a partner. Ask and answer questions about the months.

Which is the first month?   January.

1 We write: 3/4/1999 or 3 April 1999.
  We say: 'The third of April, nineteen ninety-nine.'
  or 'April the third, nineteen ninety-nine.'
2 Notice how we say these years.
  1900 nineteen hundred
  1905 nineteen oh five
  2001 two thousand and one
  2012 two thousand and twelve, or twenty-twelve

4 Practise saying the dates.

1 April	29/2/76
2 March	9/12/83
17 September	3/10/99
9 November	31/5/2005
	15/7/2015

T 6.15 Listen and check.

5 **T 6.16** Listen and write the dates you hear.

1 _____
2 _____
3 _____
4 _____
5 _____
6 _____

6 Ask and answer the questions with your partner.
1 What's the date today?
2 When did this school course start? When does it end?
3 When's Christmas Day?
4 When's Valentine's Day?
5 When's your birthday?
6 What are the dates of public holidays in your country?
7 What century is it now?
8 What were some important dates in the last century?

7 Write some important dates for you. Ask and answer questions about the dates with your partner.

Unit 6 • Life's ups and downs 53

Dates to remember

Past Simple (2) • Questions and negatives • Time expressions
Adverbs • Special occasions

STARTER

1 Work in groups. Do the history quiz. Discuss your answers with the class.

20TH CENTURY QUIZ
How much do you know about events in the last century?

1 When did Henry Ford sell the first Model-T motor car?
 a in 1903
 b in 1908
 c in 1910

2 When was the first talking movie, *The Jazz Singer*?
 a in 1903
 b in 1915
 c in 1927

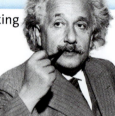

3 When did Einstein publish his theory of relativity?
 a about 100 years ago
 b about 60 years ago
 c about 50 years ago

6 How many people died in the Second World War?
 a about 20 million
 b about 60 million
 c about 80 million

5 When was the first non-stop flight around the world?
 a about 90 years ago
 b about 60 years ago
 c about 30 years ago

4 When was the Russian Revolution?
 a in 1909
 b in 1914
 c in 1917

7 When did the Berlin Wall come down?
 a in 1945
 b in 1975
 c in 1989

8 On what date in 1969 did man first land on the moon?
 a on 20 July
 b on 3 May
 c on 13 August

10 When did the twentieth century end?
 a at midnight on 31/12/1999
 b at midnight on 31/12/2000

9 How many number 1 hits did The Beatles have in the UK?
 a 12
 b 17
 c 27

2 **T 7.1** Listen and check your answers. Which group won the quiz?

THE GOOD OLD DAYS
Past Simple – questions and negatives

1 **T 7.2** Listen to Tommy talking to his grandad, Bill, about when Bill was young. Tick (✓) the things they talk about.

- [ ] programmes on TV
- [ ] sport
- [ ] pocket money
- [ ] housework
- [ ] comics
- [ ] holidays

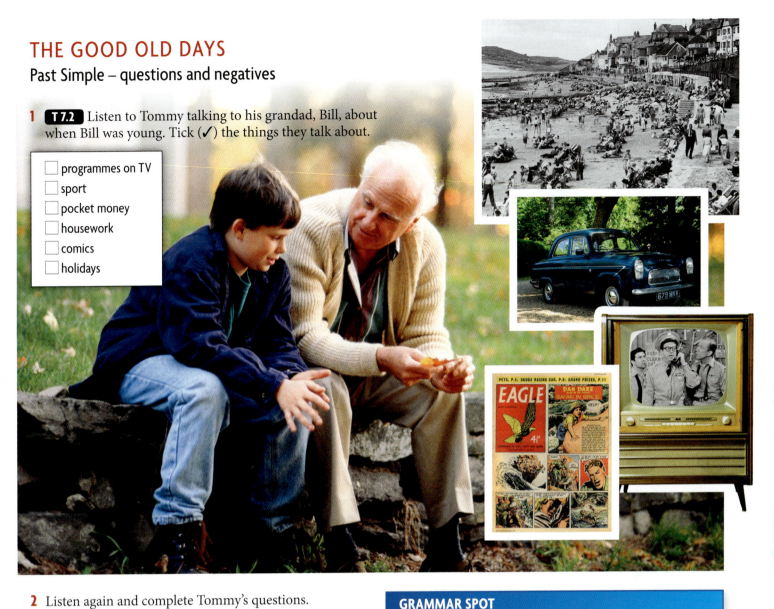

2 Listen again and complete Tommy's questions.

1 _How_ _many_ TV channels _were_ there?
2 _____ _____ did programmes begin?
3 _____ _____ pocket money _____ you get?
4 _____ _____ of comics _____ you _____?
5 _____ _____ you _____ on holiday?
6 _____ _____ you _____ there?
7 _____ _____ you go to the same place?

T 7.3 Listen and check. With a partner, ask and answer the questions.

3 What did Bill say about these things?
- colour TV   *It wasn't a colour TV like now.*
- TV programmes
- planes
- pocket money
- dishwashers
- holidays

4 Imagine what Bill said about these things.
- computers   *We didn't have computers in those days!*
- mobile phones
- fast food
- theme parks

GRAMMAR SPOT

1 Write the Past Simple forms.

Present Simple	Past Simple
I want to go.	I wanted to go.
He loves it.	
Do you watch TV?	
Where does she work?	
I don't buy sweets.	
They don't go on holiday.	

2 Complete the time expressions.

Henry Ford sold the first Model-T _____ 1908.
I was born _____ 17 April 1991.
Our lessons begin _____ nine o'clock.
Tommy saw Bill two days _____.

▶▶ Grammar Reference 7.1 – 7.2 p139

PRACTICE

1 Match a question word in **A** with a line in **B** and an answer in **C**.

A	B	C
1 Where 2 When 3 Who 4 How 5 Why 6 What 7 How many 8 How much	did you buy? did you go? did you go with? did you get there? did you pay?	A friend from work. By bus. Yesterday. £29. To the shops. Because I wanted to. A shirt. Only one.

T 7.4 Listen and check. Practise the questions and answers.

Bill's life

2 Work with a partner.

Student A Look at p150.   **Student B** Look at p153.

You have different information about Bill's life. Ask and answer questions.

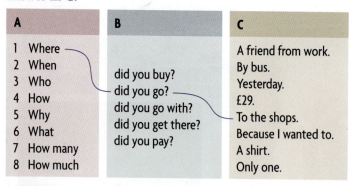

— When was Bill born?
— He was born in 1951.
— How many brothers and sisters did he have?
— He had two sisters and a brother.

Time expressions

3 Write the correct preposition.

in   at   on

___ seven o'clock   ___ the morning
___ Saturday   ___ Sunday morning
___ night   ___ July
___ 2009   ___ the weekend
___ summer   ___ the twentieth century

4 Work with a partner. Ask and answer questions with *When ... ?* Use a time expression and *ago* in your answer.

When did ...?
- you get up
- you have breakfast
- you arrive at school
- you start learning English
- you start at this school
- this term start
- you last use a computer
- you last go on holiday
- your parents get married
- you last have a coffee break

— When did you get up this morning?
— At seven o'clock, three hours ago.

— When did this term start?
— In September, two months ago.

5 Tell the class about your day up to now. Begin like this.

I got up at seven o'clock and had breakfast. I left the house at ...

Listening and pronunciation

6 **T 7.5** Listen and tick (✓) the sentence you hear.

1 a ☐ Where do you want to go?
　b ☐ Why do you want to go?
2 a ☐ I don't go to college.
　b ☐ I didn't go to college.
3 a ☐ Where is he?
　b ☐ Where was he?
4 a ☐ Do you like it?
　b ☐ Did you like it?
5 a ☐ Why did he come?
　b ☐ Why didn't he come?
6 a ☐ She doesn't work there.
　b ☐ She didn't work there.

SPEAKING
Talking about my life

1 Work with a partner. Freddy is at a party talking to Alisa. Look at Freddy's questions. Use the notes in Alisa's answers. What did she say?

> **F** You aren't English, are you, Alisa? Where are you from?
>
> **A** No – Russian – born – St Petersburg
>
> **F** Is that where you grew up?
>
> **A** Yes – lived – parents – two sisters – house near the university – father worked – university
>
> **F** Oh, how interesting! What was his job? Was he a teacher?
>
> **A** Yes – professor – psychology
>
> **F** Really? And what did your mother do?
>
> **A** doctor – worked – hospital
>
> **F** So, where did you go to school?
>
> **A** High School – ten years – 18 – university
>
> **F** What did you study?
>
> **A** philosophy and education – university – Moscow – four years
>
> **F** Wow! And did you start work after that?
>
> **A** No – travelled – States – six months – worked – summer camp – Yellowstone National Park – amazing!
>
> **F** It sounds great! And what's your job now?
>
> **A** work – junior high school – Paris – teach Russian and English
>
> **F** Your English is really good! Well, it was very nice to meet you, Alisa!
>
> **A** Nice – meet – too. Bye!

T 7.6 Listen and compare.

2 Practise the conversation with a partner. Swap roles and practise again.

3 Make some notes about your own life story.

4 Work in groups. Tell each other your life stories. Ask and answer questions.

What did you …?
How long …?
Who …?
Did you enjoy it?

Alisa as a child

Alisa
Freddy

Alisa at work

Unit 7 • Dates to remember 57

READING AND SPEAKING
Sixty years of flight

1. Look at the pictures. Who are the men? What did they do? When did they do it?

2. Read the titles. What was 'phenomenal'?

3. Work in two groups.

   Group A Read about the first air journey.
   Group B Read about the first man on the moon.

   Answer the questions.
   1. When and where did the journey begin?
   2. How long did it take?
   3. How far was the journey there?
   4. How fast did he/they go?
   5. Where did the journey end?
   6. In what way was this flight a beginning?

4. Find a partner from the other group. Compare and swap your answers to exercise 3.

5. Work with the same partner. Look again at the texts and answer these questions.

   Blériot
   1. Why was Blériot's flight difficult?
   2. Was the weather good?
   3. How did he know where to land?
   4. What did he win?

   Apollo 11
   5. Why couldn't the astronauts sleep?
   6. What did Armstrong say as he stepped onto the moon?
   7. How long did they spend walking on the moon's surface?
   8. What did they leave on the moon?

Speaking

6. Find the numbers in the texts. What do they refer to?

1909	37	4.30	40	250	1,000	
1969	three	30	8.17	600 million	one	22

   T 7.7 Listen and check.

7. Work with a partner. Use the numbers in exercise 6 to help you retell the stories.

58 Unit 7 • Dates to remember

PLANES TO

There are just 60 years between the first

1909
THE FIRST AIR JOURNEY

1969
THE FIRST MAN ON THE MOON

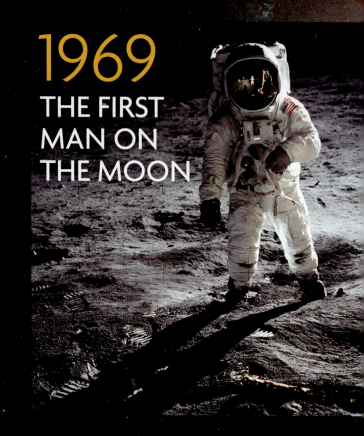

ROCKETS IN SIXTY YEARS

flight and the first man on the moon. In the 20th century, progress in aviation was phenomenal.

On July 25 1909, a Frenchman, Louis Blériot, became the first man to complete an air journey when he flew from Calais, in the north of France, to Dover, in the south of England. Blériot's flight amazed the whole of Europe. People thought that such a journey was impossible.

Louis Blériot

THE FLIGHT

The flight wasn't easy. Mr Blériot, a 37-year-old engineer, couldn't swim, so he didn't want to come down in the Channel. He couldn't walk very well because of an injury to his leg, and he didn't have a compass.

On the morning of the 25th, he took off at 4.30 from a field at the edge of a cliff. It took 37 minutes to complete the 22-mile journey. The plane flew at 40 miles per hour at an altitude of 250 feet.

Everything went well until he flew into fog. 'I continued flying for ten minutes, but I couldn't see the land, only the sky and the sea. It was the most dangerous part of the flight. I wasn't worried about the machine. It flew beautifully. Finally, I saw the land,' he told reporters.

LANDING IN ENGLAND

When he got to Dover, he saw a French journalist waving a flag. He cut the engine at 60 feet and crashed into a field.
The news quickly went round the world, and Mr Blériot's flight was celebrated in London and Paris. He won a prize of £1,000.

'The crossing was the start of modern aviation,' said Louis Blériot, the grandson of the pioneer.

On 16 July 1969, at 9.30 in the morning, Apollo 11 lifted off from the Kennedy Space Center in Florida. There were three astronauts – Neil Armstrong, Buzz Aldrin, and Michael Collins. The enormous rocket took three days to complete the 250,000 miles to the moon, travelling at six miles per second (21,600 miles an hour). Then it circled the moon 30 times, giving time to prepare for the landing.

Neil Armstrong   Michael Collins   Buzz Aldrin

THE LUNAR LANDING

The lunar module landed on a part of the moon called the Sea of Tranquillity at 8.17 in the evening on 20 July.

It was time for the astronauts to rest, but they were too excited to sleep. At 3.00 in the morning on July 21, Neil Armstrong became the first man to walk on the moon. Six hundred million people all over the world watched on TV. As Armstrong took his first steps, he said the famous words, 'That's one small step for man, one giant leap for mankind.'

WALKING ON THE MOON

Armstrong and Aldrin spent two and a half hours walking on the moon. They collected samples and set up scientific equipment. Finally, they put up a US flag. After 22 hours on the moon, the lunar module lifted off and flew up to join the rocket that took them back to Earth. They left an inscription:

> HERE MEN FROM THE PLANET EARTH FIRST SET FOOT UPON THE MOON, JULY 1969. WE CAME IN PEACE FOR ALL MANKIND.

This flight was the beginning of man's exploration of space.

VOCABULARY AND LISTENING
Adverbs

1 Look at these sentences from the texts on p59. The words in **bold** are adverbs.

> Everything went **well** …
> The plane flew **beautifully**.
> The news **quickly** went round the world …
> **Finally**, they put up a US flag.

GRAMMAR SPOT

1 Regular adverbs end in *-ly*.

   quick**ly**   slow**ly**   careful**ly**
   quiet**ly**   bad**ly**   real**ly**

2 There are some common irregular adverbs.

   drive **fast**   work **hard**
   feel **well**   get up **early/late**

▶▶ Grammar Reference 7.3 p139

2 Are the words in *italics* adjectives or adverbs?
   1 a Smoking is a *bad* habit.
     b We lost the match because we played *badly*.
   2 a Please listen *carefully*.
     b Jane's a *careful* driver.
   3 a It's a *hard* life.
     b I work *hard* and play *hard*.

3 Match a **verb** with an **adverb**. Sometimes there is more than one possible answer.

Verbs	Adverbs
work	fluently
speak English	carefully
breathe	fast
do my homework	late
drive	hard
arrive	deeply

4 Put the word in brackets into the correct place in the sentence.
   1 We had a holiday in Italy. (terrible)
   2 I lost my passport. (unfortunately)
   3 I contacted the police. (immediately)
   4 It was a journey because the traffic was bad. (long)
   5 Fortunately, Sally's a driver. (good)
   6 She speaks Italian. (well)

Telling a story

5 Complete the sentences with your own ideas.
   1 It started to rain, but fortunately, <u>I had an umbrella.</u>
   2 James invited me to his party, but unfortunately, …
   3 Suddenly, six friends arrived for lunch. Fortunately, …
   4 I saw a beautiful pair of shoes in a shop. Unfortunately, …
   5 I was fast asleep, when suddenly …
   6 I saw the accident happen. Immediately, …
   7 When I met her at the party, my heart stopped. I really …
   8 I heard a noise, got silently out of bed, and went slowly …

6 **T 7.8** Look at the picture and listen to the man. What did he hear in the middle of the night?

7 **T 7.8** Listen again. Number the adverbs 1–8 in the order you hear them.

| ☐ quickly | ☐ quietly | ☐ slowly | ☐ suddenly |
| ☐ immediately | ☐ carefully | ☐ fortunately | ☐ really |

8 Work with a partner. Take turns to retell the story. Use the adverbs to help.

▶▶ **WRITING** Telling a story *p110*

EVERYDAY ENGLISH
Special occasions

1 Look at the list of days. Which are the special days? Match them with the pictures.

| birthday | yesterday | Easter Day | Mother's Day | Hallowe'en | New Year's Eve | today |
| Monday | Valentine's Day | weekend | Friday | wedding day | tomorrow | Christmas Day |

2 Which days do you celebrate in your country? What do you do on these days?

| make a cake | wear special clothes | give cards and presents | give flowers or chocolates |
| have a special meal | have a party | go out with friends | have fireworks |

3 Complete the lines. What are the occasions?

1. Happy _____ to you,
   Happy _____ to you,
   Happy _____ , dear Grandma,
   Happy _____ to you.

2. **A** Did you get any _____ cards?
   B Yes, I did. Listen to this.
   Roses are red, violets are blue.
   You are my _____,
   And I love you.
   A Wow! Do you know who it's from?
   B No idea.

3. **C** Mummy! Daddy! Wake up! It's _____!
   D Mm? What time is it?
   C It's morning! Look. Father _____ gave me this present!
   E Oh, that's lovely! Merry _____ , darling!

4. **F** Congratulations! It's great news!
   G Thank you very much. We're both very happy.
   F So, when's the big day?
   H Pardon?
   F Your _____ day! When is it?
   G December the 12th. You'll get an invitation!

5. **I** It's midnight! Happy _____ _____, everyone!
   J/K/L _____ _____ _____ !

6. **C** Wake up, Mummy! Happy _____!
   D Thank you, darling. Oh, what beautiful flowers! And a cup of tea! Well, aren't I lucky!
   C And we made you a card! Look!
   D It's beautiful! What clever children you are!

7. **M** Thank goodness it's Friday!
   N Yeah! Have a good _____ !
   M Same to you.

4 **T 7.9** Listen and check. Work with a partner. Learn some of the conversations by heart.

8 Eat in or out?

Count and uncount nouns • *some* and *any* • *I like* and *I'd like*
How much? or *How many?* • Food and drink • Shopping in the High Street

STARTER

1 Look at the pictures. Which foods did you like as a young child? Which *didn't* you like? Were you a fussy eater? Tell the class.

2 Match the food and drink with the pictures.

T 8.1 Listen, then say the lists aloud as a class.

A	B
☐ tea	☐ bananas
☐ coffee	☐ apples
☐ wine	☐ strawberries
☐ cheese	☐ potatoes
☐ yoghurt	☐ carrots
☐ pasta	☐ peas
☐ ice-cream	☐ onions
☐ apple juice	☐ tomatoes
☐ bread	☐ eggs
☐ milk	☐ biscuits
☐ chocolate	☐ crisps
☐ broccoli	☐ chips

3 Which list, **A** or **B**, has plural nouns?
Complete these sentences with *is* or *are*.

Broccoli _____ good for you.
Tomatoes _____ good for you.
Apple juice _____ delicious.
Apples _____ delicious.

Can we count broccoli? Can we count tomatoes?

▶▶ **Grammar Reference 8.1 p139**

62 Unit 8 • Eat in or out?

WHO'S A FUSSY EATER?

Count and uncount nouns – *some, any, a lot of* ...

1 **T 8.2** Duncan and Nick are students. Listen to their conversation.
   - Who is the fussy eater?
   - What didn't Duncan like when he was a kid? What did he like?
   - Where do they go to eat?

2 **T 8.2** Listen again and complete the lines.

   1 'Oh, good, we have _some_ tomatoes.'
   2 'I didn't like a _____ of things when I was a kid.'
   3 'I didn't like _____ green vegetables.'
   4 'Did you like _____ vegetables at all?'
   5 'I liked _____ fruit, but not all.'
   6 'I drank a _____ of apple juice.'
   7 'I liked _____ the usual things kids like.'

GRAMMAR SPOT

Read the sentences. When do we use *some* and *any*?

There's **some** wine.	There are **some** tomatoes.
There isn't **any** beer.	There aren't **any** apples.
Is there **any** coffee?	Are there **any** bananas?

▶▶ Grammar Reference 8.2 p139

I like ... and *I'd like ...*

3 **T 8.3** Duncan and Nick are in Romano's Italian restaurant. Read and listen to their conversation with the waitress.

W Good evening, guys. Are you ready to order?
D I think we are. What would you like, Nick?
N Pasta, of course. I love pasta. I'd like the spaghetti Bolognese.
D Same for me, please. I really like spaghetti.
W Great! And would you like the wine list?
D No, thanks. Just a glass of red for me. Would you like some wine, Nick?
N Yes, but I don't like red wine. I'd like a glass of dry white, if that's OK.
W That's fine.
N Oh, and can we have some water too, please?
W Of course. Would you like sparkling or still?
D Just some tap water, thanks.
W No problem.

4 Read the sentences. Are the sentences true (✓) or false (✗)? Correct the false ones.

   1 Duncan and Nick both order the same meal.
   2 Duncan doesn't like spaghetti very much.
   3 They would both like some red wine.
   4 Nick only likes white wine.
   5 They don't want any water.
   6 Duncan would like some sparkling water.

5 Practise the conversation with a partner.

GRAMMAR SPOT

1 Which pair of sentences means *Do you want/I want ...*?

   | **Do** you **like** wine? | **Would** you **like** some wine? |
   | I **like** apples. | **I'd like** some red wine. |

2 We use *some*, not *any*, when we request and offer things.

   Would you like **some** wine?   Can we have **some** water?

3 We use *any*, not *some*, in other questions and negatives.

   There aren't **any** tomatoes.   Is there **any** pasta?

▶▶ Grammar Reference 8.3 p139

Unit 8 • Eat in or out?

PRACTICE

Would/Do you like …?

1 Choose *Would/Do you like …?* or *I/I'd like …*

 1 Excuse me, are you ready to order?
  Yes. *I like / I'd like* a steak, please.

 2 *Would / Do* you like a sandwich?
  No, thanks. I'm not hungry.

 3 *Do / Would* you like Ella?
  Yes. She's very nice.

 4 *Do / Would* you like a cold drink?
  Yes, please. Do you have any apple juice?

 5 Can I help you?
  Yes. *I like / I'd like* some stamps, please.

 6 What sports do you do?
  Well, *I'd like / I like* skiing very much.

 T 8.4 Listen and check. Practise with a partner.

2 **T 8.5** Listen to some questions. What are the correct replies?

 1 ☐ I like French wine, especially red wine.
   ☐ We'd like a bottle of French red wine.

 2 ☐ Just cheese, please. I don't like ham.
   ☐ I'd like a cheese and ham sandwich.

 3 ☐ I'd like a book by Patricia Cornwell.
   ☐ I like books by Patricia Cornwell.

 4 ☐ I'd like a new computer.
   ☐ I like Apple Macs more than PCs.

 5 ☐ No, but I'd like a dog.
   ☐ I like dogs, but I don't like cats much.

 6 ☐ No, thanks. I don't like ice-cream.
   ☐ I'd like some ice-cream, please.

 T 8.6 Listen and check. Practise with your partner.

a or *some*?

3 Write *a*, *an*, or *some*.

 1 __a__ banana
 2 __some__ fruit
 3 _____ egg
 4 _____ bread
 5 _____ milk
 6 _____ meat
 7 _____ apple
 8 _____ toast
 9 _____ sandwiches
 10 _____ biscuits
 11 _____ cup of coffee
 12 _____ apple juice

EATING IN

some/any, *much/many*

1 Duncan and Nick want to cook Cottage Pie for their girlfriends. Look at the recipe. What do they need?

 They need onions, minced beef, …

COTTAGE PIE

Ingredients
2 medium onions, chopped
500 g minced beef
10 ml oil
2 medium carrots, chopped
400 g tomatoes
1 tbsp thyme
Salt and black pepper

Topping
4 large potatoes
50 g butter
100 g Cheddar cheese
15 ml milk

2 Work with a partner. Look at their kitchen worktop. What is there for the recipe? Use *some/any* and *not much/not many*.

 There are some onions.   There isn't much cheese.   There aren't any carrots.

3 Complete Duncan and Nick's conversation with *some/any* and *much/many*.

N This recipe for Cottage Pie looks easy.

D But I can't cook at all.

N Don't worry. I really like cooking. Now, vegetables – do we have _any_ onions? Are there _____ carrots or potatoes?

D Well, there are _____ onions, but there aren't _____ carrots, and we don't have _____ potatoes. How _____ do we need?

N Four big ones.

D OK, put potatoes on your list.

N And how _____ tomatoes are there?

D Only two small ones. Put them on the list too.

N How _____ milk is there?

D There's a lot but there isn't _____ cheese or butter.

N OK, cheese and butter. What about herbs? Do we have _____ thyme?

D Yeah, that's fine. But don't forget the minced beef. How _____ do we need?

N 500 grams. Now, is that everything?

D Er – I think so. Do we have oil? Oh yeah, there's _____ left in the bottle.

N OK, first shopping, then I'll give you a cooking lesson!

D I'd like that. I hope the girls like Cottage Pie.

N Everyone likes Cottage Pie!

T 8.7 Listen and check. Practise with your partner.

GRAMMAR SPOT

1 We use *many* with count nouns in questions and negatives.
How **many** potatoes are there?   There **aren't many** onions.

2 We use *much* with uncount nouns in questions and negatives.
How **much** butter is there?   There **isn't much** oil.

3 In the positive we use *a lot of*.
There are **a lot of** tomatoes.   There's **a lot of** milk.

▶▶ Grammar Reference 8.4 p139

PRACTICE

much or many?

1 Complete the questions using *much* or *many*.
1 How _much_ toast would you like?
2 How _____ yoghurt do we have left?
3 How _____ people were at the wedding?
4 How _____ money do you have in your pocket?
5 How _____ petrol is there in the car?
6 How _____ children does your brother have?
7 How _____ days is it until your birthday?
8 How _____ time do you need for this exercise?

2 Choose an answer for each question in exercise 1.
a ___ Just 50p.   e ___ Two more minutes.
b ___ It's tomorrow!   f ___ Two. A boy and a girl.
c _1_ Just one slice, please.   g ___ About 150.
d ___ Not a lot. Just one   h ___ It's full.
     strawberry and one
     raspberry.

T 8.8 Listen and check. Practise with a partner.

Check it

3 Underline the correct word.
1 How many *eggs / butter / milk* do you need?
2 We don't have much *biscuits / cheese / potatoes* left.
3 I'm hungry. I'd like a *sandwich / bread / apple*.
4 I'd like *a / some / any* fruit, please.
5 I don't like *broccoli / an ice-cream / some ham*.
6 Would you like some *tea / sandwich / vegetable*?
7 How many *money / cousins / family* do you have?
8 We have *no / much / many* homework today.

Speaking

4 Work in small groups. Who can cook? Look at the picture of the Cottage Pie. How do you think it is made? You can use these verbs.

| chop | fry | boil | mix | add |

You chop the onions and the ...

Check the recipe on p155.

Project

What are your favourite recipes? Choose one. Find out the ingredients you need and how you make it. Tell the other students.

▶▶ **WRITING** Two emails *p112*

READING AND SPEAKING
Everybody likes a sandwich!

1. When did you last have a sandwich? What was in it?

2. Read the text quickly. Find these names.
   - Hillel the Elder
   - John Montague
   - Eliza Leslie
   - Dagwood Bumstead

   Who are the people? What is their connection to the sandwich?

3. Read the text again. Work with a partner to complete the lines with information from the text.

   1. Hillel the Elder made his sandwich with nuts, apples and spices, and …
   2. 'Trenchers' were the first …
   3. The Earl of Sandwich sometimes liked to … at the same time.

The Earl of Sandwich

   4. The Beef Steak Club chefs put … two slices of bread.
   5. Eliza Leslie's recipe for … was very popular in America.
   6. Sandwiches became popular worldwide because …
   7. Dagwood Bumstead is …
   8. The Dagwood sandwich is made with a … of meat, cheese, and vegetables.

4. How many kinds of sandwich can you think of? Write them down. Share ideas with the class.

The History of the Sandwich

1st Century BC
A famous rabbi, Hillel the Elder, made the first recorded sandwich. He mixed some nuts, apples, and spices with some wine, and put it between two matzohs (pieces of flat bread).

6th – 16th Century
People used bread as plates. They put meat and vegetables onto some bread and ate with their fingers. These were the first open sandwiches, and they called them 'trenchers'.

18th Century
The name 'sandwich' first appeared. An Englishman, John Montague (1718–1792), the Fourth Earl of *Sandwich, liked to eat and gamble at London's Beef Steak Club. Sometimes he stayed 24 hours at the gaming table. He was hungry, but he didn't want to stop gambling, so the chefs from the club put some beef between two pieces of bread, and he ate while he gambled. This new meal became very fashionable with other men in the club, and they called it the 'sandwich' after the Earl.

* Sandwich is a town in the South of England.

19th Century
An American writer, Eliza Leslie, introduced sandwiches to America. In 1837, she wrote a cookbook, 'Directions for Cookery'. In it she had a recipe for ham sandwiches: 'Cut some thin slices of bread and ham. Butter the bread and put the ham between two slices with some mustard. Eat for lunch or supper.' Americans loved them.

20th – 21st Century
Sandwiches became very popular indeed. They were easy to make and they were a wonderful, cheap, portable meal for workers and school children.

Did you know...?

The 'Dagwood' sandwich is the sandwich to top all sandwiches. It is enormous! Named after the American cartoon character Dagwood Bumstead, it is made with a great many layers of meat, cheese, tomatoes, egg, salad, and vegetables.

LISTENING

5 Believe it or not, there is a *World Sandwich Week*! In a survey, people were asked, *What's your favourite sandwich?*

T 8.9 Listen and complete the chart with words from the box.

bacon	beef	cheese	chips	fish fingers
~~ham~~	onions	sugar	tomatoes	peanut butter
~~mustard~~	mackerel	olives	basil	

What's your favourite sandwich?

Angus from the North
ham and mustard

Ulla from Denmark
_____

Tom from London
_____

Marianne in Italy
_____

John in Turkey
_____

6 What is your favourite sandwich? Discuss with the class.

What do you think?

- Which of the sandwiches in exercise 5 would you like to try?
- Do you eat sandwiches often? When?
- What are the most popular sandwiches in your country?

Unit 8 • Eat in or out? 67

VOCABULARY AND PRONUNCIATION
Daily needs

1 Match the words from the shopping list with the pictures.

SHOPPING LIST
- n aspirin
- __ chocolate
- __ notebook
- __ scissors
- __ adaptor
- __ envelopes
- __ plasters
- __ sellotape
- __ toothpaste
- __ shampoo
- __ batteries
- __ screwdriver
- __ magazine
- __ newspaper

2 **T 8.10** Listen to the words. Write them in the correct column.

••	••	•••	•••	•••
aspirin				

T 8.10 Listen again, and repeat the words.

3 Of course you can buy all the things in the pictures in a supermarket, but which High Street shops can you buy them in?

| newsagent's   hardware shop   chemist's   stationer's |

You can buy an adaptor in a hardware shop.

68 Unit 8 • Eat in or out?

EVERYDAY ENGLISH
Shopping in the High Street

1 **T 8.11** Listen and complete the conversations with the words in the boxes.

1 | too many   ~~sort~~   all   enough |

   A I'd like some batteries, please.
   B What _sort_ do you want?
   A AA, please.
   B Would you like a packet of four or six?
   A Six is _____. Four is _____.
   B Anything else?
   A That's _____, thanks.

2 | too big   large   else |

   C Can I have some toothpaste, please?
   D Small or _____?
   C The large is _____. The small is fine.
   D Anything _____?
   C No, thanks. How much is that?

3 | too much   better   only |

   E I'm looking for a nice pen.
   F What about this one? It's £25.
   E No, that's _____. I don't want to spend that much.
   F Well, this one is £12.
   E That's _____. And I need some pencils as well.
   F There are ten pencils in this packet.
   E But I _____ want two!
   F I'm afraid I only have packets of ten. Sorry.

2 Work with a partner. Learn two of the conversations. Act them in front of the class.

3 Have similar conversations using other things on the shopping list on p68.

Sounding polite

4 **T 8.12** Listen, and look at these lines of conversation in a café. Which sound more polite?

I'd like a coffee, please.   Can I have a sandwich?
I want a latte.   A cup of tea.
Give me some cake with that!   Could you bring me a smoothie?

5 Complete the conversation in a café.

   A Hi! What can I get you?
   B _I'd like_ a latte, please.
   A Sure. Have in or take away?
   B Have in.
   A And what size do you want? Small, medium, or large?
   B _____, please.
   A Would you like anything to eat? A croissant? Some toast?
   B _____ some toast, please?
   A No problem.
   B _____ some honey with the toast?
   A Sure. Take a seat and I'll bring it over.

T 8.13 Listen and compare. Practise the conversation. Try to sound polite.

6 Have similar conversations in a café with different things to eat and drink.

9 City living

Comparative and superlative adjectives • *have got*
Town and country • Directions

The Eiffel Tower, Paris
The Gherkin, London

STARTER

1 Think of a town or city in your country. Say where it is.
   It's in the north/south/east/west   ... near the mountains/sea   ... on the River ...

2 **T 9.1** Listen to the descriptions of two cities. Which cities are they?

LONDON AND PARIS
Comparative adjectives

1 **T 9.2** Read and listen to the conversation.

> A Which do you prefer, London or Paris?
> B Well, I'm from Paris, so of course I love Paris.
> A London's a lot **bigger than** Paris.
> B It's true. Paris is much **smaller**, but it's **more romantic**!
> A Yes, this is what people say.
> B And the food is **better**.
> A Well, I'm not so sure about that ...

Practise the conversation. What are the differences between London and Paris? **London's bigger than Paris.**

GRAMMAR SPOT

1 Regular comparative adjectives add *-er* or *more*. Write the comparative forms.
   big **bigger**   romantic _____   small _____
   What are the rules? When do we add *-er*? When do we use *more*?

2 Some adjectives are irregular.   good **better**   bad _____

▶▶ Grammar Reference 9.1 p140

2 What is the comparative form of the adjectives in the box?
   tall – taller   expensive – more expensive

   | ~~tall~~ ~~expensive~~ hot cheap nice wet warm cold polite beautiful bad good |

Work with a partner. Test each other on the comparative forms. Check the spelling.

3 Look at the pictures of London and Paris. Compare the two cities. Use *I think* … and the adjectives from exercise 2.
- the Eiffel Tower/the Gherkin
  I think the Eiffel Tower is taller than the Gherkin.
- the Métro/the Underground – €€€? £££?
  I think the Métro is …
- the weather – warm? wet?
  I think it's …
- the buildings
  I think the buildings …
- the people
  I think the people …

T 9.3 Listen and compare. Practise the lines.

4 **T 9.4** Listen to Rob, an Englishman who lives and works in Paris. Complete his sentences.

1 The Métro is _cheaper_ and _easier_ to use than the Underground.
2 Paris is certainly _____ than London.
3 Paris, in fact, is _____ than London; but in London there are _____ wet days.
4 The architecture in Paris is _____ _____, but the buildings in London are _____ _____.
5 Life is _____ in London.
6 Londoners are generally _____ _____ than Parisians.
7 People in London work _____ and they earn _____.
8 In Paris, having a good time is _____ _____.

5 Work with a partner. Close your books. Try to remember what Rob said.

PRACTICE

Comparing cities

1 Complete the conversations using the comparative form of the adjectives.

1 A New York is _older_ _than_ London. (old)
  B No, it isn't! New York is much _more_ _modern_! (modern)
2 A Tokyo is _____ _____ Bangkok. (cheap)
  B No, it isn't! Tokyo's much _____ _____! (expensive)
3 A Seoul is _____ _____ Beijing. (big)
  B No, it isn't! Seoul is much _____! (small)
4 A Johannesburg is _____ _____ Cape Town. (safe)
  B No, it isn't! It's much _____ _____! (dangerous)
5 A Taxi drivers in New York are _____ _____ taxi drivers in London. (good)
  B No, they aren't! They're much _____! (bad)

T 9.5 Listen and check.

2 Work with a partner. Practise the conversations in exercise 1. Be careful with stress and intonation.

New York is much more modern!

3 Work in small groups. Compare two capital cities you know.

… is bigger than …   … is nearer the …   …, but … is safer …

Unit 9 • City living 71

A PARISIAN IN LONDON
have got

1 **T 9.6** Listen to Chantal, a French woman. Where does she live and work? Is she married?

2 **T 9.6** Listen again and complete the questions and answers. Practise them with a partner.

Hi! I'm Chantal! I've got a good job in a bank.

Q <u>Have</u> you <u>got</u> a flat?
C We _____ a nice flat in Camden.
Q _____ André _____ a job?
C He _____ a shop in Camden. He sells French cheese!
Q _____ you _____ a car?
C No, I _____ a car. I go everywhere on public transport. It's much easier.

> **GRAMMAR SPOT**
>
> 1 *Have* and *have got* both express possession.
>   We use *have got* more in spoken English.
>
>   I **have** a good job. = I**'ve got** a good job.
>   **Do** you **have** a nice flat? = **Have** you **got** a nice flat?
>   She **doesn't have** a car. = She **hasn't got** a car.
>
> 2 The past of *have* and *have got* is *had*.
>   I **had** a boring job, so I left.
>
> ▶▶ Grammar Reference 9.2 p140

3 Rewrite the sentences with *have got*.
  1 We have a nice flat.
  2 I have a French husband.
  3 He has a business in Camden.
  4 Do you have a lot of friends?
  5 How many brothers and sisters do you have?
  6 I don't have any brothers. I have a sister called Natalie.
  7 Natalie has a big house.
  8 You have a good English accent.

T 9.7 Listen and check. Read the sentences aloud.

I've got a bigger house than you!

4 Work with a partner. Imagine you're both millionaires. Who's got the best house?
  Student A Look at p150.
  Student B Look at p153.

> *I've got a bigger house than you!*
>
> *I don't think so. I've got ten bedrooms!*
>
> *That's nothing! I've got eight bedrooms on the first floor, and . . .*

72 Unit 9 • City living

London's

Superlative adjectives

1 Look at the introduction to the text about Camden Market. Complete the chart.

Adjectives	Superlatives
1 big	biggest
2 popular	_____
3 busy	_____
4 good	_____

2 Read the rest of the text. Complete it with the adjective in the superlative.

3 What's special about …?
  • Camden   It's got the largest street market in the UK.
  • the weekend   • the food   • the clothes
  • the Electric Ballroom   • Proud

T 9.8 Listen and check.

> **GRAMMAR SPOT**
>
> 1 Look at the superlatives in exercise 1. What are the rules?
>
> 2 What are the comparative and superlative forms of these adjectives?
>
>   small   expensive   hot
>   easy   beautiful
>
> ▶▶ Grammar Reference 9.1 p140

biggest market

CAMDEN MARKET

The biggest and most popular market in London takes place every day in Camden, but it is busiest and best at the weekend.

Camden is famous all over the world for its fashion, artists, clubs, and music, but it is ¹_____ (famous) for its market. It is the ²_____ (large) street market in the UK.

More than 400,000 people come every weekend to look, shop, eat, and meet friends. There is music everywhere. The street food is delicious, and it is the ³_____ (cheap) in north London.

In every part of the market you find something interesting. It has the ⁴_____ (amazing) clothes, beautiful jewellery, music, and tattoo shops.

The Electric Ballroom is the ⁵_____ (old) nightclub in Camden. You can hear the ⁶_____ (late) rock bands before they become famous. There are hundreds of clubs, but Proud is one of the ⁷_____ (cool).

Camden Market rocks!

PRACTICE

It's the biggest!

1 Complete these sentences with a superlative adjective.
 1 The _tallest_ building in London is Canary Wharf. It's 235 metres.
 2 The _____ hotel is the Lanesborough. It costs £7,000 per night!
 3 The _____ park in central London is Hyde Park. It's 142 hectares.
 4 The _____ tourist attraction is the London Eye. It has 10,000 visitors a day.
 5 The _____ building is Buckingham Palace. Everyone knows who lives there.
 6 The _____ restaurant for spotting celebrities is *The Ivy*. They all go there.

T 9.9 Listen and check. Make sentences about your town.

Making comparisons

2 Complete the sentences with an opposite comparative adjective.
 1 The music here is too **loud**. Can we go somewhere _quieter_ ?
 2 The 10.00 train is too **slow**. Is the 11.30 train a _____ one?
 3 You're **late**. Why weren't you here _____ ?
 4 This flat is too **far** from the town centre. I need somewhere _____ .
 5 Five minutes is too **short** for a break. We need a _____ one.
 6 This exercise is too **easy**. Can I do something _____ ?

Check it

3 Tick (✓) the correct sentence.
 1 ☐ Yesterday was more hot than today.
    ☐ Yesterday was hotter than today.
 2 ☐ She's taller than her brother.
    ☐ She's taller that her brother.
 3 ☐ I am the most young in the class.
    ☐ I am the youngest in the class.
 4 ☐ This exercise is most difficult in the book.
    ☐ This exercise is the most difficult in the book.
 5 ☐ I've got three sisters.
    ☐ I got three sisters.
 6 ☐ Do you got any money?
    ☐ Have you got any money?
 7 ☐ She hasn't got a good job.
    ☐ She no got a good job.

Unit 9 • City living 73

READING AND LISTENING
Megacities

1 Look at the list of cities. Put them in order of size of population: 1 = the biggest.
- ☐ Mumbai   ☐ Shanghai   ☐ Tokyo
- ☐ New York   ☐ Mexico City

T 9.10 Listen. Were you right? What is a megacity? What happened in 2008?

2 Look at the photos. What can you see? Look at the title of each article. Which city …?
- is very fast   • has a mix of cultures   • has a lot of poverty

3 Work in three groups.

Group A   Read about **Tokyo**.
Group B   Read about **Mumbai**.
Group C   Read about **Mexico City**.

Make notes about your city under these headings:

> The city and its people
> Money and business
> Buildings and history
> Climate
> Transport

4 Work with students from the other two groups. Exchange and compare information about the cities.

Listening

5 **T 9.11** Listen to these people from the three megacities. What do they like about their capital city? What do they say about …?
- the people   • the climate   • transport   • things to do

Makiko from Tokyo

Vimahl from Mumbai

Lourdes from Mexico City

Project

Research another megacity. Make some notes. Present your findings to the rest of the class.

74 Unit 9 • City living

HIGH-SPEED TOKYO

Tokyo has a population of 35 million people. It is the largest city in the world. It is also one of the most exciting. Everything moves fast here. It has one of the biggest and busiest railway systems in the world. Every day, 11 million commuters use it to get to and from work. People earn the highest salaries, and they spend the most money. They wear the latest fashions, and have the most up-to-date phones. It is the world's most expensive city.

Old and new

Tokyo was originally a small fishing village called Edo. The name changed in 1868 when the Emperor moved there.
The architecture is very modern. There are not many old buildings because of the 1923 earthquake and the Second World War. But traditional Japan is always near, with many Shinto shrines and public baths around the city.

Visiting Tokyo

Tokyo is on the east coast of Japan. The summers are hot and humid. The most beautiful time of year is spring, when the famous cherry blossom is on the trees.
The city is huge, but it is one of the safest cities in the world.
Japan is mysterious. It is difficult for foreigners to understand.

MUMBAI
A CITY OF EXTREMES

Mumbai is India's largest city with a population of 22.8 million. It is also India's most important commercial centre. Mumbai was part of the British Empire until independence in 1947. It was called Bombay until 1995, when it was renamed Mumbai after a Hindu goddess, Mumba Devi.

Rich and poor

Mumbai is both old and modern, rich and poor. The streets are full of people doing business, selling snacks and clothes, or just living there.

Money is everywhere in modern Mumbai. India's most important businesses and banks have their headquarters there. The Bollywood film industry produces more films than Hollywood in Los Angeles.

Modern skyscrapers and new shopping malls are right next to slums. Sixty percent of the population live with no running water, no electricity, and no sanitation.

Visiting Mumbai

Mumbai is on the west coast. The wet season is from June to September. Between November and February it is a little cooler and dryer.

The city is best at sunrise and sunset, when the colour of the stone buildings changes from gold to orange and pink. The cheapest and easiest transport is by bus. Trains can be crowded and dangerous.

Because of its poverty, Mumbai can be a difficult place to live, but the experience is unique.

MULTICULTURAL MEXICO CITY

Mexico City has a population of 23.4 million. It is the largest city in both North and South America. The Aztecs called it Tenochtitlan, and it was already an important city when the Spanish invaded in 1521. The country became independent in 1821.

Indian and European

Mexico City offers a variety of experiences. In the Zócalo, the main square, you can see the Spanish cathedral, an Aztec temple, and a modern skyscraper. The city has a lot of museums and theatres. European squares and colonial houses sit next to busy markets selling Mexican food and Indian handicrafts.

It is the richest city in Latin America. There are elegant shops selling high-class goods, expensive restaurants, and supercool bars. There are also many people who live in poor houses.

Visiting Mexico City

Mexico City is in a valley in the south central area of the country. It is surrounded by mountains.

The rainy season is from June to October. The warmest months are April and May. It has the largest and cheapest subway system in Latin America. Traffic moves so slowly that it is often faster to walk. The air quality is not good, and visitors need to be careful, but the city offers a rich cultural mix.

VOCABULARY AND SPEAKING

Town and country

1. Look at the pictures. Which is the town? Which is the village?

2. Find the words in the box in the pictures.

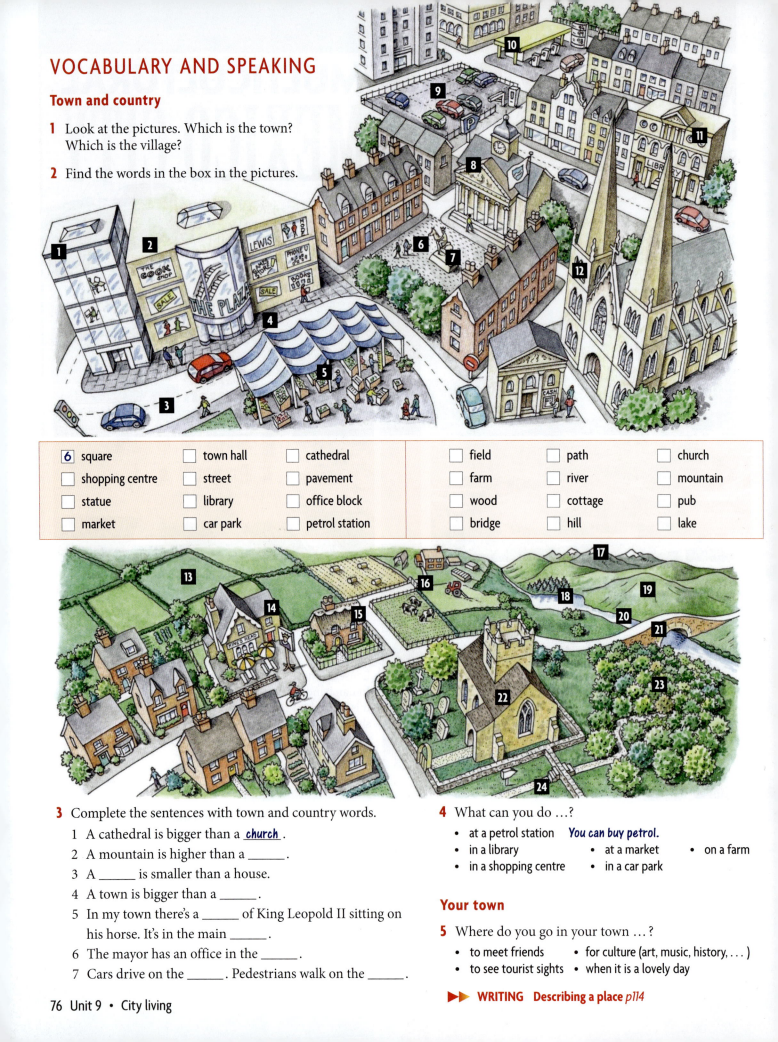

☑ 6 square	☐ town hall	☐ cathedral	☐ field	☐ path	☐ church
☐ shopping centre	☐ street	☐ pavement	☐ farm	☐ river	☐ mountain
☐ statue	☐ library	☐ office block	☐ wood	☐ cottage	☐ pub
☐ market	☐ car park	☐ petrol station	☐ bridge	☐ hill	☐ lake

3. Complete the sentences with town and country words.
   1. A cathedral is bigger than a _church_.
   2. A mountain is higher than a _____.
   3. A _____ is smaller than a house.
   4. A town is bigger than a _____.
   5. In my town there's a _____ of King Leopold II sitting on his horse. It's in the main _____.
   6. The mayor has an office in the _____.
   7. Cars drive on the _____. Pedestrians walk on the _____.

4. What can you do …?
   - at a petrol station   _You can buy petrol._
   - in a library   • at a market   • on a farm
   - in a shopping centre   • in a car park

Your town

5. Where do you go in your town …?
   - to meet friends   • for culture (art, music, history, …)
   - to see tourist sights   • when it is a lovely day

▶▶ **WRITING** Describing a place p114

76 Unit 9 • City living

EVERYDAY ENGLISH
Directions

1. Look at the map of Kingston. Find these things.

   | a roundabout | traffic lights | a pedestrian crossing | a traffic sign |

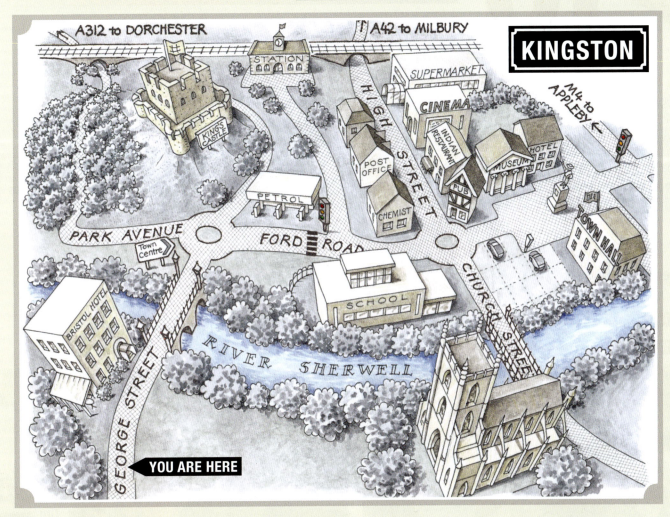

2. **T 9.12** Listen. Complete the directions from **YOU ARE HERE** to the A312 to Dorchester. Use the prepositions.

   | over | ~~along~~ | past | round | up | down | through | under |

   Go _along_ George Street, _____ the Bristol Hotel on your left, and _____ the bridge. At the roundabout, turn left and go _____ Park Avenue. Go _____ the corner, _____ the wood, and _____ the hill. Then go _____ the railway bridge and you are on the A312 to Dorchester.

3. **T 9.13** Start from **YOU ARE HERE**. Listen to the directions. Where do you finish?

   1 _____   2 _____   3 _____

4. Work in pairs. Ask for and give directions to …
   - the railway station
   - the M4 to Appleby
   - a supermarket
   - the Town Hall
   - the church
   - a chemist's
   - a car park
   - the A42 to Milbury

   > Excuse me! Can you tell me how to get to … ?

   > Is there a … near here?

5. Give directions to places in your town from your school.

   > Go out of the school. Turn right and …

Unit 9 • City living 77

10 Where on earth are you?

Present Continuous • something/nothing… • Describing people
Social expressions (2)

STARTER

Work with a partner. Which preposition *in*, *at*, or *on* goes with these places?   at a party   in a meeting

| a party | a meeting | my car | work | my way home | the train | bed | holiday | a café | home |
| the airport | the bus stop | my office | town | the pub | school | university | the kitchen | Jenny's house | the bus |

I'M SITTING ON THE TRAIN
Present Continuous

1 **T 10.1** Look at the pictures. Listen. Who is speaking?   *I'm cooking.*   1 Fiona   2 _____   3 _____   4 _____

2 **T 10.2** Listen and complete the conversations. Practise them with a partner.

Tony Hello?
Nina Hi, Tony! It's Nina. Where are you?
Tony We're on the train. We're going to Birmingham for the weekend.
Nina Oh, great! How's the journey?
Tony Fine. I _____ the paper and Alice _____ something on her laptop …

Fiona Hello?
Pete Fiona, hi! It's Pete. How are you? What _____ you _____?
Fiona Fine. We're at home. I _____ just _____ some dinner.
Pete What _____ Tim _____?
Fiona He _____ the football. Can't you hear?
Pete Ah, right!

3 Ask and answer questions about the people in the pictures.
• What/doing?   • Where/going?   • What/cooking?   • What/watching?

T 10.3 Listen and check.

78 Unit 10 • Where on earth are you?

Negatives

4 Look at the picture of Beth and Ellie.

T 10.4 Listen to Beth's phone conversation with her father. Is she telling the truth?

What *is* the truth?

They aren't sitting in Ellie's bedroom.
They … working …   She isn't …   … aren't …

5 **T 10.5** Listen to six false sentences about Alice, Tony, Fiona, Tim, Beth, and Ellie. Correct them.
   1 'Alice is sleeping.'
   Alice isn't sleeping! She's working on her laptop!

GRAMMAR SPOT

1 The Present Continuous (*to be* + *-ing*) describes activities happening now.
2 Complete the chart.

I	_____	
You	_____	learning English.
He/She	_____	sitting in a classroom.
We	_____	listening to the teacher.
They	_____	

What are the questions and the negatives?

3 What's the difference between these sentences?
   She **speaks** Spanish.   She**'s speaking** Spanish.
▶▶ Grammar Reference 10.1 – 10.2 p141

PRACTICE

Questions and negatives

1 Look at the replies. Use the verbs to make the questions.

1 (read) What are you reading? — A romance.
2 (watch) _____? — The news.
3 (go) _____? — To my bedroom.
4 (talk to) _____? — My girlfriend.
5 (wear) _____? — Jeans and a T-shirt.
6 (cry) _____? — Because it's a sad film.

2 Make a negative sentence about each picture in exercise 1.
   1 She/a detective story   She isn't reading a detective story.
   2 He/a film
   3 He/out with his friends
   4 He/his mother
   5 She/a dress
   6 She/a romantic comedy

Talking about you

3 Write sentences that are true for you at the moment.
   1 I/learn/English   I'm learning English.
   2 We/learn/Chinese
   3 I/sit next to a clever student
   4 It/rain
   5 The teacher/talk to us
   6 The students/listen to the teacher

4 Look out of the window of your classroom. What can you see? What's happening?   Some people are walking in the street.
   Nothing's happening.

Unit 10 • Where on earth are you?

PRESENT SIMPLE OR CONTINUOUS?
Who's who?

1 **T 10.6** Listen to a man and a woman talking about the people in the room. Write the names in the boxes.

2 **T 10.6** Listen again and complete the chart.

	What's he/she doing?	What does he/she do?
Paul	He's talking to Sophie.	He's a banker. He works in New York.
Sophie		
Helena		
Roger		
Sam and Penny		

3 Complete the two questions about the people.

1 Where _does_ Paul _work_ ?   *In New York.*
   Who _'s_ he _talking_ to?   *Sophie.*

2 Why _____ Sophie _____?   *Because Paul is funny.*
   Where _____ she _____?   *At Bristol University.*

3 What _____ Helena _____?   *Champagne.*
   What _____ she _____?   *Stories for children.*

4 Who _____ Roger _____ for?   *The British Museum.*
   What _____ he _____?   *Crisps.*

5 What _____ Sam and Penny _____?   *Clothes for kids.*
   What _____ they _____ at?   *A photo on Sam's phone.*

4 Put the verbs in **bold** in the Present Simple or Continuous.

work

1 My father _____ in a bank.
2 I _____ very hard at the moment. I need the money.

go

3 Hi, Dave! Are you on the train? Where _____ you _____?
4 I always _____ to the cinema every Friday.

have

5 Let's have lunch tomorrow. I usually _____ lunch at 1.00.
6 I'm sorry! _____ you _____ lunch? I'll phone you back later.

do/make

7 Sh! I _____ my homework. You _____ too much noise!
8 In my house, my mum usually _____ the dinner, and my dad usually _____ the washing-up.

SOMETHING'S HAPPENING
something/nothing ...

1 Look at the pictures. Complete the sentences with the words in the box.

| anything | something | nothing | everything |

1 He's doing _____ on the computer.
2 He isn't wearing _____.
3 She's buying _____.
4 'What are you having for breakfast?'
   '_____. I'm not hungry.'

GRAMMAR SPOT
Complete the chart.

some	any	every	no
something	_____	_____	_____
somebody	anybody	_____	nobody
_____	anywhere	everywhere	_____

▶▶ Grammar Reference 10.3 p141

2 Underline the correct word.
1 I'm hungry. I want *something* / *anything* to eat.
2 I can't find my phone *nowhere* / *anywhere*.
3 *Anybody's* / *Everybody's* enjoying the party!
4 Oh, dear! I don't know *anybody* / *somebody*.
5 The lights are off. *Nobody's* / *Somebody's* at home.
6 My brother is so intelligent. He knows *nothing* / *everything*!

PRACTICE
Everything was too expensive!

1 Complete the conversations with words from the boxes.

1 | everything   nothing   ~~anything~~   something |

A Did you buy *anything* at the shops?
B No. _____.
A Why not?
B _____ was too expensive.
A What a pity!
B But I bought _____ for you. Happy Birthday!

2 | nobody   anybody   somebody   everybody |

C Did you talk to _____ interesting at the party?
D No. _____.
C Why not?
D _____ was dancing and the music was really loud!
C Oh!
D But I danced with _____ beautiful – a girl called Kate.

3 | somewhere   everywhere   anywhere   nowhere |

E Did you go _____ on Saturday night?
F No. _____.
E Why not?
F _____ was closed. There wasn't one club open.
E That's incredible!
F So next weekend I'm going _____ more interesting.

T 10.7 Listen and check.

2 In pairs, learn two of the conversations. Act them to the class.

Check it

3 Tick (✓) the correct sentence.
1 ☐ Anybody is on the phone for you.
  ☐ Somebody is on the phone for you.
2 ☐ I don't have anything for your birthday.
  ☐ I don't have nothing for your birthday.
3 ☐ I want to go somewhere hot for my holidays.
  ☐ I want to go everywhere hot for my holidays.
4 ☐ I learning English.
  ☐ I'm learning English.
5 ☐ She isn't working hard.
  ☐ She is no working hard.

READING AND LISTENING
The International Space Station

1 Look at the pictures. Talk about what you can see.

2 Read the first part of the article on this page. Are the sentences true (✓) or false (✗)? Correct the false ones.
   1 The ISS is flying very fast.
   2 It's flying a long way from Earth.
   3 It goes round the Earth every 90 minutes.
   4 New supplies arrive once a month.
   5 The Americans are competing against Russians and Europeans.
   6 They are doing a lot of scientific experiments.
   7 They are learning about the Earth and its history.
   8 They are looking for life on other planets.

3 Imagine you are talking to one of the astronauts. What questions would you like to ask him/her?
   - work every day?
   - wake up?
   - free time?
   - eat?
   - sleep?
   - wash?
   - exercise?

4 Read the rest of the article on page 83. Did you find answers to your questions?

5 What is the future of the ISS?

6 What do these numbers from the article refer to?

| 100 billion | 1998 | six | 200 | 15 | eight | zero |

Listening

7 **T 10.8** Listen to the interview with Soichi Noguchi, an ISS astronaut who is on board the space station. Answer the questions.
   1 Who does he work for?
   2 What did he study? Where?
   3 Where is he from? Is he married?
   4 What are his interests on Earth?
   5 What is he doing on the space station?
   6 What does he do when he isn't working?
   7 What does he think about?

Project

Find out who is on board the ISS at the moment. Choose one of the astronauts and do some research. Answer some of the questions from exercise 7 about them.

Tell the rest of the class.

LIVING

A science laboratory 360 kilometres from Earth? A preparation for a flight to Mars? A cathedral in the sky? The International Space Station, or ISS, is all of these.

At this very moment, the ISS is orbiting the Earth at a distance of 360 kilometres. It is flying at 28,000 km/hr. It goes round the Earth 16 times a day. It took more than $100 billion and 14 years to develop. It is the most expensive thing ever built.

The station
The first part of the station went into space in 1998. Astronauts started to live on it in November 2000. There are usually three astronauts on board, and they stay for about six months at a time. Over the years there have been over 200 visitors from 15 different countries. Supply ships arrive about eight times a year.

Aims
Space agencies in the United States, Russia, Japan, Canada, and Europe are working together. They are using the zero gravity of space to do experiments in biology, physics, and astronomy. They are learning about living in space over a long time, and the effects of this on the human body. The astronauts are growing plants to make oxygen. They are studying the Earth's weather and geography. And they are looking at planets and stars to understand the origin of the universe.

IN SPACE

An astronaut's day

Astronauts work for ten hours a day during the week and five hours on Saturday. The rest of the time they are free.

They wake up at 6.00 and have breakfast. There is a meeting, and they decide the day's plans. They have an hour for lunch, then more work till dinner at 7.00. Lights out is at 9.30. They do two hours' exercise every day, because weightlessness affects the body's muscles and bones.

Food

There isn't a real kitchen, but there is a kitchen table. All food comes in tins or packets. There is fresh fruit only when a supply ship comes.

Astronauts eat with a spoon. It is a good idea to have food with a sauce so that it stays on the spoon and doesn't float away! They like spicy food because in space the sense of taste isn't very strong.

Personal lives

They have their own sleeping compartment. They sleep in bags attached to the wall. Because there is no up or down in space, they sleep 'standing up'. They have their own clothes and books and laptops. The temperature is always 72°F, so astronauts usually wear shorts and a T-shirt.

There isn't a shower, but there are two toilets. In their free time they send emails home, read, and play games. But what they like to do best is look out of the windows at Earth below.

Future of the ISS

The ISS is the first of many space stations. There isn't a date yet for a manned trip to Mars, but space agencies are already talking about it. One thing is sure – at some time in the 21st century it will certainly happen.

VOCABULARY AND LISTENING
Describing people

1 **T 10.9** Look at the pictures. Listen to four descriptions. Who is being described?

2 Work in groups. Describe the people in the pictures.

Who …?
- is pretty
- is handsome
- isn't very tall
- is good-looking
- is tall

Who's got …?
- long hair
- blond hair
- red hair
- blue eyes
- short hair
- dark hair
- brown eyes

Who's wearing …?
- a suit
- a hat
- trainers
- a scarf
- a T-shirt
- a dress
- shoes
- jeans
- glasses
- a coat
- boots
- a shirt and tie
- shorts

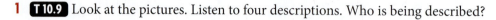

3 Take turns. Choose a person in the pictures, but don't say who it is. Describe him/her to your group. Can they guess who it is?

4 Work as a class. Take turns. Choose someone in the room but don't say who it is. Ask and answer *Yes/No* questions to find out who it is.

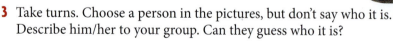

- Is it a boy or a girl?
- Is she sitting near the window?
- Is she wearing trainers?

The famous person game!

5 In your groups, think of someone in the news at the moment. The other groups ask questions until they guess the name.

- Is he an actor?
- Does he work on TV?
- Is he very good-looking?

▶▶ **WRITING** Comparing and contrasting *p115*

EVERYDAY ENGLISH
Social expressions (2)

1 Look at the pictures and the first lines of the conversations. What do you think are the replies?

A Patrick and I are getting married.
B Wow! That's fantastic! Congratulations!

C Can I help you?
D _____

E Don't forget it's a bank holiday on Monday.
F _____

G We're going to the cinema tonight.
H _____

I Excuse me! This machine isn't working.
J _____

K Hi. Can I speak to Dave, please?
L _____

M Thanks for the invitation to your party, but I'm afraid I can't come.
N _____

O/P Bye! Have a safe journey!
Q/R _____

2 Match these replies to the lines in exercise 1.

> I'm sorry. Let me have a look. Ah! It isn't switched on. That's why!
>
> What a pity! Never mind!
>
> Sorry, what does that mean?
>
> ~~Wow! That's fantastic! Congratulations!~~
>
> I'm afraid he isn't here at the moment. Can I take a message?
>
> No, I'm just looking, thanks.
>
> Thanks. We'll see you in a couple of days!
>
> Oh, lovely! Well, I hope you enjoy the film!

T 10.10 Listen and check. What are the extra lines in the conversations?

3 Work with a partner. Choose some conversations and practise them.

Unit 10 • Where on earth are you? 85

11 Going far

going to future • Infinitive of purpose • What's the weather like?
Making suggestions

STARTER

How many sentences can you make?

I'm going to India	soon.
I went to India	when I was a student.
	next month.
	in a year's time.
	two years ago.
	when I retire.

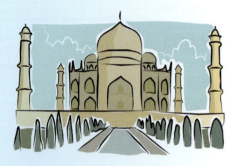

PLANNING MY FUTURE
going to

1 Look at the pictures. What are the people doing? What are they thinking about?

Alan — 'When I get home ...'

Brendan — 'When I get a pay rise ...'

George — 'When I retire ...'

Leila — 'When I arrive on Koh Samui island ...'

Yvonne — 'When the kids are in bed ...'

86 Unit 11 • Going far

2 Whose future plans are these? Match them with the people in exercise 1.

1 Alan   'I'm going to relax with my wife.'
2 _____ 'I'm going to be a racing driver.'
3 _____ 'I'm going to sit down and have a glass of wine.'

Complete these plans. Whose are they?

4 _____ '… buy my girlfriend a ring.'
5 _____ '… lie on the beach.'
6 _____ '… learn to play golf.'
7 _____ '… meet my friends for coffee.'

T 11.1 Listen and check.

Jason

'When I grow up …'

Ayesha

'When this lesson ends …'

3 **T 11.2** Listen and repeat. Then ask and answer questions about *all* the people with a partner.

> What's Alan going to do?
> He's going to relax.
> What's Jason going to do?
> He's going to be a racing driver.

4 **T 11.3** What *aren't* the people going to do? Listen, then talk to a partner about them.

> Alan isn't going to talk about work. He's going to relax.

Talking about you

5 Work in small groups. What are you going to do after the lesson? Ask and answer questions.

- watch TV
- have a coffee
- see your friends
- cook a meal
- do some shopping
- wash your hair
- do your homework
- go on the Internet

> Are you going to watch TV?
> Yes, I am.
> No, I'm not.

6 Tell the class some of the things you and your partner *are* or *aren't* going to do.

> We're both going to have coffee.
> I'm going to cook, but Anna isn't. She's going to have a pizza.

GRAMMAR SPOT

1 The verb *to be* + *going to* expresses future plans. Complete the chart.

I	_____	
He/She	_____	going to cook tonight.
You/We/They	_____	

2 Make the question and negative.
   What **am** I **going to cook** tonight?

3 Is there any difference in meaning between these sentences?
   I'm leaving tomorrow.   **I'm going to leave** tomorrow.

▶▶ Grammar Reference 11.1 – 11.2 p142

Unit 11 • Going far 87

PRACTICE

Careful! You're going to drop it!

1 Look at the pictures. Write what is going to happen. Use the verbs in the box.

> We also use *going to* when we can see now something that is sure to happen in the future.

drop
have
~~rain~~
sneeze
win
be late
kiss
fall

1. It's going to rain.
2.
3.
4.
5.
6.
7.
8.

T 11.4 Listen and check.

2 Work with a partner. Can you remember the lines? **T 11.4** Listen again. Practise them.

Check it

3 Tick (✓) the correct sentence.
   1. ☐ He's go to watch the football.
      ☐ He's going to watch the football.
   2. ☐ We going to the cinema tonight.
      ☐ We're going to the cinema tonight.
   3. ☐ She isn't going to cook.
      ☐ She no going to cook.
   4. ☐ Is going to rain?
      ☐ Is it going to rain?
   5. ☐ When are they going to get married?
      ☐ When they going to get married?
   6. ☐ I'm going the pub.
      ☐ I'm going to the pub.

a

b

e

f

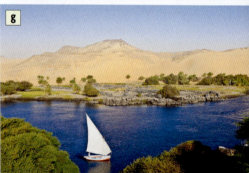
g

h

WE'RE OFF TO SEE THE WORLD!
Infinitive of purpose

GRAMMAR SPOT

1 With the verbs *to go* and *to come*, we usually use the Present Continuous for future plans.

We**'re going to** Egypt soon.   We**'re coming** home in June.
NOT   ~~We're going to go~~ …   ~~We're going to come~~ …

2 Do these sentences mean the same?

We're going to Egypt **to see** the pyramids.
We're going to Egypt **because we want to see** the pyramids.

The infinitive can answer the question *Why …?*

▶▶ Grammar Reference 11.3 p142

1 Match the places and activities. Find them in the photos.

Australia	take a cruise down the River Nile
The US	climb Mount Kilimanjaro
Peru	fly over the coldest place on earth
Antarctica	take photos of Ayers Rock at sunset
Egypt	visit Machu Picchu
Cambodia	go on a tiger safari
Tanzania	see the supervolcano at Yellowstone Park
India	visit the temples of Angkor Wat

2 Rob and Becky are planning a world trip. Complete their conversation with a friend with lines from exercise 1.

Rob   First, we're going to Egypt.
Friend   Why? To see the pyramids?
Becky   Well, yes, but also we want to _____ down the Nile.
Friend   Fantastic! Where are you going after that?
Rob   Well, then we're going to Tanzania to _____ .

T 11.15 Listen and check. Practise the conversation with a partner.

PRACTICE

Listening and speaking

1 **T 11.6** Listen to Rob and Becky's whole conversation. Write down the order of places on their journey.
Egypt, Tanzania, …

2 Talk about their journey. Use *first*, *then*, *next*, *after that*.
First, they're going to Egypt to see the pyramids and to take a cruise down the Nile.
Then, they're …

When …? Why …?

3 Write down the names of some places you went to in the past. Ask and answer questions about the places with a partner.

When did you go to England?   Two years ago.
Why did you go?   To learn English.

Tell the class about your partner.

▶▶ **WRITING**   **T 11.7** Describing a holiday *p116*

Unit 11 • Going far 89

READING AND SPEAKING
Meet Ed, Will, and Ginger

1 **T 11.8** Close your eyes and listen to a traditional folk song. Write down any of the words you remember from it.

2 Look at the photos of three young men.
   - Where are they?
   - What are they wearing?
   - What are they doing?
   - What are they carrying?

3 Read the first part of the text. Correct these false statements.

   1 It's a rainy Sunday morning in Petersfield.
   2 The three young men are carrying suitcases and wearing suits and ties.
   3 They start singing pop songs.
   4 The people of Petersfield aren't interested. They don't stop to listen.
   5 They don't give the men any money.

4 Read the rest of the text. Ask and answer these questions with a partner.

   1 How old are the three young men?
   2 Which two are brothers?
   3 When do they walk? In which seasons?
   4 Where do they sleep?
   5 Where did they meet?
   6 What jobs did they have?
   7 Where do they sing?
   8 What do their families think?
   9 What did they do last year?
   10 What are they going to do this year?

What do you think?
- Will says he doesn't really know why they are walking. Why do you think they are doing it?
- What is meant by 'simple human activities'? Give examples.
- What kind of activities are not so simple?

Roleplay

5 Work with a partner.

   Student A
   You are a newspaper journalist.
   Interview one of the singers.
   Use questions from exercise 4 to help.

   Student B
   You are one of the singers, Will, Ed, or Ginger.
   Answer the journalist's questions.

   What ... your names?
   Why ... in Petersfield?
   How old ... ?

Project

What popular traditional songs are there in your country? Choose your favourite. Does it tell a story? Tell the class.

90 Unit 11 • Going far

It's a sunny Saturday afternoon in the small market town of Petersfield. Three young men arrive in the High Street with backpacks and walking sticks. They're wearing green and brown jackets, hats, and boots. Is it Robin Hood with his Merry Men? Passers-by are interested. Who are these young people? What are they going to do? One of the young men puts his hat down on the pavement, and puts up a sign:

'We're walking to Wales – singing for our supper'

And they start singing. People stop to listen and smile. They are singing in perfect harmony, not pop songs, but traditional folk songs. The hat is soon full, and the people of Petersfield look and feel happier.

Singing

Ed, Will, and Ginger

for their supper

Meet the singers

Ed, 27, his brother Ginger, 25, and their friend Will, 26, are three young men who decided to leave their comfortable homes without any money or mobile phones and walk round the whole of Britain, in all seasons, in good and bad weather. They are singing for their supper and sleeping anywhere they can find, in woods, fields, and sometimes houses – when people offer hospitality.

Ed and Ginger started singing with Will when they were all at school together in Canterbury. After school, Ed went to study art in Paris and London and became an artist; Ginger became a gardener, and Will a bookseller. They were still friends and liked walking together, but weren't very happy with their lives. One day they had an idea. 'Why don't we start walking and just not stop?' And so they did.

They love the freedom and the simple life. Walking and singing are simple human activities in a busy, stressful world. They sing in streets, pubs, and market squares. Sometimes people they meet teach them new songs.

Why are they doing this?

'People ask us why we're doing this, and we don't really have an answer,' says Will. 'It's a great life and we're learning so much on our journey.'

Their families worry about their futures, but they don't. Last year they started a website, www.awalkaroundbritain.com, and they made a CD of 16 of their songs. This year they are going to make podcasts to tell more stories of their walks, and they're going to make another CD. They also plan to start a charity to help traditional country activities. The future looks good.

VOCABULARY AND LISTENING
What's the weather like?

1 Look at the weather map of Europe and name some of the countries.

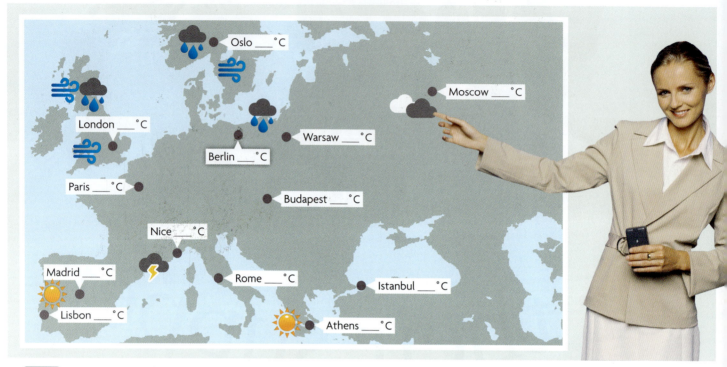

T 11.9 Listen to a weather forecast. Write the temperatures on the map. Which season is it?

2 Match the weather adjectives with their symbols on the map. Which two adjectives are not in the forecast?

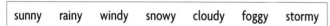

sunny   rainy   windy   snowy   cloudy   foggy   stormy

3 Look at these adjectives. Which words in exercise 2 can they go with? Make some sentences.

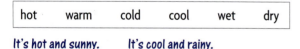

hot   warm   cold   cool   wet   dry

It's hot and sunny.   It's cool and rainy.

> **T 11.10** Listen and repeat the question.
> **What's the weather like?**
> *What ... like?* asks for a description.
> *What's the weather like?* means *Describe the weather*.

4 Work with a partner. Ask and answer questions about the weather. Use sentences from exercise 3 in your answers.

What's the weather like?

It's hot and sunny.

5 **T 11.11** Listen and complete the conversation. Practise it with your partner.

A What's the weather like today?
B It's _____ and _____.
A What was it like yesterday?
B Oh, it was _____ and _____.
A And what's it going to be like tomorrow?
B I think it's going to be _____ and _____.

Ask and answer questions about the weather where you are for today, yesterday, and tomorrow.

6 Work with a new partner to find out about world weather tomorrow.

Student A   Look at p151.
Student B   Look at p154.

Ask and answer questions to complete the information.

What's the weather going to be like in Berlin?

Rainy and cold. Seven degrees.

7 Write a short weather forecast for the coming weekend. Read it to your partner.

EVERYDAY ENGLISH
Making suggestions

1. Make a list of things you can do in good weather and things you can do in bad weather. Compare your list with a partner and the class.

Good weather	Bad weather
play tennis	watch a DVD

2. **T 11.12** Listen and complete the conversations.

   1 **A** What a lovely day!
      B Yeah! It's really _____ and _____. What shall we do?
      A Let's _____!

   2 **A** What an awful day! It's raining again.
      B I know. It's so _____ and _____! What shall we do?
      A Let's _____ and _____.

---

1. We use *shall* with *I* and *we* to ask for and make suggestions.
   What **shall we** do?
   Shall we go swimming? = I suggest that we go swimming.

2. We use *Let's* to make a suggestion for everyone.
   Let's go! = I suggest that we all go. (Let's = Let us)
   Let's have a pizza!

---

3. Continue the two conversations in exercise 2 with these lines in the correct order.

   Oh no, that's boring! We did that last night.
   Oh no! It's too hot to walk.
   OK, let's go to the beach.
   OK then, shall we go out for a coffee?
   Great! I'll get my coat and an umbrella!
   Good idea! Why don't we take a picnic?

   T 11.13 Listen and check. Practise the conversations with your partner.

4. Have more conversations suggesting what to do when the weather is good or bad. Use your lists of activities in exercise 1.

Unit 11 • Going far 93

12 Never ever!

Present Perfect • ever, never, yet, and just • take and get
Transport and travel

STARTER

1 Match the countries and flags. What are their capital cities?

Australia	Hungary
Brazil	Italy
China	Japan
Egypt	Spain
Great Britain	Switzerland
Greece	the US

 a b
 c d
 e f
 g h
 i j
 k l

2 Tick (✓) the countries that you have visited.

BEEN THERE! DONE THAT!
Present Perfect + ever and never

1 **T 12.1** Lara and her friend, Kyle, are from Australia. Listen to their conversation. Answer the questions.
- What are they talking about?
- Who is Mel?
- Why does Lara want to end the conversation?

2 Read these lines from the conversation. Who is each line about, Lara, Kyle, or Mel?
1 I've been to Rome many times. **Kyle**
2 I've never been there.
3 She's been to London and Paris.
4 She hasn't been to Rome.
5 I haven't travelled much at all.
6 I've been to North and South America.

T 12.2 Listen and repeat the lines.

I've = I have   She's = She has

3 Work in groups. Tell each other which countries in the Starter you *have* or *haven't* been to.

> I've been to Hungary, but I've never been to Australia or the US.

> I haven't been to any of those countries!

4 **T 12.3** Listen to the conversation. Complete the replies.

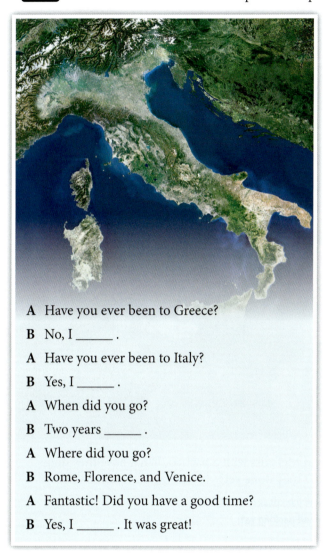

A Have you ever been to Greece?
B No, I _____ .
A Have you ever been to Italy?
B Yes, I _____ .
A When did you go?
B Two years _____ .
A Where did you go?
B Rome, Florence, and Venice.
A Fantastic! Did you have a good time?
B Yes, I _____ . It was great!

Practise the conversation with a partner.

5 Write down the names of two countries or cities. Have similar conversations with your partner.
Start: **Have you ever … ?**

6 Tell the class about your partner.

> Maria's been to Berlin. She went there two years ago.

> Mikel hasn't been to Paris. / He's never been to Paris.

GRAMMAR SPOT

1 The Present Perfect can express experiences.
   I've **been** to Paris.
   Have you **ever** (*at any time in your life*) **been** to Paris?

2 The Past Simple expresses exactly when something happened.
   I **went** to Paris **last year**.
   'When **did** you **go** to Madrid?' 'In 2009.'

3 The Present Perfect is formed with *have/has* + past participle. Complete the charts.

Positive

I/You/We/They	_____	been to Paris.
He/She	_____	

Negative

I/You/We/They	_____	been to Paris.
He/She	_____	

4 Write *ever* and *never* in these sentences.
   Has he _____ been to London?
   He's _____ been to Paris.

▶▶ Grammar Reference 12.1 – 12.2 p142

7 Here are the past participles of some verbs. Write the infinitive. Which two are regular verbs?

been	_____	run	_____
lived	_____	bought	_____
flown	_____	given	_____
met	_____	made	_____
eaten	_____	had	_____
failed	_____	taken	_____
seen	_____	done	_____
slept	_____		

8 What are the Past Simple forms of the verbs in exercise 7?

9 Work with a partner. Take turns to test each other.

> see

> saw, seen

▶▶ Irregular verbs p158

PRACTICE

Talking about you

1. Have you ever done these things in your life?
   - flown in a jumbo jet
   - worked through the night
   - lived in a foreign country
   - seen the sun rise
   - slept in a tent
   - met a famous person
   - run a marathon
   - eaten Chinese food
   - failed an exam

2. Work in small groups. Ask and answer questions.

3. Tell the class about the people in your group.

    José has been to the US. He went to Disneyland with his family.

GETTING READY TO GO!

Present Perfect + *yet* and *just*

1. **T 12.4** Lara and Mel are getting ready for their trip to Europe. Read their 'Things to do' list and listen to their conversation. Tick (✓) the things they have done.

2. Look at Lara and Mel's list with a partner. What have they done and what haven't they done yet?

   They've bought new backpacks.
   They haven't finished packing yet.

   T 12.4 Listen again and check. Practise the conversation.

   ### GRAMMAR SPOT

   1. Complete the sentences.
      1. They _____ finished packing **yet**.
      2. _____ you emailed your aunt **yet**?
      3. She _____ **just** emailed back.

   2. Where do we put *yet* in a sentence? Where do we put *just* in a sentence?

   3. We can only use *yet* with two of the following. Which two?
      ☐ positive sentences   ☐ questions   ☐ negative sentences

   ▶▶ Grammar Reference 12.3 p142

PRACTICE

Tense revision

1 Work with a partner. Read what Lara says about her trip. Put the verbs in brackets in the correct tense.

> I'm really excited about my trip to Europe. I ¹_____ (not travel) much outside Australia before. Just once, two years ago, I ²_____ (go) on holiday to Bali with my family, but I ³_____ (never be) to Europe or the US. I often ⁴_____ (travel) inside Australia. Last year I ⁵_____ (fly) to Perth to visit my cousin, who ⁶_____ (live) there. It's a five-hour flight from Sydney, where I ⁷_____ (live). Australia's a big country! Also, I ⁸_____ (go) up to Cairns in the north three times. I ⁹_____ (learn) to scuba dive there on the Great Barrier Reef.
>
> We ¹⁰_____ (just finish) packing, and now we ¹¹_____ (wait) for the taxi to take us to the airport. I ¹²_____ (never fly) on a 747 before. It's a very long flight. It ¹³_____ (take) 20 hours to get to Rome. I ¹⁴_____ (watch) films all the way. I can't wait!

T 12.5 Listen and check.

2 Answer the questions about Lara. Then ask and answer with a partner.
1. Why is she excited?
2. Has she ever travelled outside Australia?
3. Does she often travel?
4. Why did she go to Perth?
5. Where does Lara live?
6. How many times has she been to Cairns?
7. What did she do there?
8. How are they going to the airport?
9. How long does the flight to Rome take?
10. What is she going to do on the flight?

No, not yet!

3 Work with a partner. Ask and answer the questions about you.
1. check your emails
2. do the shopping
3. wash your hair
4. clean the car
5. make the dinner
6. do the washing-up
7. meet the new student
8. finish the exercise

> Have you checked your emails yet?
>
> Yes, I've just checked them.
>
> No, I haven't. / No, not yet.

T 12.6 Listen and compare. Practise again.

Check it

4 Tick (✓) the correct sentence.
1. ☐ I saw Kyle yesterday.
   ☐ I've seen Kyle yesterday.
2. ☐ Did you ever met my cousin?
   ☐ Have you ever met my cousin?
3. ☐ When did she go to Bali?
   ☐ When has she been to Bali?
4. ☐ What are you going to do in Rome?
   ☐ What do you going to do in Rome?
5. ☐ He doesn't like flying.
   ☐ He isn't liking flying.
6. ☐ Has Lara yet finished packing?
   ☐ Has Lara finished packing yet?
7. ☐ Did you ever been to a rock concert?
   ☐ Have you ever been to a rock concert?

Unit 12 • Never ever! 97

READING AND LISTENING
The Glastonbury festival

1 Have you ever been to a music festival? Where? When? Did you enjoy it?

Have you heard of the Glastonbury Music Festival?

2 **T 12.7** Listen to part of a song called *They can't buy the sunshine*. It was sung at Glastonbury by a group called Turin Brakes.

3 Read the facts about Glastonbury. Answer the questions.
  1 Where and when does Glastonbury take place?
  2 How many hours of music are there every day?
  3 What are some differences between Glastonbury in 1970 and today?
  4 Who do you know from the list of performers? Who do you like?
  5 What happened in 2009?
  6 What happened in 2005? Why is the song *They can't buy the sunshine* a good song for the festival?

I've been to

The world's biggest

Some facts

The festival covers 1,000 acres of farmland in south-west England. It takes place in June and lasts four days.

About 700 acts play on over 80 stages. There is continual music from 9 o'clock in the morning until 6 o'clock the next morning.

1,500 people attended the first festival in September 1970. They paid £1 a ticket. Last year 190,000 people attended. They paid £200 for a ticket.

Hundreds of famous names have performed at Glastonbury: singers such as Paul McCartney, Bruce Springsteen, Robbie Williams, Jay Z, and Amy Winehouse, and bands such as REM, Radiohead, Coldplay, and Arctic Monkeys.

In 2009, news of Michael Jackson's death hit in the middle of the festival. Immediately T-shirts with the slogan 'I was at Glastonbury when Michael Jackson died' were on sale.

The festival is famous for its rain! In 1997, 1998, and 2005 it rained every day, and the festival-goers danced in the mud.

Glastonbury!

open air music festival

Some experiences

Marina M, Scotland 'My first Glastonbury was 2005. The year of rain and MUD! We took off our shoes and danced in it up to our knees! I loved it! I've now been six times! It's always great fun, even though you don't sleep much! This year's festival was fantastic – I didn't want to go home. A definite highlight for me was an Icelandic band called Sigur Rós. I've never heard of them, but I loved their music. And well done for all the toilets this year! Much better!'

Dave Chow, London 'Well, I don't know what to say – my first time, and it was the most amazing experience! I'm now sitting at work thinking about the best four days of my life. We didn't see any rubbish bands, and the DJs rocked all night. We saw the sun rise at 5.15 on Sunday morning – an amazing experience. Only one complaint – there were so many mobile phones. Why? I thought Glasto was about getting away from it all.'

Len Ferris, Gloucester 'I've taken my kids to Glastonbury twice. It really is an education for kids. The atmosphere is amazing. I think this is because of the mix of people of all ages. It's great to see them – from babies, toddlers, and teenagers, to people my parents' age and older. Everyone gets on so well. On Saturday night we watched Radiohead with my 11-year-old son, and the crowd moved back so he could see better. We loved everything.'

Izzi, Christchurch, New Zealand 'This was my first year at Glastonbury. I travelled 10,000 miles to be there. I've been to other festivals in Australia and Europe. I went to the Sonar Festival in Barcelona two years ago – it was brilliant, but I've always wanted to come to Glastonbury. It was amazing. Radiohead was the best thing I have ever seen at a festival ever, and I'm going to come next year if I can. Long live Glastonbury!!'

---

4 Read four people's experiences of Glastonbury very quickly. Answer the questions.
1. Who has been there often?
2. Who has been only once?
3. Which people loved it all?
4. Who had one complaint. What about?
5. Who took his child?
6. Who travelled a long way to get there?

5 Read the experiences again. Are these statements true (✓) or false (✗)? Correct the false ones.
1. **Marina** slept in her tent when it rained.
2. She thought the Icelandic band was very good and the toilets were cleaner.
3. **Dave** stayed up all night listening to the music.
4. He had no complaints. He loved everything and everybody.
5. **Len** loves the festival because it brings people of all ages together.
6. His son couldn't see the stage because of the crowds.
7. **Izzi** has never been to a music festival before.
8. She travelled from Barcelona to be there.

Listening

6 **T 12.8** Listen to two more people, Elsa and Daniel. What do they say about ...?
- the food
- the drink
- the music
- the people

Who had the best experience?

What do you think?

- Why do you think so many people love the Glastonbury experience?
- Why do bands like playing there?
- Would you like to go to Glastonbury? Why/Why not?

VOCABULARY AND SPEAKING
take and *get*

1 The verbs *take* and *get* have a lot of uses in English. Look at these sentences from the experiences at Glastonbury.

> *It **takes place** in June.*   *Everyone **gets on** so **well**.*
> *We **took off** our shoes.*   *I **got** really **bored**.*
> *It **took a long time** to **get to** the stages.*

2 Complete the conversations with an expression from exercise 1 in the correct tense.

A It's really hot in here.
B Why don't you _____ _____ your jumper?

A Is your office near where you live?
B No, it _____ _____ time to _____ _____ work.

A What are your work colleagues like?
B Great! We all _____ _____ really _____ .

A How often are there exhibitions in the museum?
B They _____ _____ regularly, every two months.

A Do you like learning English?
B It's OK, but sometimes I _____ really _____ !

T 12.9 Listen and check. Practise with a partner.

3 Here are some more expressions. Which go with *take* and which with *get*? Complete the chart.

~~a test~~	married	it easy	better soon
home late	photos	ready	a taxi
on/off the bus	a long time	a lot of emails	very wet

take	get
a test	

4 Complete the sentences with *take* or *get* in the correct form.
1 The best way to _____ to the airport is to _____ a taxi.
2 How long _____ it _____ if you go by train?
3 I haven't _____ a camera. I _____ photos with my iPhone.
4 Sue _____ her driving test three times and she's failed every time.
5 Are you still _____ ready? We're going to be so late!
6 The doctor told me to _____ it easy if I want to _____ better soon.
7 It rained on the day we _____ married. We _____ very wet, but still had a great day.
8 You can't _____ on the bus with that big dog. Please, _____ off!

T 12.10 Read the sentences aloud. Then listen and check.

Talking about you

5 Work with a partner. Complete the questions then ask and answer them about you.
1 How long does it _____ you to _____ to school?
2 What time do you _____ back home after school/work?
3 What time do you usually _____ up in the morning?
4 Have you _____ any exams recently?
5 Does it _____ you a long time to _____ ready before you go out?
6 Are you _____ tired of this exercise?

EVERYDAY ENGLISH
Transport and travel

1 Write the words in the chart. Some words can go in more than one column.

airport	railway station	bus stop	flight		bus	train	plane
return ticket	ticket office	platform	departures				
arrivals	customs	hand luggage					
boarding pass	security check						

2 **T 12.11** Listen to three travel announcements. Are they for bus, train, or plane?

3 Listen again. Write down all the numbers you hear. What do they refer to? Which places can you remember?

4 Read these lines. Are they for bus, train, or plane?
1. The number 360 stops near the museum.
2. The platform number has just gone up on the departures board.
3. Does the number 24 go to the Natural History Museum?
4. How many pieces of hand luggage have you got?
5. You board from Gate 9 at 10.20.
6. You'll want a day return.

5 Work with a partner. Put the lines in **A** and **B** in the correct order to make two conversations.

Conversation 1

A	B
☐ At 9.55. The platform number has just gone up on the departures board.	☐ Oh, yes. I can see. Thank you very much.
☑ Next, please!	☐ A day return to Oxford, please.
☐ Have a good journey!	☐ Thank you. What time does the next train leave?
☐ That's £12.70.	

Conversation 2

A	B
☐ Oh, thanks for your help.	☐ From that bus stop over there.
☐ Where can I get it?	☐ Don't mention it.
☐ Excuse me, does the number 24 go to the Natural History Museum?	☐ No, it doesn't. You need the 360.

T 12.12 Listen and check. Practise the conversations with your partner.

6 **T 12.13** Listen and complete this conversation. Where are Lara and Mel?

A Have you _____ _____ online?
M Yes, we have.
A Fine. How many _____ have you got?
L We haven't got _____, just _____.
A Oh, yes. Can you put them on the scales?
M Here you are …
A They're fine. And how many pieces of _____ _____?
L Just these _____.
A They're fine, too. You _____ from Gate 9 at 10.20.
L Where do we go now?
A To the departure gate and _____. They're over there. Have a nice _____.
M Thanks very much. Goodbye.

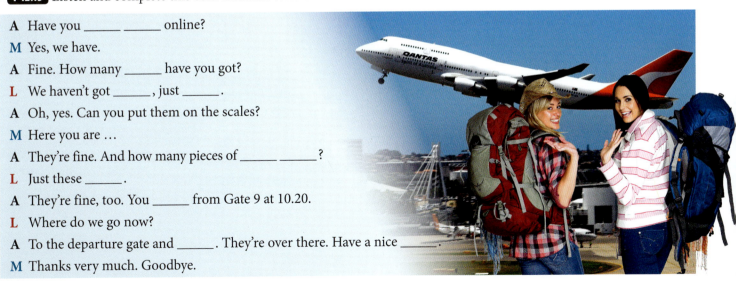

7 Practise the transport and travel conversations with your partner. Act some of them to the class.

▶▶ WRITING **T 12.14** A poem *p117*

Writing and reference materials

▶ **WRITING SECTION** p103

▶ **TAPESCRIPTS** p118

▶ **GRAMMAR REFERENCE** p134

▶ **WORD LIST** p143

▶ **PAIRWORK STUDENT A** p149

▶ **PAIRWORK STUDENT B** p152

▶ **EXTRA MATERIALS** p155

▶ **IRREGULAR VERBS / VERB PATTERNS** p158

▶ **PHONETIC SYMBOLS** p159

Writing contents

▶	UNIT 1	**A BLOG** p104	Keeping an online journal
▶	UNIT 2	**IMPROVING STYLE** p105	Using pronouns
▶	UNIT 3	**FORM FILLING** p106	An application form
▶	UNIT 4	**DESCRIBING YOUR HOME** p107	Linking words *and, so, but, because*
▶	UNIT 5	**A FORMAL EMAIL** p108	Applying for a job
▶	UNIT 6	**A BIOGRAPHY** p109	Combining sentences
▶	UNIT 7	**TELLING A STORY** p110	Using time expressions
▶	UNIT 8	**TWO EMAILS** p112	Informal and more formal
▶	UNIT 9	**DESCRIBING A PLACE** p114	Relative pronouns *which, who, where*
▶	UNIT 10	**COMPARING AND CONTRASTING** p115	Linking words *but, however, although*
▶	UNIT 11	**DESCRIBING A HOLIDAY** p116	Writing a postcard
▶	UNIT 12	**A POEM** p117	Choosing the right word

UNIT 1 A BLOG – Keeping an online journal

▶ p11

1 What is a blog? Are you a blogger?

2 Complete the blog about you.

My English Blog   **Blog posts**   Images   Links

Day 1 Welcome to my blog!   POSTED ON _____ BY _____.

Hello! My name's _____. I'm from _____ and
I'm _____ years old. I'm a student. I go to _____.
I want to learn English because _____
_____.

Day 2 Meet my family!   POSTED ON _____ BY _____.

I want to tell you about my family. It is/isn't very _____.
My _____'s name is _____. He's/She's _____.
My _____'s name is _____. He's/She's _____.
I have _____
_____.
We live in _____ near _____.

Day 3 Come to my school!   POSTED ON _____ BY _____.

My school is in _____. It's very _____
and it's near _____. My teacher's name is _____.
The students' names are _____.
They are from _____.
After class, I _____
_____.

3 Talk about your blog to a partner.

4 Choose a topic and think of a title. Write your blog entry for Day 4. Read it aloud to the class.

Day 4 _____   POSTED ON _____ BY _____.

Hello again! _____
_____
_____
_____
_____.

UNIT 2   IMPROVING STYLE – Using pronouns

1 Complete the charts.

Subject pronouns	Object pronouns	Possessive adjectives
I	me	my
___	you	___
he	him	his
___	her	___
it	it	its
we	us	___
___	them	their

2 Circle the possessive adjectives and underline the pronouns in the sentences.

1 (Her) son is in my class. I like him.
2 Our grandmother has a new TV. She doesn't like it.
3 They like their teacher. He helps them.

▶▶ Grammar Reference 2.3 p135

3 Complete the sentences with the correct pronoun.

1 I like my brother's new girlfriend, but _she_ doesn't like _me_ .
2 Tom has two sons. _____ often plays football with _____ .
3 That's my dictionary. Can I have _____ back, please?
4 Mr Banks is our new teacher. We like _____ a lot.
5 Rosa and I are good students. _____ like our teacher and she likes _____ .
6 Our teacher gives _____ a lot of homework.
7 Kate likes Joanna, but Maria doesn't like _____ at all.
8 Mike buys a newspaper every day. _____ reads _____ on the train.
9 Look! This is a photo of _____ with my family.
10 Sally works with Paul and Sue. _____ has lunch with _____ every day.

4 Read the text about David Guetta. Answer the questions.
- What is his job?
- Who does he work with?
- Who does he want to work with?
- Where does his wife come from? What does she do?
- How many YouTube hits does David have?

5 Rewrite the text to make it more natural. Begin like this:
David Guetta is French. He lives in Paris, but he works ...

T 2.12 Listen and check.

DAVID GUETTA
The superstar DJ with 70 million hits on YouTube!

David Guetta is French. David lives in Paris, but David works all over the world. David is a very famous DJ. David is number 3 in the 'Top 100 DJs' poll. David works with a lot of pop stars, such as Britney Spears, Celine Dion, and Madonna. David sometimes writes songs for the pop stars. David really likes Lady Gaga, and David wants to work with Lady Gaga. David's job is very exciting, and David likes David's job a lot. David is married to Cathy. Cathy comes from Senegal. Cathy is a businesswoman and an actress. Cathy and David often go to Ibiza. Every year, Cathy and David have parties there. People love Cathy and David's parties. Cathy and David have two young children, and they love to spend time with the two children.

UNIT 3 FORM FILLING – An application form

◀◀ *p25*

1 Work with a partner. Read Lena's application form for a sports and leisure centre.

Use the information to talk about Lena.

| Her name's … | She … married. | She's … years old. | She's … | She … | Her (email) address/phone numbers … | She likes … |

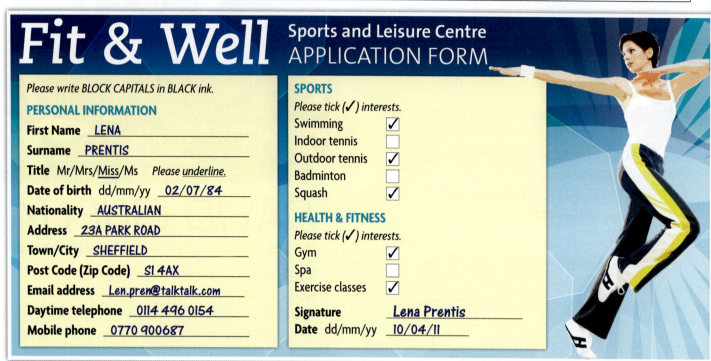

2 Fill in the same form for you. Compare your form with your partner's.
   I like playing squash, but Thomas doesn't.   We both like swimming.

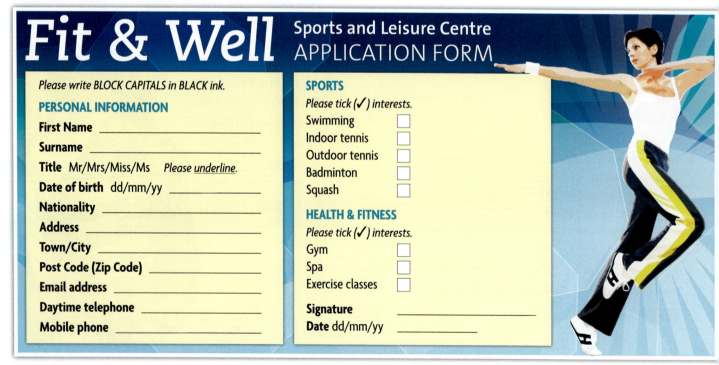

3 Discuss as a class which sports are popular.

106 Writing   Unit 3

UNIT 4 DESCRIBING YOUR HOME – Linking words *and, so, but, because*

▶▶ p35

1 Match **A**, **B**, and **C** to make four sentences.

A	B	C
I love my new flat	and so but because	I like your flat too. it's very beautiful. please come and see it soon. unfortunately there isn't a garden.

2 Make similar sentences about where you live using *and*, *so*, *but*, or *because*.

I like my house/flat/room ...

3 Complete the sentences with *and*, *so*, *but*, or *because*.

1 I don't have a TV in my bedroom __because__ I don't want one.
2 Our flat's really small, _____ it's comfortable.
3 The rent is cheap _____ it's above a busy restaurant.
4 My wife and I like sailing _____ we live near the sea.
5 We like living here _____ it's opposite the park.
6 We don't have a garden, _____ we have a small balcony.
7 There's a lot to do _____ a lot to see in our town.
8 Our best friends live in the next street _____ we often see them.

4 Read about Megan's new flat. Choose the correct linking words.

T 4.9 Listen and check.

5 Write some notes about where you live.
- Where is it?
- Is it old or new?
- How many rooms are there?
- Is there a garden?
- Who do you live with?
- Do you like it? Why? What is the best thing?

Talk to a partner about your notes.

6 Write a description of your home. Use linking words to join ideas. Read it aloud to the class.

My new flat

My new flat is near the centre of town, **(1)** *but / so* I often walk to work. It's not very big, **(2)** *but / because* it's very comfortable! There's just one bedroom, a living room, **(3)** *because / and* quite a big kitchen with a table in the centre. This is good **(4)** *because / so* I love cooking, **(5)** *because / and* I can invite my friends to dinner. The living room has one big window. It faces south, **(6)** *but / so* it's always very sunny. I have two comfortable, old armchairs, **(7)** *but / so* I don't have a sofa **(8)** *because / and* the room is quite small.

There isn't a garden, **(9)** *because / but* there's a small balcony in my bedroom. I want to put a chair there **(10)** *and / so* I can sit in the sun on summer evenings.

I love my new flat for many reasons: the big kitchen, the sunny living room, **(11)** *but / so* most of all I love it **(12)** *and / because* it's my first home!

Writing Unit 4 107

UNIT 5 A FORMAL EMAIL — Applying for a job   p41

1 Carl is a student. He wants a holiday job.
   Read the information about him.
   Ask and answer some questions with a partner.

   What's …?   How old …?   What was …?
   Can he …?   What … like doing?

NAME	CARL HAMPTON
AGE	22
Address	17 Park Street, BATH, BA2 4EE
Email address	carl.ham6@yoohoo.com
Mobile phone	07557 888453
Present job	Student
Last job	Ski instructor in Austria
Languages	French, German
Interests	Skiing, travel, guitar

2 Read the advertisement for a tourist guide.
   Why do you think Carl is interested in this job?

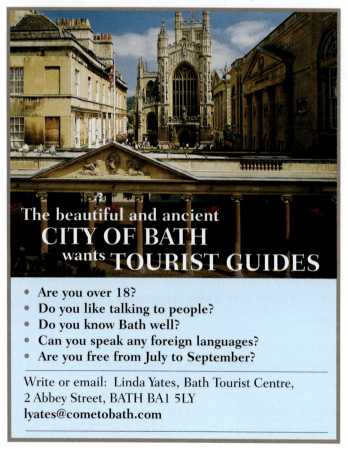

The beautiful and ancient
CITY OF BATH
wants **TOURIST GUIDES**

- Are you over 18?
- Do you like talking to people?
- Do you know Bath well?
- Can you speak any foreign languages?
- Are you free from July to September?

Write or email: Linda Yates, Bath Tourist Centre,
2 Abbey Street, BATH BA1 5LY
lyates@cometobath.com

3 Read and complete Carl's email applying for the job.

   Job as tourist guide
   from: carl.ham6@yoohoo.com
   to: "Linda Yates" <lyates@cometobath.com>

   Dear Ms Yates

   I am interested in the job of **(1)** _____ .
   I am **(2)** _____ years old and I **(3)** _____ in
   Bath. I am a **(4)** _____ at Durham University,
   so I am **(5)** _____ from mid-June until the
   end of September.

   Last winter I was a **(6)** _____ in a
   holiday resort in Austria. I **(7)** _____ speak two
   (8) _____ quite well, French and German, and
   I **(9)** _____ working with people very much.
   I **(10)** _____ born in Bath, so I know the city
   very well indeed.

   I look forward to hearing from you.
   Yours sincerely
   Carl Hampton

4 Read this advertisement for a job. What is the job?
   Answer the questions about you.
   Write a similar email to Carl's.

   The *International School* in
   your town:

   wants a receptionist.

   - Do you like working with people?
   - Can you speak two languages, and English?
   - Do you have experience working in an office?
   - Can you use a computer?
   - Do you know (your town) well?

   Email Anne Watson, Director, at
   awatson@international.school.com

5 Compare your email with a partner's.

108 Writing Unit 5

UNIT 6   A BIOGRAPHY – Combining sentences   ▶▶ *p49*

1 Work with a partner. Join the lines in **A** and **C** about Ben Way with a linking word from **B**.

The multi-millionaire Ben Way

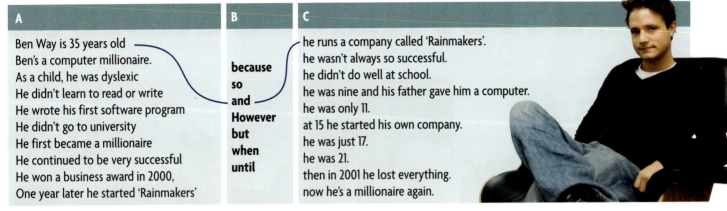

A	B	C
Ben Way is 35 years old Ben's a computer millionaire. As a child, he was dyslexic He didn't learn to read or write He wrote his first software program He didn't go to university He first became a millionaire He continued to be very successful He won a business award in 2000, One year later he started 'Rainmakers'	because so and However but when until	he runs a company called 'Rainmakers'. he wasn't always so successful. he didn't do well at school. he was nine and his father gave him a computer. he was only 11. at 15 he started his own company. he was just 17. he was 21. then in 2001 he lost everything. now he's a millionaire again.

T 6.10 Listen and compare. Take turns to read the sentences about Ben aloud.

2 Write some notes about someone you know who is successful.
   Talk to your partner about him or her.

   • What's his/her name? How old is he/she?
   • What does he/she do?
   • How do you know him/her?
   • Was he/she clever at school?

   • How did he/she become successful?
   • Did he/she have any ups and downs?
   • When and where do you see him/her?

3 Complete the text about Gabriella with linking words from exercise 1.

My successful cousin Gabriella

My cousin Gabriella is only 24 years old **(1)** _____ she is already a very successful dress designer.
Gabriella and I played a lot together **(2)** _____ we were children **(3)** _____ we are the same age. We also went to the same school **(4)** _____ we were 18 years old. **(5)** _____, after school we didn't see each other very often.
Gabriella was always very artistic **(6)** _____ she went to a fashion school in London. I went to Oxford University and studied Law **(7)** _____ I wanted to be a lawyer.
Four years later, I'm still a poor student, **(8)** _____ my cousin Gabriella is rich and famous. She won a major fashion award **(9)** _____ she was just 22. Our family is very proud of her.
Gabriella and I now have very different lives **(10)** _____ we don't meet very often. **(11)** _____, we still stay in touch by email and texting. She's in Milan this week for a fashion show. I love hearing about her life **(12)** _____ it is very exciting.

4 Write about a successful person that you know. Use your notes.

Writing   Unit 6   109

UNIT 7 TELLING A STORY — Using time expressions

1 Work with a partner. Do you know anything about Christopher Columbus? Look at the pictures and share what you know.

CHRISTOPHER COLUMBUS

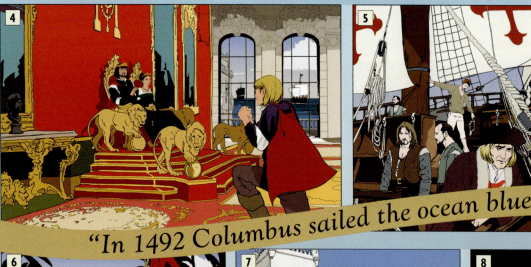

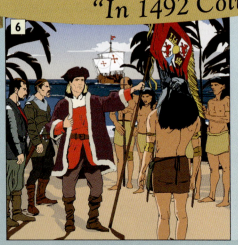

"In 1492 Columbus sailed the ocean blue!"

Christopher Columbus was a great explorer. For a long time people believed that he discovered America. However, we now know that (1) _____

EARLY LIFE
Columbus was born in 1451 in Genoa, Italy. He was one of five children. He didn't go to school, (2) _____
However, he always wanted to go to sea.

LIFE AT SEA
He became a sailor. Between 1477 and 1485 he visited many countries, including Spain, Iceland, Ireland, Madeira, and West Africa. (3) _____

Columbus wanted to be rich and famous. For eight years (4) _____
Finally they agreed and he got three ships, the *Santa Maria*, the *Pinta*, and the *Niña*, and enough food for a voyage of one year.

He left Spain on 3 August, 1492 and sailed west. After three months at sea, (5) _____

They wanted to go home. 'Give me just three more days,' said Columbus. Two days later, they saw land. It was an island. (6) _____
Next, they sailed to Cuba. Columbus thought he was in China or Japan. The world was a lot bigger than he thought.

Then, unfortunately, near Haiti the *Santa Maria* hit rocks, so Columbus returned to Spain on the *Niña*, leaving 40 sailors on the island to look for gold. (7) _____

FINAL YEARS
Between 1492 and 1504 Columbus made three more voyages across the Atlantic. He took his 13-year-old son Ferdinand with him on the last voyage. He became famous, but not very rich. In the last years of his life, (8) _____.
He died on 20 May, 1506.

2 Read these lines about Columbus. Match them with the pictures.

a ☐ He learned to read and write Spanish during his early travels.
b ☐ the Norseman, Leif Ericson, landed there 500 years before Columbus.
c ☐ he worked with his father, who was a wool worker.
d ☐ The Spanish people gave Columbus a hero's welcome.
e ☐ his sailors became tired and ill.
f ☐ he begged King Ferdinand and Queen Isabella of Spain to give him money to discover new lands.
g ☐ he was in great pain with arthritis and couldn't leave his bed.
h ☐ Columbus named it San Salvador, and its people, Indians.

3 Read the story of Christopher Columbus. Complete it with lines a–h.

4 What do the highlighted time expressions in the story refer to?

5 Work with a partner. Use the pictures to retell the story of Christopher Columbus in your own words.

Project

Research and make notes about a historical character from your country. Discuss them with your partner. Write the story.

- give an introduction
- include information about his/her early life
- include facts about his/her life
- write about his/her final years

UNIT 8 TWO EMAILS – Informal and more formal

1 Duncan is a student in Manchester and Sally is a student in Edinburgh. Read the email Sally wrote after visiting Duncan. Answer the questions.

1 Did Sally enjoy the weekend?
2 Is Duncan a good cook?
3 Why does Sally want the recipe?
4 How did Sally travel back to Edinburgh?
5 Why did she sleep on the journey?
6 Why is Duncan 'a star'?
7 When would she like to see Duncan again?
8 Is the email formal or informal?
9 Did she visit Duncan before or after their exams?

💬 Last Weekend   ↩ Reply | ▽

from: Sally.bates4@chatchat.co.uk
to: dunk.dude@garglemail.com
date: Mon 3 May

Hi Duncan,

Thanks for last weekend. It was really great. The meal was fantastic – didn't know you could cook! Just kidding ;-) Email me the recipe. I'd like to make cottage pie for my friends here – they're always starving hungry!

The journey was sooooooooooo long and boring – the coach stopped at a motorway service station where I had a disgusting cheese sandwich and a cold coffee. Yuk!

I slept for the rest of the journey – not surprising really – we did dance ALL night! House Rules was a brilliant club, but going to bed at 4 and getting up at 8 to go back to Edinburgh was awful! You're a star for getting up early to take me to the coach station!

Everyone here is worried about the exams. They start next week, like yours. It was good to forget about them for the weekend! I miss you a lot. Come and visit me soon – it's cheap on the coach.

Can't wait to see you again. Email me, or send a text.

Lots of love
Sal xxxx

Attachments:

duncan in kitchen 003.jpg

house rules 005.jpg

▶▶ *p65*

2 Sally also stayed with Duncan's parents for a weekend. Read her thank-you email. Answer the questions.
  1 When did she visit his parents?
  2 Was it the first time?
  3 What did she do there?
  4 Did she wait until after the exams to see Duncan?

3 The email to Duncan's parents is more formal than the email to Duncan. Compare the beginnings and endings, then compare line by line. What other differences can you find?

THANK YOU

from: Sally.bates4@chatchat.co.uk
to: owenandowen@gmail.uk
date: Mon 21 April

Dear Mr and Mrs Owen,

I'd like to thank you so much for having me to stay last weekend. I had a really lovely time, and I was so pleased to meet you at last. The meal you made was delicious. Duncan told me that his mother was an excellent cook – and he was right. I also enjoyed our walk – the countryside and woods near your house are beautiful.

The journey back was long and I slept for most of the way. It was very kind of you to drive me to the station so early in the morning. I was very grateful!

It's good to be back at university. I have a lot of work at the moment before the exams start. I know Duncan has exams too, so we can't see each other until the end of June – we are just too busy!

I'd love to visit again in the summer holidays with Duncan.

Thank you again for everything.

Best wishes,
Sally

---

4 Write an informal thank-you email after a visit to a friend. Show it to a partner. Discuss ways you could change it to a more formal style.

UNIT 9 DESCRIBING A PLACE – Relative pronouns *which*, *who*, *where*

▶◀ *p76*

1 Read and complete the Grammar Spot.

2 Join the sentences with *which*, *who*, or *where*.

1 Jack wrote the letter. It arrived this morning.
_____

2 There's the park. We play football in it.
_____

3 This is the hotel. I always stay here.
_____

4 Barbara's got a car. It's faster than yours.
_____

5 I met the man. He lives in the house on the corner.
_____

> **GRAMMAR SPOT**
>
> **Relative pronouns**
>
> Which relative pronoun is for 'people', for 'things', for 'places'? Complete the sentences.
>
> 1 We use *which* for _____:
> This is the book. It has the information.
> This is the book **which** has the information.
>
> 2 We use *where* for _____:
> There's the house. John and Mary live in it.
> There's the house **where** John and Mary live.
>
> 3 We use *who* for _____:
> I like the girl. She sits next to me.
> I like the girl **who** sits next to me.

3 Read about London and complete the text with the words from the box.

| a where the Queen lives | c which are much bigger | e where the Romans landed | g which costs £8 a day |
| b which is the biggest | d who want to drive | f where you can buy anything | h where you can see |

My capital city: LONDON

London has a population of about 7,000,000. It lies on the River Thames, (1) _____ nearly 2,000 years ago. From about 1800 until World War Two, London was the biggest city in the world, but now there are many cities (2) _____.

London is famous for many things. Tourists come from all over the world to visit its historic buildings, such as Buckingham Palace, (3) _____, and the Houses of Parliament, (4) _____ and hear the famous clock, Big Ben. They also come to visit its theatres, its museums, and its many shops, such as Harrods, (5) _____. And of course they want to ride on the London Eye next to the river!

Like many big cities, London has problems with traffic and pollution. Over 1,000,000 people a day use the London Underground. People (6) _____ into the city centre pay the Congestion Charge, (7) _____, but there are still too many cars on the streets. The air isn't clean, but it is cleaner than it was 100 years ago.

For me, the best thing about London is the parks. There are five in the city centre. But my children's favourite place is Hamleys, (8) _____ toy shop in the world!

4 Write four paragraphs about your capital city. Begin each paragraph in the same way as the text about London. Answer the questions below. Write 100–150 words.

Paragraph 1 How big is it? Where is it?
Paragraph 2 What is it famous for?
Paragraph 3 Does it have any problems?
Paragraph 4 What do you like best about it?

UNIT 10 COMPARING AND CONTRASTING – Linking words *but*, *however*, *although* ◀◀ p84

1 *But*, *however*, and *although* have similar meanings. Notice how they join these sentences.

1 I love travel, **but** I don't like flying – I prefer the train.
2 I love travel. **However**, I don't like flying – I prefer the train.
3 **Although** I love travel, I don't like flying – I prefer the train.

Which two sentences are the most formal?

2 Join each sentence in three different ways, with *but*, *However*, and *although*.

1 I like Peter. I don't love him.
2 My flat has a balcony. It doesn't have a garden.
3 My brother's older than me. He's smaller than me.

3 Complete the text with these linking words.

| but | so | because | however | although | when |

My Brothers

I have twin brothers, Nick and Chris. They're 20 years old and (1) _____ they're twins, they are not identical twins (2) _____ they are different in many ways.

For a start they don't look alike. Nick's got blond hair and blue eyes, and he's quite tall. (3) _____ , Chris isn't very tall and he's got red hair and brown eyes. Also, they never wear the same clothes. This is (4) _____ our mother always dressed them alike (5) _____ they were children and they hated it.

Something else that they don't like is (6) _____ people talk about 'the twins', not 'Nick' and 'Chris'. They want to be individuals. (7) _____ , they do have some interests in common. For example, they love being outdoors (8) _____ they often go for long walks together in the countryside. Also, they both have great computer skills. In fact, they're both studying IT at university, (9) _____ in different towns. Another thing is that they both hate football, which is very unusual for boys of their age.

Finally, I must say that I love my brothers very much. (10) _____ they have different personalities, they are both lovely brothers. Nick is quiet and quite shy, (11) _____ Chris loves going to parties and telling jokes. (12) _____ , both of them are always very kind to me, their little sister. I can tell them all my problems.

4 Compare two people in your family, or two friends. Try to use some of the highlighted expressions. Include:
- an introduction
- what they look like
- their personalities
- what they like doing

UNIT 11 DESCRIBING A HOLIDAY – Writing a postcard

▶▶ p89

1 Luke and Tina are going on holiday. Read the information about it.

QUESTIONS	LUKE AND TINA
Where/go?	South of France
When/go?	21 May
How/travel?	plane and hired car
How long/stay?	10 days
Where/stay?	a house in a village
What/do?	swim, shop in the markets, read and relax, eat in good restaurants

2 Complete the questions in exercise 1 about Luke and Tina's holiday. Ask and answer with a partner.

> Where are they going?

> To the South of France

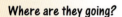 Listen and compare.

GRAMMAR SPOT

The Present Continuous can describe future arrangements.

I**'m seeing** the doctor tomorrow.
They**'re going** on holiday next week.
What **are** you **doing** this evening?

▶▶ Grammar Reference 11.2 p142

3 It's now 28 May. Luke and Tina are in France. Read the postcard that they are sending to friends.

Complete it with the adjectives from the box. Use each adjective once only.

delicious	wonderful	hot	old
beautiful	relaxed	warmer	loud
huge	busy	frightened	sunny
colourful	expensive	peaceful	

4 Do you sometimes send or receive postcards? What was the last postcard you received or sent? Where from? Who to/from?

5 Write a holiday postcard to a friend. Write about some of these things:

- where you are
- where you are staying
- the journey
- the weather
- your activities, past, present, and future

Read it aloud to a partner.

Wednesday, May 28th

Dear Toby and Mel,

We're having a really (1) _____ time here in the South of France. We're renting a lovely, (2) _____ house in a (3) _____ village. It's got a swimming pool, which is great because the weather is quite (4) _____ for May. We usually swim in the afternoons when the water is (5) _____. Yesterday there was a (6) _____ storm – the thunder was so (7) _____ we were quite (8) _____ and ran into the house. Today it's (9) _____ again and we're going to the market in a town called St Rémy. We love the markets here, they're so (10) _____, but the things are quite (11) _____. This evening we're having dinner in a local restaurant called 'Le Provençale' – their food looks (12) _____!

It's so (13) _____ here. We feel very (14) _____. We're reading a lot – we never have time to read at home, we're always too (15) _____. Only three more days! See you soon.

Lots of love,
Luke and Tina

UNIT 12 A POEM – Choosing the right word

▸▸ *p101*

1 Work with a partner. Match the question words and answers.

What …?	Nobody.
Where …?	Because I needed a holiday.
When …?	Last September.
Why …?	Spain.
Who …?	A suitcase.
How …?	The small brown one.
Which …?	It's mine.
Whose …?	By boat.

Complete the questions to suit the answers.

2 Read the poem called *Why did you leave?* It has lots of questions in it. Who do you think is asking the questions? Who is answering them? What is the poem about?

3 Discuss with your partner which words best complete the lines of the poem. Read some verses aloud to the class.

4 **T 12.14** Listen to the poem. Compare your choices. Do you think any of your ideas are better than those in the poem?

5 Write more verses. Complete these lines.

> *Who* did you meet?
> I met …
> Who did you meet?
> I met …
>
> *How* can we help you?
> You …
> How can we help you?
> You …
>
> *What* have you learned?
> I've learned …
> What have you learned?
> I've learned …

Read your verses to the class. Whose lines are most interesting?

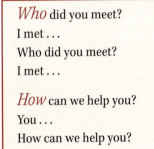

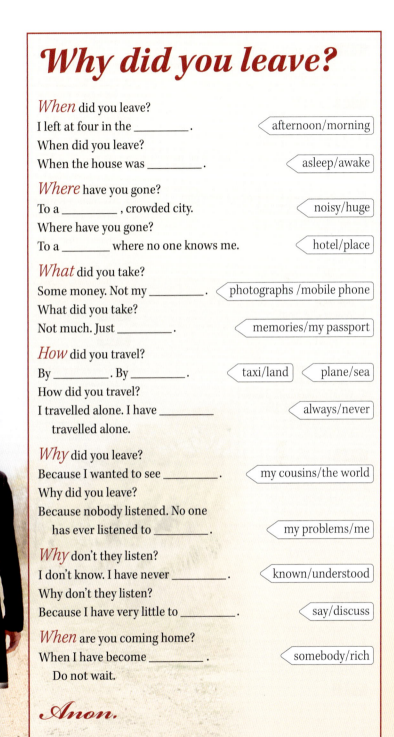

Why did you leave?

When did you leave?
I left at four in the _____ .   ⟨ afternoon/morning ⟩
When did you leave?
When the house was _____ .   ⟨ asleep/awake ⟩

Where have you gone?
To a _____ , crowded city.   ⟨ noisy/huge ⟩
Where have you gone?
To a _____ where no one knows me.   ⟨ hotel/place ⟩

What did you take?
Some money. Not my _____ .   ⟨ photographs/mobile phone ⟩
What did you take?
Not much. Just _____ .   ⟨ memories/my passport ⟩

How did you travel?
By _____ . By _____ .   ⟨ taxi/land ⟩ ⟨ plane/sea ⟩
How did you travel?
I travelled alone. I have _____ travelled alone.   ⟨ always/never ⟩

Why did you leave?
Because I wanted to see _____ .   ⟨ my cousins/the world ⟩
Why did you leave?
Because nobody listened. No one has ever listened to _____ .   ⟨ my problems/me ⟩

Why don't they listen?
I don't know. I have never _____ .   ⟨ known/understood ⟩
Why don't they listen?
Because I have very little to _____ .   ⟨ say/discuss ⟩

When are you coming home?
When I have become _____ .   ⟨ somebody/rich ⟩
Do not wait.

Anon.

Tapescripts

UNIT 1

T 1.1 The alphabet
A-B-C-D-E-F-G-H-I-J-K-L-M-N-O-P-Q-R-S-T-U-V-W-X-Y-Z

T 1.2 see p6

T 1.3
C = Carla   D = David
C Hello. My name's Carla. What's your name?
D David.
C Where are you from, David?
D I'm from Bristol. Where are you from?
C I'm from Bristol, too!
D Oh! Nice to meet you!

T 1.4
1 What's his surname?
   Frasier
2 What's his first name?
   Bill
3 Where's he from?
   Chicago
4 How old is he?
   30
5 What's his phone number?
   312 555 0749
6 What's his email address?
   bfrasier@gmail.com
7 Is he married?
   No, he isn't.

T 1.5
1 What's her surname?
2 What's her first name?
3 Where's she from?
4 How old is she?
5 What's her phone number?
6 What's her email address?
7 Is she married?

T 1.6 see p8

T 1.7
1 I go to Kingston University.
2 I have a brother and a sister.
3 I live with my parents in a house in West London.
4 My family really like Lily!

T 1.8
1 Where are you from?
2 'Are you from London?' 'Yes, I am.'
3 'How old are you?' 'I'm 15.'
4 'Are your sisters married?' 'No, they aren't.'
5 I like you. You're my friend.
6 Hans isn't from Germany, he's from Switzerland.
7 'Is your mother a doctor?' 'No, she isn't.'
8 I'm not Italian. I'm French.

T 1.9
1 She's from Italy.
2 What's his name?
3 Your English is good.
4 Where's she from?
5 He's a teacher from England.
6 We aren't English.

T 1.10 Spelling
1 My name's Vanessa. That's V-A-N-E-S-S-A. Vanessa.
2 My first name's Joseph. That's J-O-S-E-P-H. My surname's Bowen. That's B-O-W-E-N. Joseph Bowen.
3 My name's Katie Matthews. That's Katie, K-A-T-I-E, Matthews M-A-T-T-H-E-W-S.
4 My email address is g.hunt8@yahoo.com. That's G dot H-U-N-T eight at yahoo dot com.
5 My email address is zac.yates@gmail.co.uk. That's Zac, Z-A-C, dot Yates, Y-A-T-E-S, at gmail dot co dot UK.

T 1.11 see p11

T 1.12
1 Where's Annalisa from? Italy.
2 Where's her school? In the centre of London.
3 What's her teacher's name? Charlotte.
4 What's her family's name? Wilson.
5 Where's their house? In Notting Hill, in West London.
6 How old are the two brothers? Edward's 16 and Rick's 19.
7 Is the weather OK? Yes, it is. It's cold and sunny.

T 1.13
1 P Goodbye, Annalisa! Have a good day at school!
   A Thank you, Peter. And you have a good day at work!
2 C Good morning, Annalisa. Where's your homework?
   A It's here, Charlotte.
3 A Hello, Cristo. Where are you from?
   C I'm from Mexico.
4 A A ticket, please.
   B The National Gallery is free.
   A Oh, good! Thank you!
5 A A coffee, please.
   B Certainly. Here you are.

T 1.14
Joseph My family isn't very big. I have a sister, Andrea, she's 18, and a brother Richard, he's 25. They're not married. I'm married, erm, my wife's name is Isabel. We have two children, a daughter, Nancy, that's N-A-N-C-Y, she's 4, and a son, Tom, he's only six months old. We live near my parents. My dad's name is John, and my mum's is Odile, that's O-D-I-L-E. She's French. My grandmother lives with them, her name's Marie. She's my mum's mum.

T 1.15
1 A Hello, Sally. How are you?
   B OK, thank you. And you?
   A Fine, thanks.
2 A Hi, Pete. How are you?
   B All right, thanks. And you?
   A Not bad, thank you.
3 A Good morning, Mr Simpson. How are you?
   B Very well, thank you. And you?
   A Fine, thank you.
4 A Hello, Mrs Brown. How are you?
   B Fine, thank you. And you?
   A Not bad.

T 1.16
1 A Bye, Mum! It's time for school.
   B Goodbye darling. Have a good day!
   A Thanks. See you later.
2 C Good morning!
   D Good morning! Can I have a coffee, an espresso, please?
   C Yes, of course! Anything else?
   D No, thank you.
3 E Good afternoon! Can I help you?
   F No, thank you. We're just looking.
   E That's OK.
4 G Frank. This is Gina. She's from our New York office.
   H Hello, Gina. Nice to meet you.
   I Hello, Frank. Pleased to meet you, too.
5 J Thank goodness it's Friday! Bye, Ian.
   K Bye, Derek. Have a good weekend.
   J Thanks. Same to you.
   K See you on Monday!
6 L Good night! Sleep well.
   M Good night! See you in the morning.

UNIT 2

T 2.1 see p14

T 2.2
/s/ likes works writes walks
/z/ comes goes earns plays
/ɪz/ teaches

T 2.3
1 Andrew is an engineer. Claudia is a zoologist.
2 She comes from the US. He comes from New Zealand.
3 He lives in Scotland. She lives in California.
4 She works in the desert. He works on an oil rig.
5 He earns £200 a day. She earns $60,000 a year.
6 She likes her job, and he likes his job, too.
7 He goes to the gym in his free time. She walks her dog. Her dog's name is Brewer.
8 She's married. Her husband's name is Jim. Andrew isn't married.

T 2.4 Questions and negatives
What does Andrew do? He's an engineer.
Where does he come from? New Zealand.
Does he live in Scotland? Yes, he does.
Does he live in New Zealand? No, he doesn't.
He isn't married. He doesn't have any children.

T 2.5 see p15

T 2.6
1 Where does Andrew work?
  On an oil rig.
2 Does he work hard?
  Yes, he does.
3 How much does he earn?
  £200 a day.
4 What does he do in his free time?
  He goes to the gym and he plays snooker.
5 Does he like his job?
  Yes, he does.
6 Does he have a dog?
  No, he doesn't.

T 2.7 Stress and intonation
1 Darcey comes from London.
2 She lives in England.
3 She has two children.
4 She plays tennis a lot.
5 David's English.
6 He works in Paris.
7 His wife comes from Miami.
8 He writes songs in his free time.

T 2.8
1 A Darcey comes from London.
  B Yes, that's right.
2 A She lives in England.
  B No, she doesn't. She lives in Australia.
3 A She has two sons.
  B No, she doesn't. She has two daughters.
4 A She writes stories for children.
  B Yes, that's right.
5 A David's English.
  B No, he isn't. He's French.
6 A He works all over the world.
  B Yes, that's right.
7 A His wife comes from Miami.
  B No, she doesn't. She comes from Senegal.
8 A He writes songs in his free time.
  B Yes, that's right.

T 2.9 Talking about family and friends
1 A My husband comes from Belgium.
  B Where exactly in Belgium?
  A From the capital, Brussels.
2 A My grandmother lives in the next town.
  B Does she visit you often?
  A Yes, she does. Every Sunday.
3 A My mother loves reading.
  B What does she read?
  A Detective stories.
4 A My father travels a lot in his job.
  B Where does he go?
  A He's in Berlin this week.
5 A My sister speaks Spanish very well. She wants to learn French too.
  B Does she want to be an interpreter?
  A No, she doesn't. She wants to be a teacher.
6 A My little brother watches TV a lot.
  B What does he like watching?
  A Sport, sport, sport and er- football!
7 A My friend Tom writes a blog on the Internet.
  B What does he write about?
  A Everything and everybody!

T 2.10
1 A What does your sister do?
  B She's a student. She wants to be a doctor so she studies a lot.
2 A Does Peter like his new job?
  B No, he doesn't. He works very hard and he doesn't earn a lot of money.
3 A Is that your dog?
  B No, he isn't. He's my mother's. He goes with her everywhere. She loves him a lot. His name's Boris.
4 A Your friend Ella speaks English very well.
  B Yes, she does. She goes to England every summer.
5 A What does your grandfather do all the time?
  B Well, he watches TV a lot, but on Saturdays he plays golf with friends, and on Sundays he visits us.

T 2.11
1 He likes his job.
2 She loves working.
3 He isn't married.
4 Does he have three children?
5 Where does he go?

T 2.12 Improving style
David Guetta – The superstar DJ with 70-million hits on YouTube!
David Guetta is French. He lives in Paris, but he works all over the world. He's a very famous DJ. He's number 3 in the "Top 100 DJs" poll. He works with a lot of pop stars, such as Britney Spears, Celine Dion, and Madonna. He sometimes writes songs for them. He really likes Lady Gaga, and he wants to work with her. His job's very exciting, and he likes it a lot. He's married to Cathy. She comes from Senegal. She's a businesswoman and an actress. They often go to Ibiza. Every year, they have parties there. People love their parties. Cathy and David have two young children, and they love to spend time with them.

T 2.13 An interview
I = Interviewer S = Student
I Can I ask you some questions about your school?
S Yes, of course.
I How many students are in your school?
S There are 650 now.
I That's quite a lot. And how many teachers?
S Ten teachers.
I And what time do your classes start?
S Five o'clock every day.
I How much does it cost?
S Oh, the school is free.
I Very good! And your teacher, what's your teacher's name?
S Babur Ali. He's only sixteen.
I Sixteen! That's amazing! Is he a good teacher?
S He is very good indeed.
I What does he teach?
S He teaches English, Bengali, history, and maths.
I That's a lot of subjects. Does he work hard?
S Oh, yes, very hard. He studies all day and he teaches us every evening. He's the best teacher in the world!

T 2.14 Jobs
1 She's a hairdresser. She cuts hair.
2 He's a pilot. He flies from Heathrow airport.
3 She's a receptionist. She works in a hotel.
4 He's an architect. He designs buildings.
5 She's a lawyer. She works for a family law firm.
6 He's a taxi driver. He knows all the streets of London.
7 She's a journalist. She writes news stories.
8 He's a dentist. He looks after people's teeth.
9 She's a nurse. She works in the City Hospital.
10 He's an accountant. He likes working with money.

T 2.15

1. A What does your brother do?
   B He's a journalist. He writes for *The Times* newspaper.
   A Oh, that's a good job.
2. C What does your father do?
   D He's an accountant. He works for a big firm in the city.
   C And your mother? What does she do?
   D She's a teacher. She teaches French and Spanish.
3. E Does your sister work in the centre of town?
   F Yes, she does. She's a receptionist. She works in the Ritz Hotel.
   E Oh, that's near where I work.
4. G Are you a doctor?
   H No, I'm not. I'm a nurse.
   G Oh, but I want to see a doctor.
5. J I want to be a pilot when I'm big.
   K I want to be a lawyer. They earn lots of money.
   J Pilots earn a lot too, *and* they travel the world.

T 2.16 What time is it?

It's five o'clock.
It's eight o'clock.
It's half past five.
It's half past eleven.
It's quarter past five.
It's quarter past two.
It's quarter to six.
It's quarter to nine.
It's five past five.
It's ten past five.
It's twenty past five.
It's twenty-five past five.
It's twenty-five to six.
It's twenty to six.
It's ten to six.
It's five to six.

T 2.17 see p21

T 2.18

1. A Excuse me. Can you tell me the time, please?
   B Yes, of course. It's just after six o'clock.
   A Thank you very much.
2. C Excuse me. Can you tell me the time, please?
   D I'm sorry. I don't have a watch.
   C Never mind.
3. E Excuse me. What time does the bus leave?
   F At ten past ten.
   E Thank you. What time is it now?
   F It's about five past.
   E Five past ten?
   F No, no, five past *nine*. You're OK. No need to hurry.
4. G When does this lesson end?
   H At four o'clock.
   G Oh dear! It's only quarter past three!

UNIT 3

T 3.1 Lisa's two jobs!

'Hi, I'm Lisa Parsons. I'm 24 years old and I live in New York City. I'm always very busy, but I'm very happy. From Monday to Friday I work in a bookstore, the Strand Bookstore in Manhattan. Then on Saturdays I have another job – I'm a singer with a band. It's great because I love books and I love singing. On weekdays I usually finish work at 6 o'clock, but sometimes I stay late, until 9 or 10 o'clock at night. On Saturday evenings, I sing in nightclubs in all parts of the city, I don't go to bed until 3 or 4 o'clock in the morning. On Sundays, I don't do much at all. I often eat in a little restaurant near my apartment. I never cook on a Sunday. I'm too tired.'

T 3.2

1. Where do you live?
   In New York.
2. Do you like your job?
   Yes, I do.
3. Do you relax at weekends?
   No, I don't.
4. Why don't you relax at weekends?
   Because I sing in nightclubs.

T 3.3

I = Interviewer   L = Lisa
I Hi, Lisa. Nice to meet you.
L Nice to meet you too.
I Now, I hear you often sing in nightclubs here in New York
L That's right. I love singing.
I And how old are you Lisa?
L I'm 24.
I And do you live in New York?
L Yes, I do. I live downtown near the river.
I And where do you work?
L I work in a bookstore. The Strand Bookstore in Manhattan.
I What time do you finish work?
L Well, I usually finish at 6 o'clock but sometimes I stay late, until 9 or 10 o'clock, but I always finish at 6 on Saturdays because I sing in the evening.
I How many jobs do you have?
L Just two! The bookstore and singing.
I And do you like your jobs?
L Oh, yes! I love them both.
I Why do you like them?
L Because I love singing and I love books. I'm lucky. I love my work.
I What do you do on Sundays?
L I don't do much at all. I often eat in a little restaurant near my apartment.
I Do you sometimes cook on Sundays?
L Never! I'm too tired.
I I understand that! Thank you very much for your time, Lisa.
L My pleasure.

T 3.4

1. Lisa, why do you like your job?
2. Where do you live in New York?
3. What do you do on Tuesday evenings?
4. She really loves singing.
5. She eats a lot.
6. What does she do on Sundays?

T 3.5 Talking about you

1. What time do you get up?
   At about 7 o'clock on weekdays.
2. Where do you go on holiday?
   To Turkey or Egypt.
3. What do you do on Sundays?
   I always relax.
4. When do you do your homework?
   When I get home.
5. Who do you live with?
   My mother and brothers.
6. Why do you like your job?
   Because it's interesting.
7. How do you travel to school?
   Usually by bus.
8. Do you go out on Friday evenings?
   Yes, I do sometimes.

T 3.6 In my free time

1. Andy
   A I play tennis a lot. I'm no good but I like playing.
   B When do you play?
   A Oh, summer usually but sometimes in spring and autumn if it's sunny.
2. Roger
   R My favourite sport is skiing. I go skiing with my family every year. We all love it.
   B When do you go?
   R Always in January or February, after Christmas. We go to France.
   B And are you a good skier?
   R I'm OK. My wife's good, the kids are really good – but I'm just OK.
3. Linda
   B Do you go to the gym every day?
   L Yes, I do, every day, every morning before work.
   B And do you go swimming there?
   L Yes. I swim every morning too. Do you go to the gym?
   B Well -er no, I don't. I like my bed in the morning!
4. Ben & Josh
   B You like a lot of sports, don't you?
   B&J Oh yeah, my favourite is windsurfing. Me and my brother go to surf school every summer and … and we play golf and football of course.
   B All outdoor sports?
   B&J Er- no, we watch sport a lot on TV, and we play computer games after school.
   B Not a lot of time for homework then?
   B&J Well …

5 **Sandra & Brian**
S In winter we love evenings at home.
B What do you do? Watch TV?
S Well, yes, sometimes. We like all the cookery programmes. I love cooking.
B Oh, we love those programmes too, but we often play cards on winter evenings.
S We like cards too, but we only play when we're on holiday in summer. It's a 'holiday thing' in our family.
B What do you play?
S Well, usually we play …

T 3.7
1 I often watch TV.
2 I sometimes watch French films.
3 I always listen to music in the car.
4 I don't play the piano.
5 I sometimes play cards with friends.
6 I go dancing a lot.
7 I go shopping every Saturday.
8 I get up late on Sundays.
9 I often cook dinner for my friends.

T 3.8 Song Extract from *20-something* by Jamie Cullum

T 3.9 Dr Susan Hall – The work–life balance

Of course, work is important for us all, it gives us money to live, it gives structure to our everyday lives. But, for a happy, balanced life, it's also important to 'play' sometimes. It's important to find time to relax with friends and family. It's not good to think about work all the time. I know from my work as a doctor that it's sometimes difficult not to take your work problems home – but if you take your problems home you never relax, and it's difficult for your family, and bad for your health. Don't live to work, work to live! Life is more than work.

T 3.10 Social expressions
1 A Bye! Have a nice day!
 H Thanks. Same to you. See you later.
2 H I'm sorry I'm late. The traffic's very bad this morning.
 B Never mind. Come and sit down.
3 B What's the matter, Hakan? Do you have a problem?
 H Yes. I don't understand this exercise.
4 H Can I open the window? It's really warm in here.
 B Sure. Good idea. It is hot in here, isn't it?
5 H Can you help me? What does *bilingual* mean?
 B It means *in two languages*.
6 C Do you want a macchiato?
 H Pardon? Can you say that again?
7 H Excuse me! Is this seat free?
 D Yes, it is. Do sit down if you want.
8 F *Parlez-vous français?*
 H I'm sorry. I don't speak French.
9 A Hi, Hakan! How was your day?
 H Good, thanks. Really interesting. How about you?

T 3.11
1 see p29
2 H I'm sorry I'm late. The traffic's very bad this morning.
 B Never mind. Come and sit down.
 H Thanks.
 B We're on page 28.
3 B What's the matter, Hakan? Do you have a problem?
 H Yes, I don't understand this exercise.
 B Don't worry. I'll help you with it.
 H Oh, thank you very much.
4 H Can I open the window? It's really warm in here.
 B Sure. Good idea. It is hot in here, isn't it?
 H Very. Thanks a lot.
 B That's all right. I think we all need some fresh air.
5 H Can you help me? What does *bilingual* mean?
 B It means *in two languages*.
 H Oh, right, of course. I need to buy a bilingual dictionary!
 C Yeah, that's a very good idea!
6 D Do you want a macchiato?
 H Pardon? Can you say that again?
 D A macchiato. Do you want a macchiato?
 H Sorry. What is 'a macchiato'?
 D It's a strong white coffee.
 H Er – yes, OK. Fine. I'll try one. Thank you!
7 H Excuse me! Is this seat free?
 D Yes, it is. Do sit down if you want.
 H Thanks very much. That's very kind.
 D Not at all. Are you a new student?
 H Yes, I am.
 D Are you having a good time?
 H Yes. It's getting better, thanks.
8 E *Parlez-vous français?*
 H I'm sorry. I don't speak French.
 E Oh! It's OK. It doesn't matter.
 H Can I help you?
 E No. Don't worry. I need some help with my homework, but I can do it.
 H All right.
9 A Hi, Hakan! How was your day?
 H Good, thanks. Really interesting. How about you?
 A Oh, not bad. Just another day at work.
 H Well, tomorrow's the weekend.
 A Yes, thank goodness!

UNIT 4

T 4.1
living room
 sofa
 DVD player
 armchair
 bookshelves
 mirror
kitchen
 cooker
 fridge
 table
 oven
 washing machine
street
 bus stop
 post office
 café
 pavement
 chemist's
 traffic lights

T 4.2 A flat to rent
J = Josie E = Emily
J Here's a flat in Queen's Road!
E Is it nice?
J There's a big living room.
E Mmm!
J And there are two bedrooms.
E Great! What about the kitchen?
J There's a new kitchen.
E Wow! How many bathrooms are there?
J Er … there's just one bathroom.
E Is there a garden?
J No, there isn't a garden.
E It doesn't matter. It sounds great!

T 4.3
Is there a shower?
Yes, there is.

Is there a fridge?
Yes, there is.

Is there a dining room?
No, there isn't.

How many bedrooms are there?
Two.

How many bathrooms are there?
One.

How many armchairs are there?
Two.

Are there any pictures?
No, there aren't.

Are there any bookshelves?
Yes, there are.

Are there any carpets?
No, there aren't.

T 4.4 Prepositions
1. The flat's in Queen's Road.
2. It's on the first floor.
3. It's above a chemist's.
4. The chemist's is next to a clothes shop.
5. There's a mobile phone shop opposite the clothes shop.
6. There's a post office near the flat.
7. The bus stop is outside the café.
8. There's a bench under a tree.

T 4.5 What's in your picture?
The flat is near the centre of town. It has four bedrooms, a lovely living room with views over the town, and two bathrooms. The kitchen is very big, and there's a dining room next to it.

The flat is on the second floor. In the living room there are two sofas and an armchair. There are a lot of pictures on the wall. There's a carpet in front of the fire, and there's a TV and a DVD player. There is a table in front of the sofa.

T 4.6 A new flat
1. She has some plates.
2. She has a lot of clothes.
3. She doesn't have any glasses.
4. She has some pictures.
5. She has a lot of CDs.
6. She doesn't have any mugs.
7. She has a lot of shoes.
8. She doesn't have any towels.
9. She has some cups.

T 4.7 this/that/these/those
J = Josie   A = Shop assistant   E = Emily
1. J How much is this lamp, please?
   A It's £45.
2. J I like that picture.
   E Yes, it's lovely!
3. J How much are these glasses?
   A They're £15.
4. J I love those towels!
   E They're fabulous!
5. J Look at those flowers!
   E They're beautiful!
6. E Do you like this kettle?
   J Yeah! It's a great colour!
7. J How much are these mugs?
   A £5 each.
8. J Look at that coat!
   E You don't need any more clothes!

T 4.8 What's in your bag?
Christina What's in my bag? Well, there's my phone, and my purse, of course. I have some pens. I always have some pens. A blue one, and a red one. And there's my diary. I need to know what appointments I have. And I have a lipstick … . Oh, and keys. I have some keys, my house keys and my car keys. And that's all!

T 4.9 Describing your home
My new flat
My new flat is near the centre of town, so I often walk to work. It's not very big, but it's very comfortable! There's just one bedroom, a living room, and quite a big kitchen with a table in the centre. This is good because I love cooking, and I can invite my friends to dinner. The living room has one big window. It faces south, so it's always very sunny. I have two comfortable, old armchairs, but I don't have a sofa because the room is quite small.

There isn't a garden, but there's a small balcony in my bedroom. I want to put a chair there so I can sit in the sun on summer evenings.

I love my new flat for many reasons: the big kitchen, the sunny living room, but most of all I love it because it's my first home!

T 4.10 see p36

T 4.11
1. A Do you know Alice has a new boyfriend?
   B Really? Is he OK?
   A Mm! He's lovely!
   B Ooh! What's his name?
   A James.
   B Good for Alice!
2. C Ben has a new flat.
   D Wow! Where is it?
   C In the centre of town.
   D Is it nice?
   C Oh, yes. It's fantastic! The living room is fabulous!
3. E What a horrible day!
   F Yes, it is! Rain, rain, rain. It's terrible weather at the moment.
   E Oh, well! Tomorrow's another day!
4. G Mmm! This is an excellent meal!
   H Thank you! I'm pleased you like it.
   G And the wine is wonderful! Where's it from?
   H I think it's French. Yes, it is. French.
5. I I love your shoes! They're great!
   J They're nice, aren't they? They're Italian.
   I The colour's amazing! Red! Wow!
6. K We have a new teacher. Her name's Nancy.
   L Is she nice?
   K No, she's awful! I hate her.
   L Why?
   K I don't understand her. She talks, and talks, and talks all the time!

T 4.12 Adverb + adjective
1. A Look at Angela's car! It's a Mercedes!
   B Wow! They're really expensive! Is it fast?
   A Very fast.
2. A Does Tom have a lot of money?
   B Well, he has a really beautiful house with a very big garden, and a swimming pool.
   A Mm. He's very rich, isn't he?
3. C Do you like my new jeans?
   D Yeah! They're really nice! What make are they?
   C They're Prada.
   D How much were they?
   C They weren't expensive. Well, not *very* expensive.
4. E Look! That's Peter's new girlfriend!
   F Mmm! She's pretty. How old is she?
   E Twenty-eight.
   F Wow! That's old!
   E Twenty-eight? That isn't very old!
5. G Maria's very clever, isn't she?
   H Oh, yes. She's really intelligent. She knows everything.
   G Do you like her?
   H No, not really. She isn't very nice to talk to.
   G No, I don't like her either.

T 4.13 see p37

T 4.14
one and a half
two and a quarter
six point eight
seventeen point five
oh two oh, seven four eight one, six four nine oh
oh seven eight six one, five double six seven eight

T 4.15
1. There are thirty students in my class – seventeen boys and thirteen girls.
2. I live at number 62, Station Road. My mobile number is 07629 34480.
3. My father works in a big hotel. There are 460 rooms on sixteen floors.
4. The population of my town is 280,000.

T 4.16 Numbers and prices
1. 'How much is this book?' 'Six pounds fifty.'
2. 'How much are these pictures?' 'Twenty-four pounds each.'
3. I only earn £18,000 a year.
4. 'How much is this car?' '£9,500.'
5. 'Just this postcard, please.' 'That's 60p, please.'
6. 'Can I have these jeans, please.' 'Sure, that's $49.'
7. 'How much is a return ticket from Paris to Madrid?' '€150.'
8. There are about 1.4 dollars to the euro.

UNIT 5

T 5.1 Superman!

Superman comes from the Planet Krypton. He can fly at the speed of light; he can see through walls; he can jump 250 metres; he can speak every language; he can turn back time. There's nothing Superman can't do!

T 5.2 Superman is fantastic!

A = Alfie   I = Ivy
A Superman's fantastic!
I Hmm! What can he do?
A He can do everything!
I No, he can't!
A Yes, he can. He can fly at the speed of light, he can see through buildings, *and* he can speak every language in the world!

T 5.3

A = Alfie   I = Ivy
A He can speak every language in the world!
I Really? I don't believe that.
A Well, he can! Can you speak any languages?
I Yes, I can. I can speak French and Spanish a little bit. We learn them at school.
A Well, I can speak French too.
I Oh, yeah?!
A I can say 'Bonjour' and 'Merci'.
I That's nothing! You can't speak French at all!
A Well, I can skateboard! You can't!
I I don't want to skateboard. I like other things. What about skiing? Can you ski?
A Yeah, I can ski a bit, but my mum and dad can ski brilliantly!
I I love skiing. I can ski really well.
A OK, OK, we can do some things, but Superman can do everything. There's nothing Superman can't do.
I Oh, you and Superman! Remember he's not real, he's only a …

T 5.4

1 'Can you speak any languages?'
  'Yes, I can. I can speak French and Spanish.'
2 'You can't speak French at all!'
3 'I can skateboard! You can't!'
4 'Can you ski?'
  'I can ski a bit, but my mum and dad can ski brilliantly!'
5 'Superman can do *everything*. There's nothing Superman can't do.'

T 5.5 see p39

T 5.6 Ivy can't cook. Can you?

Ivy: So what can I do? Speak a foreign language … Hmm. Well, yes, I can speak French, and Spanish a little bit, but just holiday Spanish! Cooking? No, I can't cook at all. My mum can, she's a fantastic cook! Hmm. Sports – well, I think I'm quite good at sports – my cousin Alfie says I'm not because I can't skateboard, but skateboarding's not a sport. I can swim of course. Everyone can swim, can't they? I can swim very well, I like swimming, and I like tennis. I can play tennis quite well. But skiing is my best sport, I love it, and I can ski really well, really fast. Musical instruments? Er … well, no, I can't play any musical instruments. My dad can play the guitar brilliantly, and my mum can play the piano a bit, but I can't play anything at all.

T 5.7

1 She can speak Spanish a little bit.
2 She can't cook at all.
3 She can swim very well.
4 She can play tennis quite well.
5 She can ski really well.
6 Her dad can play the guitar brilliantly.
7 Her mum can play the piano a bit.
8 She can't play anything at all.

T 5.8 *can* or *can't*?

1 She can cook.
2 I can't hear you.
3 They can't come to the party.
4 Can you see my glasses anywhere?
5 You can't always get what you want.
6 Can you do the homework?

T 5.9 see p40

T 5.10 Pronunciation

1 It was Monday.
2 We were at school.
3 'Was it sunny?' 'Yes, it was.'
4 'Was it cold?' 'No, it wasn't.'
5 'Were you at school?' 'Yes, we were.'
6 'Were they at school?' 'No, they weren't.'

T 5.11 Marc Yu – Pianist

1 He was born on January 5, 1999, in California, USA.
2 He can play the piano and the cello.
3 He could play the piano when he was three.
4 He could play the cello when he was four.

Last year he played with Lang Lang, the famous Chinese pianist, in New York. They were a big success.

T 5.12 Cleopatra Stratan – Singer

Cleopatra Stratan is a singer. She was born on October 7th, 2002 in Moldova, near Romania. She could sing beautifully when she was just two years old. When she was three, she made an album, *La vârsta de trei ani*. Her album was a big success. 150,000 were sold round the world.

T 5.13 Pablo Picasso
25 October, 1881 – 8 April, 1973

A Hey, look at that painting! It's a Picasso!
B Oh yes! Fantastic!
A Where was Picasso born?
B In Málaga.
A Ah! So he was Spanish?
B Yes, he was.
A Were his parents rich?
B Well, they weren't rich and they weren't poor. His father, Don José, was a painter and a professor of art. His mother, Doña Maria, was a housewife.
A So was Picasso good at drawing when he was young?
B Oh, yes. He was a child prodigy. He could draw before he could speak. His first word was *lápiz*, which is Spanish for *pencil*.
A Wow! What a story!

T 5.14 Noun + noun

1 A Excuse me! Is there a post office near here?
  B Yes. Can you see the bus stop over there?
  A Yes, I can.
  B Well, it's next to the bus stop. Near the traffic lights.
  A Thanks.
2 A I can't find my sunglasses.
  B Not again! Look in your handbag.
  A Where's my handbag?
  B It's in the living room.
  A Oh yes! There it is, and there they are!
3 A Excuse me! Is there a petrol station near here?
  B A petrol station? Yeah. Go past the railway station and the car park. It's just before the motorway.
  A That's very kind. Thank you.

T 5.15 Verb + noun

1 A You send a lot of text messages!
  B I know. My mobile phone is my best friend!
2 A Do you earn a lot of money?
  B What a question! Mind your own business!
3 A Do you live on the third floor?
  B Yes, I have a great view. I can see right over the town.
4 A Do you wear a suit and tie when you go to work?
  B No, no. Where I work is very casual. I wear jeans and a T-shirt.
5 A Can you play the guitar?
  B Yes, I can. And the piano. And the violin.
6 A Can you ride a motorbike?
  B I can. Do you want to come for a ride? You can sit on the back.
7 A Can you drive a car?
  B Of course not! I'm only 16!
8 A You have a full-time job. Who looks after your children?
  B They go to playschool.
9 A Do you watch TV a lot?
  B No, not really, just in the morning, and in the evening, and sometimes in the afternoon.
10 A I can't speak any foreign languages.
   B I can. German and Spanish.

T 5.16 Prepositions

1. A Do you like listening to music?
   B Yes, of course. I have it all on my iPod.
2. A What sort of music do you like?
   B All sorts but especially jazz.
3. A Where's your girlfriend from? Is she Mexican?
   B No, she isn't. She's from Brazil. She speaks Portuguese.
4. A Is Paula married to Mike?
   B That's right. Do you know her?
5. A Do you want to come shopping with me?
   B Oh, yes. Can you wait a minute? I'll get my coat.
6. A Were there any good programmes on television last night?
   B I don't know. I was on the Internet all evening.
7. A What do you want for your birthday?
   B Can I have an iPhone? Or is that too expensive?
8. A Can I speak to Dave? Is he at work today?
   B Sorry, he's on holiday all this week. He's back next week.

T 5.17 Polite requests

1. A Can I have a coffee, please?
   B Yes, of course.
2. A Can you open the door for me, please?
   C Sure. No problem.
   A Thanks.
3. A Could I have the menu, please?
   D Certainly, madam.
4. A Could you tell me the time, please?
   E It's 10.30.
   A Thanks a lot.

T 5.18

Can I …?   Can I have a …?
Can I have a coffee, please?

Could you …?   Could you tell me …?
Could you tell me the time, please?

T 5.19

1. A Can I have a cheese sandwich, please?
   B In white or brown bread?
2. A Could you post this letter for me, please?
   B Yes, of course. No problem.
3. A Can you give me your email address?
   B I think you have it already.
4. A Can I speak to you for a moment?
   B Can it wait? I'm a bit busy.
5. A Could you lend me £20 till tomorrow?
   B I can lend you ten but not twenty.
6. A Can you give me a hand with this box?
   B Of course. Do you want it upstairs?

UNIT 6

T 6.1 Oprah – TV Star and Billionaire

A The woman
Oprah Winfrey is a famous American TV star. She lives in California but she also has an apartment in Chicago, where she works. Oprah is one of the richest women in America. She earns millions of dollars every year. She gives a lot of money to charity.

T 6.2 see p46

T 6.3

watched   interviewed   studied   talked
moved   started   earned   opened

T 6.4

C Her success
In 1984, Oprah moved to Chicago to work on a TV talk show called *A.M. Chicago*. She talked to lots of interesting people about their problems. Oprah says, 'People's problems are my problems.' The show was very successful, so in 1985, it was renamed *The Oprah Winfrey Show*. 49 million people in 134 countries watched it every week. In 1993, she interviewed Michael Jackson and 100 million people watched the programme. Last year, she earned $260,000,000.

Her charity work
In 1998, Oprah started the charity *Oprah's Angel Network* to help poor children all over the world. In 2007, she opened a special school in Johannesburg, *The Oprah Winfrey Academy for Girls*. She says, 'When I was a kid, we were poor and we didn't have much money. So what did I do? I studied hard.' There are 152 girls at the school, and Oprah calls them her daughters – the children she didn't have in real life.

T 6.5

1. Where did her father work?
   In a coal mine.
2. What did her mother do?
   She cleaned houses.
3. Who did Oprah live with?
   Her grandmother.
4. What did she study?
   Drama.
5. When did she interview Michael Jackson?
   In 1993.
6. How much did she earn last year?
   $260 million.
7. When did she open the girls' school?
   In 2007.
8. Did her parents earn much money?
   No, they didn't.

T 6.6 see p48

T 6.7

cleaned   received   studied   wanted
moved   talked   watched   interviewed
opened   decided

T 6.8 Interview with Ben Way

I = Interviewer   B = Ben Way

I Hi Ben. Nice to meet you. Can you tell us a bit about your life?
B Well, I was born on September 28th 1980 in Devon in the south-west of England.
I And what did your parents do?
B My dad was an accountant and my mum was an artist.
I Did you go to school in Devon?
B Yes, I did. I went to a small village school.
I Did you enjoy school?
B No, I didn't enjoy it at all. I had problems because I was dyslexic and couldn't read and write …
I Ah, that's difficult …
B Yes, but when I was nine, my dad gave me a computer and it changed my life. I loved it, I took it everywhere with me. I helped my friends and my parents' friends with their computers.
I Very good – and then …?
B Then, I wrote my first software programme when I was just 11, and when I was 15, I began my own computer company.
I That's fantastic! Was it successful?
B Yes, very successful – so successful that, I left school at 16 and …
I Yes, I know … you were a millionaire at 17!
B Yes, I made my first million at 17 and at 19, I had £18.5 million.
I And at 20 you won 'Young Entrepreneur of the Year'.
B Yes, I did. I often went on TV and radio and talked about it. It was amazing!
I And then one year later …?
B Yes, and then just a year later, when I was 21, I lost everything. Disaster! Dotcom businesses everywhere went down.
I Yeah, but now you're up again! Another company, another £1 million!
B I know. I work hard but I'm also very lucky!

T 6.9 Regular and irregular verbs

1. My grandad was born in 1932. He died in 2009.
2. My parents met in London in 1983. They got married in 1985.
3. I arrived late for the lesson. It began at 2 o'clock.
4. I caught the bus to school today. It took just 40 minutes.
5. I had a very busy morning. I sent 30 emails before 10 o'clock.
6. Our football team won the match 3–0. Your team lost again.
7. My brother earned a lot of money in his last job but he left because he didn't like it.
8. I studied Chinese for four years, but when I went to Shanghai, I couldn't understand a word.

T 6.10 A biography
The multi-millionaire Ben Way
Ben Way is 35 years old and he runs a company called 'Rainmakers'. Ben's a computer millionaire. However, he wasn't always so successful. As a child, he was dyslexic so he didn't do well at school. He didn't read or write until he was nine and his father gave him a computer. He wrote his first software program when he was 11. He didn't go to university because at 15 he started his own company. He first became a millionaire when he was just 17. He continued to be very successful until he was 21. He won a business award in 2000, but then in 2001 he lost it all. One year later he started 'Rainmakers' and now he's a millionaire again.

T 6.11 The businessman and the fisherman
B = Businessman   F = Fisherman
B Good morning. What beautiful tuna! How long did it take to catch them?
F Oh, about two hours.
B Only two hours! Amazing! Why didn't you fish for longer and catch more?
F I didn't want to fish for longer. With this I have enough fish for my family.
B But what do you do with the rest of your day? Aren't you bored?
F I'm never bored. I get up late, play with my children, watch football, and take a siesta with my wife. Sometimes in the evenings, I walk to the village to see my friends, play the guitar, and sing some songs.
B Really? That's all you do? Look, I am a very successful businessman. I went to Harvard University and I studied business. I can help you. Fish for four hours every day and sell the extra fish you catch …
F But …
B … Then, you can buy a bigger boat, catch more, and earn more money.
F But …
B … Then buy a second boat, a third, and so on, until you have a big fleet of fishing boats.
F But …
B … and you can export the fish, and leave this village, and move to Mexico City, or LA or New York, and open a fishing business.
F OK, OK, but how long will all this take?
B Er- let me think -er probably about 15 to 20 years.
F 15 to 20 years! And then what, Señor?
B Why, that's the exciting part! You can sell your business and become very rich, a millionaire.
F A millionaire? Really? But what do I do with all the money?
B Well, let me think. Erm- I know, you can stop work, and -er, move to a lovely, old fishing village where you can sleep late, play with your grandchildren, watch football, take a siesta with your wife, and walk to the village in the evenings where you can play the guitar, and sing with your friends all you want.
F Mmmm – well …

Fisherman's children Papa, Papa, did you catch many fish?
F I caught enough for us today and tomorrow, and also some for this gentleman. Please, Señor, have some of my beautiful fish. Goodbye Señor. Come on children, let's go home.

T 6.12 Describing feelings
1 I went to bed late last night, so I'm very tired today.
2 My football team lost again. I'm really annoyed!
3 I won £20,000 in the lottery! I'm so excited!
4 I can't find my house keys. I'm really worried.
5 I have nothing to do and nowhere to go. I am so bored!
6 The professor gave a great lecture. I was really interested.

T 6.13
1 A Did you enjoy the film?
   B No, I didn't. It was boring.
   A Oh, I loved it. It was really interesting, and very funny.
   B I didn't laugh once!
2 C How was your exam?
   D Awful. I'm very worried.
   C But you worked really hard.
   D I know, I studied until two in the morning, but then I was so tired today, I couldn't read the questions.
   C Don't worry. I'm sure you'll be OK.
3 E That was a great match! Really exciting!
   F Only because your team won. I was bored.
   E But it wasn't boring at all! It was a fantastic game!
   F Well, I didn't enjoy it, and now I'm annoyed because I paid £45 for my ticket.
4 G When's Nina's birthday?
   H You mean 'When was her birthday?' It was last Friday, March 24th.
   G Oh no! Was she annoyed that I forgot?
   H No, no, she was just worried that you didn't like her any more.

T 6.14 see p53

T 6.15 What's the date?
1 The first of April. April the first.
2 The second of March. March the second.
3 The seventeenth of September. September the seventeenth.
4 The ninth of November. November the ninth.
5 The 29th of February, 1976.
6 December the nineteenth, 1983.
7 The third of October, 1999.
8 May the 31st, 2005.
9 July 15th, 2015.

T 6.16
1 October the 31st.
2 The 23rd of June.
3 July the 15th.
4 March the 4th, 2012.
5 The 18th of February, 2020.
6 The 17th of September, 1960.

UNIT 7

T 7.1 20th Century Quiz
1 Henry Ford sold the first Model-T in 1908.
2 The first talking movie, *The Jazz Singer*, was in 1927.
3 Einstein published his theory of relativity about 100 years ago.
4 The Russian Revolution was in 1917.
5 The first non-stop flight around the world was about 60 years ago.
6 About 60 million people died in the Second World War.
7 The Berlin Wall came down in 1989.
8 Man first landed on the moon on July 20, 1969.
9 The Beatles had 17 number 1 hits in the UK.
10 The twentieth century ended at midnight on 31st December, 2000.

T 7.2 The good old days
T = Tommy   B = Bill
T Grandad, when you were a boy did you have television?
B Of course we had television! But it wasn't a colour TV like now, it was black and white.
T And were there lots and lots of channels? How many TV channels were there?
B Only two. But that was enough! We loved it! And there weren't programmes all day long. Nothing in the morning and nothing in the afternoon!
T Oh, no! What time did programmes begin?
B At 4.30, when children's TV started. There were some great programmes for us children, I can tell you! We had real stories in those days!
T Did your mum and dad give you pocket money?
B Yes, but I worked for it! I cleaned the kitchen and did the washing-up. We didn't have dishwashers in those days!
T That's terrible! How much pocket money did you get?
B My dad gave me sixpence a week. That's two and a half p these days! He didn't give me much, did he? But we bought comics and sweets.
T What sort of comics did you buy?
B Well, I bought a comic called the *Eagle*, and it was full of adventure stories. And *Superman*! That was really exciting!
T Wow! Did you have holidays?
B Yes, but not like nowadays. People didn't go abroad. I never took a plane like people do now! It was too expensive!
T Where did you go on holiday?
B To the seaside, in England.
T How did you get there?
B My father drove. We had a Ford car, a Ford Prefect it was. We went to the same place every year.
T Why did you go to the same place? Why didn't you go somewhere different?
B Because we all liked it there!
T I'm pleased I wasn't alive then! It sounds really boring!
B Oh, no! That's where you're wrong! It was the best fun ever!

T 7.3

1 How many TV channels were there?
2 What time did programmes begin?
3 How much pocket money did you get?
4 What sort of comics did you buy?
5 Where did you go on holiday?
6 How did you get there?
7 Why did you go to the same place?

T 7.4

1 Where did you go?
   To the shops.
2 When did you go?
   Yesterday.
3 Who did you go with?
   A friend from work.
4 How did you get there?
   By bus.
5 Why did you go?
   Because I wanted to.
6 What did you buy?
   A shirt.
7 How many did you buy?
   Only one.
8 How much did you pay?
   £29.

T 7.5 Listening and pronunciation

1 Where do you want to go?
2 I didn't go to college.
3 Where was he?
4 Do you like it?
5 Why did he come?
6 She doesn't work there.

T 7.6 Alisa's life

A = Alisa   F = Freddy

F You aren't English, are you, Alisa? Where are you from?
A No, I'm Russian. I was born in St Petersburg.
F Is that where you grew up?
A Yes, I lived with my parents and two sisters in a house near the university. My father worked at the university.
F Oh, how interesting! What was his job? Was he a teacher?
A Yes, he was a professor of psychology.
F Really? And what did your mother do?
A She was a doctor. She worked in a hospital.
F So, where did you go to school?
A I went to a Catholic High School. I was there for ten years, then, when I was 18, I went to university.
F What did you study?
A I studied philosophy and education at university in Moscow. I was there for four years.
F Wow! And did you start work after that?
A No, I travelled in the States for six months. I worked in a summer camp near Yellowstone National Park. It was amazing!
F It sounds great! And what's your job now?
A I work in a junior high school in Paris. I teach Russian and English.
F Your English is really good! Well, it was very nice to meet you, Alisa!
A Nice to meet you too. Bye!

T 7.7

In 1909 Bleriot made the first air journey from Calais to Dover.

Blériot was just 37 years old when he flew across the Channel. It took him just 37 minutes.
He took off from France at 4.30 in the morning.
He flew his plane at 40 miles per hour.
He flew at 250 feet above the sea.
He won a prize of £1,000.

In 1969 Neil Armstrong became the first man to walk on the moon.

Three astronauts flew in Apollo 11. The rocket took three days to get to the moon.
It circled the moon 30 times.
It landed at 8.17 a.m. on 20 July, 1969.
Six hundred million people watched on TV.
Neil Armstrong said, 'That's one small step for man, one giant leap for mankind.'
The astronauts spent 22 hours on the moon.

T 7.8 Noises in the night

It was about two o'clock in the morning, and … suddenly I woke up. I heard a noise. I got out of bed and went slowly downstairs. There was a light on in the living room. I listened carefully. I could hear two men speaking very quietly. 'Burglars!' I thought. Immediately I ran back upstairs and phoned the police. I was really frightened. Fortunately the police arrived quickly. They opened the front door and went into the living room. Then they came upstairs to see me. 'It's all right now, sir,' they explained. 'We turned the television off for you!'

T 7.9 Special occasions

1 *Happy birthday to you,*
  Happy birthday to you,
  Happy birthday, dear Grandma,
  Happy birthday to you.
2 A Did you get any Valentine cards?
  B Yes, I did. Listen to this.
    Roses are red, violets are blue,
    You are my Valentine,
    And I love you.
  A Wow! Do you know who it's from?
  B No idea.
3 C Mummy! Daddy! Wake up! It's Christmas!
  D Mm? What time is it?
  C It's morning! Look. Father Christmas gave me this present!
  E Oh, that's lovely! Merry Christmas, darling!
4 F Congratulations! It's great news!
  G Thank you very much. We're both very happy.
  F So when's the big day?
  H Pardon?
  F Your wedding day! When is it?
  H December the 12th. You'll get an invitation!
5 I It's midnight! Happy New Year, everyone!
  JKL Happy New Year!
6 C Wake up, Mummy! Happy Mother's Day!
  D Thank you, darling. Oh, what beautiful flowers! And a cup of tea! Well, aren't I lucky!
  C And we made you a card! Look!
  D It's beautiful! What clever children you are!
7 M Thank goodness it's Friday!
  N Yeah! Have a good weekend!
  M Same to you.

UNIT 8

T 8.1 see p62

T 8.2 Who's a fussy eater?

D = Duncan   N = Nick

N Oh, good, we have some tomatoes.
D Sorry Nick. I don't like them.
N Come on Duncan! Tomatoes are good for you. I didn't like them much when I was a child, but I love them now.
D Hmm – I didn't like a lot of things when I was a kid.
N Ah – you were a fussy eater! What didn't you like?
D I didn't like any green vegetables.
N Did you like any vegetables at all?
D Only potatoes. I loved chips.
N What about fruit? Did you like fruit?
D I liked some fruit, but not all. I didn't like bananas. I liked fruit juice. I drank a lot of apple juice.
N And now you drink beer and wine!
D Yeah – and coffee. But I didn't like coffee or tea when I was a kid.
N So what were your favourite foods?
D I liked ice-cream, chocolate, crisps, biscuits, especially chocolate biscuits. -er- you know, I liked all the usual things kids like.
N All the unhealthy things!
D I liked pasta too. Pasta with tomato sauce. I love that!
N Tomato sauce!? But you don't like tomatoes.
D Tomato sauce is different. Hey, let's not eat in tonight. Let's go out to Romano's.
N Romano's – a great idea! It's my favourite Italian restaurant.

T 8.3 see p63

T 8.4

1 A Excuse me, are you ready to order?
   B Yes. I'd like a steak, please.
2 A Would you like a sandwich?
   B No, thanks. I'm not hungry.
3 A Do you like Ella?
   B Yes. She's very nice.
4 A Would you like a cold drink?
   B Yes, please. Do you have any apple juice?
5 A Can I help you?
   B Yes. I'd like some stamps, please.
6 A What sports do you do?
   B Well, I like skiing very much.

T 8.5

1 What kind of wine do you like?
2 Would you like a cheese and ham sandwich?
3 Who's your favourite author?
4 What do you want for your birthday?
5 Do you have any pets?
6 Do you want some ice-cream for dessert?

T 8.6

1 A What kind of wine do you like?
   B I like French wine, especially red wine.
2 A Would you like a cheese and ham sandwich?
   B Just cheese, please. I don't like ham.
3 A Who's your favourite author?
   B I like books by Patricia Cornwell.
4 A What do you want for your birthday?
   B I'd like a new computer.
5 A Do you have any pets?
   B No, but I'd like a dog.
6 A Do you want some ice-cream for dessert?
   B No, thanks. I don't like ice-cream.

T 8.7 Eating in

N = Nick   D = Duncan

N This recipe for Cottage Pie looks easy.
D But I can't cook at all.
N Don't worry. I really like cooking. Now, vegetables – do we have any onions? Are there any carrots or potatoes?
D Well, there are some onions, but there aren't any carrots, and we don't have many potatoes. How many do we need?
N Four big ones.
D OK, put potatoes on your list.
N And how many tomatoes are there?
D Only two small ones. Put them on the list too.
N How much milk is there?
D There's a lot, but there isn't much cheese or butter.
N OK, cheese and butter. What about herbs? Do we have any thyme?
D Yeah, that's fine. But don't forget the minced beef. How much do we need?
N 500 grams. Now, is that everything?
D Er- I think so. Do we have oil? Oh, yeah, there's some left in the bottle.
N OK, first shopping, then I'll give you a cooking lesson!
D I'd like that. I hope the girls like Cottage Pie.
N Everyone likes Cottage Pie!

T 8.8 *much* or *many*?

1 A How much toast would you like?
   B Just one slice, please.
2 A How much yoghurt do we have left?
   B Not a lot. Just one strawberry and one raspberry.
3 A How many people were at the wedding?
   B About 150.
4 A How much money do you have in your pocket?
   B Just fifty p.
5 A How much petrol is there in the car?
   B It's full.
6 A How many children does your brother have?
   B Two. A boy and a girl.
7 A How many days is it until your birthday?
   B It's tomorrow!
8 A How much time do you need for this exercise?
   B Two more minutes.

T 8.9 What's your favourite sandwich?

Angus
I come from the north of England and we often call sandwiches 'butties'. My favourite butty is made with thick slices of white bread and thick slices of warm ham with hot mustard. Yes, warm ham! Mmmm, delicious. Would you like to try one?

Ulla
I'm from Denmark, so for me it's the open sandwich – of course, and my favourite is with beef – thin slices of beef, rare beef, with some crispy fried onions on the top. I love this!

Tom
Oh, the best sandwich in the world is definitely a bacon sandwich. Hot bacon between thin slices of white bread, and with lots of tomato ketchup. Simple, and very, very tasty. There's a café near where I work in London, I sometimes buy one for breakfast – mm, I'd like one right now.

Marianne
I live in Italy so my best is Italian – a ciabatta with chopped tomatoes, mozzarella cheese – with black olives, and basil. Mozzarella's my favourite cheese and I like cooking with it, I make my own pizza.

John
I was in Turkey by the sea, and a fisherman called to me 'Come, try a 'Balik Ekmek.' I think this means 'fish in bread'. He gave me a sandwich – it was fresh mackerel grilled and in a bread roll with raw onions. Fabulous!

T 8.10 Daily needs

aspirin
chocolate
notebook
scissors
adaptor
envelopes
plasters
sellotape
toothpaste
shampoo
batteries
screwdriver
magazine
newspaper

T 8.11 **Shopping in the High Street**

1 A I'd like some batteries, please.
   B What sort do you want?
   A AA, please.
   B Would you like a packet of four or six?
   A Six is too many. Four is enough.
   B Anything else?
   A That's all, thanks.
2 C Can I have some toothpaste, please?
   D Small or large?
   C The large is too big. The small is fine.
   D Anything else?
   C No, thanks. How much is that?
3 E I'm looking for a nice pen.
   F What about this one? It's £25.
   E No, that's too much. I don't want to spend that much.
   F Well, this one is £12.
   E That's better. And I need some pencils as well.
   F There are ten pencils in this packet.
   E But I only want two!
   F I'm afraid I only have packets of ten. Sorry.

T 8.12 see p69

T 8.13 **Sounding polite**

A Hi! What can I get you?
B I'd like a latte, please.
A Sure. Have in or take away?
B Have in.
A And what size do you want? Small, medium, or large?
B Large, please.
A Would you like anything to eat? A croissant? Some toast?
B I'd like some toast, please.
A No problem.
B Can I have some honey with the toast?
A Sure. Take a seat, and I'll bring it over.

UNIT 9

T 9.1 **City living**

1 This city is in the south-east of the country. It's very big, and very old. It's about 50 kilometres from the sea and it's on a famous river, the River Thames.
2 This city is in the north and centre of the country. It's about 200 kilometres from the sea and it's on the River Seine. It's one of the most popular tourist destinations in the world.

T 9.2 see p70

T 9.3

1 The Eiffel Tower is taller than the Gherkin.
2 The Underground is more expensive than the Métro.
3 Paris is warmer than London.
4 Paris is wetter than London.
5 I think the buildings in Paris are more beautiful.
6 I think the people in London are nicer.

T 9.4

Well, I like both London and Paris. But they are very different cities. Take transport for example. The Métro is cheaper and easier to use than the Underground. And the weather … well, Paris is certainly hotter than London. And Paris, in fact, is wetter than London; but in London there are more wet days. What about the buildings? Well, … people say that the architecture in Paris is more beautiful, but the buildings in London are more interesting. And living in the two cities? Well … life is faster in London. And the people? … Mmm, Londoners are generally more polite than Parisians. People in London work harder, and they earn more. In Paris, having a good time is more important.

T 9.5 **Comparing cities**

1 A New York is older than London.
   B No, it isn't! New York is much more modern!
2 A Tokyo is cheaper than Bangkok.
   B No, it isn't! Tokyo's much more expensive!
3 A Seoul is bigger than Beijing.
   B No, it isn't! Seoul is much smaller!
4 A Johannesburg is safer than Cape Town.
   B No, it isn't! It's much more dangerous!
5 A Taxi drivers in New York are better than taxi drivers in London.
   B No, they aren't! They're much worse!

T 9.6 **A Parisian in London**

I = Interviewer   C = Chantal

I Hello Chantal!
C Hi!
I Now, you're French, but you live in London. Is that right?
C Yes, that's right.
I And are you … on your own here in London?
C No, no! I'm here with my husband, André.
I Ah, OK. Do you work in London?
C Yes, I do. I've got a good job. I work in a bank.
I And … Where do you live in London? Have you got a flat?
C Yes. We've got a nice flat in Camden.
I Oh, great! Has André got a job?
C Yes, he has. He's got a shop in Camden. He sells French cheese!
I Wow, that's good! And tell me, have you got a car here?
C No, I haven't got a car. I go everywhere on public transport. It's much easier.
I OK! Thank you very much! I hope you enjoy your stay here!

T 9.7

1 We've got a nice flat.
2 I've got a French husband.
3 He's got a business in Camden.
4 Have you got a lot of friends?
5 How many brothers and sisters have you got?
6 I haven't got any brothers. I've got a sister called Natalie.
7 Natalie's got a big house.
8 You've got a good English accent.

T 9.8 **Camden**

It's got the largest street market in the UK.
The market's busiest at the weekend.
The food is the cheapest in north London.
It's got the most amazing clothes.
The Electric Ballroom is the oldest nightclub in Camden.
Proud is one of the coolest clubs in Camden.

T 9.9 **It's the biggest!**

1 The tallest building in London is Canary Wharf. It's 235 metres.
2 The most expensive hotel is the Lanesborough. It costs £7,000 per night!
3 The biggest park in central London is Hyde Park. It's 142 hectares.
4 The most popular tourist attraction is the London Eye. It has 10,000 visitors a day.
5 The most famous building is Buckingham Palace. Everyone knows who lives there.
6 The best restaurant for spotting celebrities is *The Ivy*. They all go there.

T 9.10

A megacity is a city with more than ten million inhabitants.
The largest megacity is in fact Tokyo. The next biggest is Mexico City. Third is Mumbai. Fourth is New York, with about 22 million people. And last, the smallest is Shanghai, which has about 18.4 million.
Some time in 2008, for the first time in the history of the world, more people on earth lived in cities than in rural areas.

T 9.11

Makiko from Tokyo
The first thing to say about Tokyo is that it is very safe. Women can walk everywhere anytime day or night. Little children walk to school. You can leave something on the table in a restaurant while you go out for a minute and nobody will take it.
   Tokyo is also very clean, and it is very easy to travel around. All the trains and buses run on time.
   Personally, my favourite time of year is spring, when it's dry and the cherry blossom is out.
   Tokyo is a very exciting city, because there are always new things to do, new places to go, new things to eat. It changes very quickly!

Vimahl from Mumbai
I have two strong impressions of Mumbai. First, it is a city that is so full of activity! It is busy busy busy all day long and all night long! It's a city that doesn't sleep much. The day begins early because it is so hot. It's a noisy place. There are cars going beep beep, auto rickshaws by the thousand, fast trains rushing past, vendors shouting and trying to get you to buy their food, their drinks, their clothes. And people, people everywhere trying to get to work.
   The second thing to say is that the people are very, very enthusiastic. Life isn't easy in Mumbai for a lot of people, but we really work hard and we really want to do our best. Every new day brings new possibilities! The future is exciting for us!

Lourdes from Mexico City
There are three things I like about living in Mexico City. First, the weather. It is warm and sunny most of the year. The second is the fresh fruit and vegetables – the markets are wonderful, the colours and smells are great! And the third is that I'm never bored because there is so much to see and do! We have museums, theatres, art exhibitions, parks, restaurants, bars … everything!
   My favourite time of year in Mexico City is the end of December, from the 16th to the 31st. The city is full of lights, there are parties everywhere, and we eat and drink and give presents. Everyone's really happy! I love it!

T 9.12 Directions

Go along George Street, past the Bristol Hotel on your left, and over the bridge. At the roundabout turn left and go up Park Avenue. Go round the corner, through the wood, and down the hill. Then go under the railway bridge and you are on the A312 to Dorchester.

T 9.13

1 Go along George Street, past the hotel and over the River Sherwell. Go straight over the roundabout, and it's in front of you on the hill to your left.
2 Go straight past the hotel and over the bridge until you get to a roundabout. At the roundabout follow signs to the town centre. Go past a petrol station on your left, over a pedestrian crossing, and past a set of traffic lights. At the roundabout turn right. You're in … Street.
3 Go over the bridge, the River Sherwell, and turn right into the town centre. Go straight on, past the traffic lights, and over a roundabout. When you are in the square, it's on the left-hand side, next to the museum, opposite the Town Hall.

UNIT 10

T 10.1

1 'I'm cooking.'
2 'I'm reading the paper.'
3 'I'm watching the football.'
4 'I'm working on my laptop.'

T 10.2 I'm sitting on the train

1 T = Tony   N = Nina
T Hello?
N Hi, Tony! It's Nina. Where are you?
T We're on the train. We're going to Birmingham for the weekend.
N Oh, great! How's the journey?
T Fine. I'm reading the paper, and Alice is doing something on her laptop …

2 F = Fiona   P = Pete
F Hello?
P Fiona, hi! It's Pete. How are you? What are you doing?
F Fine. We're at home. I'm just cooking some dinner.
P What's Tim doing?
F He's watching the football. Can't you hear?
P Ah, right!

T 10.3

1 What's Tony doing?
   He's reading the paper.
2 What's Alice doing?
   She's doing something on her laptop.
3 Where are Tony and Alice going?
   They're going to Birmingham.
4 What's Fiona cooking?
   She's cooking dinner.
5 What's Tim watching?
   He's watching the football.

T 10.4

B = Beth   D = Dad
B Oh, hi Dad! You OK?
D Yes. Fine. Are you all right? Where are you?
B Yeah, great! I'm … at Ellie's house. We're sitting in her bedroom.
D Ah, OK. And what are you doing at Ellie's house?
B We're er … working on the Internet.
D Oh, right. Is this school work?
B Yeah, I'm doing my homework.
D Who's that shouting?
B That's … Ellie's sister. We're looking after her.
D Hm. Really! OK. Well, see you later, then. Bye!
B I'll be home about 6.00, Dad. Bye!

T 10.5

1 Alice is sleeping.
2 Alice and Tony are going to Manchester.
3 Fiona's cooking lunch.
4 Tim's watching a film.
5 Beth's doing her homework.
6 Beth and Ellie are sitting in Ellie's bedroom.

T 10.6 Who's who?

A Oh, dear! I don't know anybody. Who are they all?
B Don't worry. They're all very nice, I'll tell you who everybody is. Can you see that man over there?
A The man near the window?
B Yes. That's Paul. He's talking to Sophie. He's a banker. Very rich. And very funny. He works in New York.
A Wow! So he's Paul. OK. And that's Sophie next to him?
B Yes. She's laughing at Paul's jokes. She's lovely. She's a professor at Bristol University. She teaches business studies.
A And who's that woman on the left?
B That's Helena. She's drinking champagne. She's a writer. She writes stories for children. They're excellent. A very nice lady.
A And who's that man she's talking to?
B Helena's talking to Roger. Roger's eating crisps. He's an interesting man. He's an art dealer. He works for the British Museum.
A Really? Wow! What a job! So that's Paul and Sophie … Helena and Roger … Now there are two more. Who are they?
B They're Sam and Penny. They're looking at a photo on Sam's phone.
A And what do they do?
B They're designers. They make clothes for children.
A OK. So that's everybody. Thanks.
B That's all right.

T 10.7 Everything was too expensive!

1 A Did you buy anything at the shops?
   B No. Nothing.
   A Why not?
   B Everything was too expensive.
   A What a pity!
   B But I bought something for you. Happy Birthday!
2 C Did you talk to anybody interesting at the party?
   D No. Nobody.
   C Why not?
   D Everybody was dancing and the music was really loud!
   C Oh.
   D But I danced with somebody beautiful – a girl called Kate.
3 E Did you go anywhere on Saturday night?
   F No. Nowhere.
   E Why not?
   F Everywhere was closed. There wasn't one club open.
   E That's incredible!
   F So next weekend I'm going somewhere more interesting.

T 10.8 An interview with an astronaut

I = Interviewer   S = Soichi

I Soichi, what exactly is your job?
S I'm an aeronautical engineer, and I'm a JAXA astronaut.
I What is JAXA?
S JAXA is the Japan Aerospace Exploration Agency.
I What did you study at university?
S Well, I studied engineering, of course! Aeronautical engineering.
I Where did you study? Which university?
S I studied at the University of Tokyo, and I graduated in 1991.
I Which part of Japan are you from?
S I'm from Yokohama, Kanagawa, which is part of Tokyo.
I Are you married?
S Yes, and I have three children.
I What do you like doing when you're on Earth?
S Well, I guess my hobbies are jogging and basketball. And I like skiing and camping with my kids.
I What are you doing on the space station at the moment?
S I'm doing quite a few space walks. I'm going out into space, and I'm checking the instruments on the outside of the space station, to make sure they're working properly.
I You're part of the Russian crew. What does this mean?
S It means that my commander is Oleg Kotov, from Roscosmos, and I'm working in his team. We're studying weather conditions in space, and we're doing experiments with plants to see how they grow in zero gravity.
I What do you do when you aren't working?
S Well, I spend a lot of time just looking down at you on Earth! And I think how lucky I am to be here. And I wish that everyone could see the Earth from space. Maybe people would stop fighting if they could see how beautiful our planet is.

T 10.9 Who is it?

1 She's got dark brown hair and she's quite pretty. She's wearing boots, and a hat, and a red scarf, and she's jumping in the air. She looks really happy!
2 He's got short dark hair. He's wearing trainers, and a purple T-shirt, and he's carrying a ball. He isn't very tall.
3 She's wearing a scarf. She's pretty, and she's got long, blond hair, and blue eyes. She isn't smiling. She doesn't look very friendly.
4 He doesn't look very happy. Perhaps he's a businessman. He's wearing a white shirt and a striped tie. He's also wearing black glasses.

T 10.10 Social expressions

1 A Patrick and I are getting married.
   B Wow! That's fantastic! Congratulations!
   A Thanks. We're both very excited. And a bit nervous.
2 C Can I help you?
   D No, I'm just looking, thanks.
   C Just tell me if you need anything.
   D That's very kind.
3 E Don't forget it's a Bank Holiday on Monday.
   F Sorry, what does that mean?
   E It means it's a national holiday. The garage is closed – most places are closed.
4 G We're going to the cinema tonight.
   H Oh, lovely! Well, I hope you enjoy the film!
   G Thanks. I'll tell you all about it.
   H Great!
5 I Excuse me! This machine isn't working.
   J I'm sorry. Let me have a look. Ah! It isn't switched on. That's why!
   I Oh, great! Thank you very much.
   J No problem.
6 K Hi. Can I speak to Dave, please?
   L I'm afraid he isn't here at the moment. Can I take a message?
   K Yes. Could you ask him to phone Kevin?
   L Sure. I'll do that.
7 M Thanks for the invitation to your party, but I'm afraid I can't come.
   N What a pity! Never mind!
   M I'm going away that weekend.
   N It's OK. Another time.
8 O/P Bye! Have a safe journey!
   Q/R Thanks. We'll see you in a couple of days!
   O/P I hope you have a good time.
   Q/R We'll try.

UNIT 11

T 11.1 Planning my future

1 When I get home, I'm going to relax with my wife.
2 When I grow up, I'm going to be a racing driver.
3 When the kids are in bed, I'm going to sit down and have a glass of wine.
4 When I get a pay rise, I'm going to buy my girlfriend a ring.
5 When I arrive on Koh Samui Island, I'm going to lie on the beach.
6 When I retire, I'm going to learn to play golf.
7 When this lesson ends, I'm going to meet my friends for coffee.

T 11.2 see p87

T 11.3

1 When I get home, I'm going to relax with my wife. I'm not going to talk about work.
2 When I grow up, I'm going to be a racing driver. I'm not going to work in an office like my dad.
3 When the kids are in bed, I'm going to sit down and have a glass of wine. I'm not going to do the washing.
4 When I get a pay rise, I'm going to buy my girlfriend a ring. I'm not going to buy a new car.
5 When I arrive on Koh Samui Island, I'm going to lie on the beach. I'm not going to check emails for a week.
6 When I retire, I'm going to learn to play golf. I'm not going to stay at home and do nothing.
7 When this lesson ends, I'm going to meet my friends for coffee. I'm not going to do my homework.

T 11.4 Careful! You're going to drop it!

1 What a pity! It's going to rain. He can't play tennis.
2 Look at the time. He's going to be late for his meeting.
3 Come on! Come on! She's going to win. Fantastic!
4 Oh no! Jack's on top of the wall! He's going to fall.
5 Careful! She's going to drop the vase. Too late!
6 They're so excited. They're going to have a baby. It's due in July.
7 There's my sister and her boyfriend! Yuk! They're going to kiss.
8 He's going to sneeze. 'Aaattishooo!' 'Bless you!'

T 11.5 see p89

T 11.6

R = Rob   F = Friend   B = Becky
R First we're going to Egypt.
F Why? To see the pyramids?
B Well, yes, but also we want to take a cruise down the Nile.
F Fantastic! Where are you going after that?
R Well, then we're going to Tanzania to …
F Wow! You're going to climb Kilimanjaro.
R Yes, and then we're flying to India.
F Are you going to visit the Taj Mahal?
B Of course, but we're also going on a tiger safari.
F You're going to see tigers!
R Well, we hope so. Then we're going to Cambodia to visit the temples of Angkor Wat and …
B … then to Australia to see Ayers Rock. We want to take photographs of it at sunset. Did you know it turns from pink to purple at sunset?
F Really! And are you going to Sydney?
R Oh, yes we're taking a flight from Sydney to Antarctica.
B Yeah, it's a day trip to see the coldest place on earth.
F I can't believe this. How many more places?
R Two. We're flying from Sydney to Peru to …
F … to see Machu Picchu of course.
R Yes, and then from Peru to the US to Yellowstone Park to see the supervolcano and perhaps some grizzly bears.
B Then home!
F Amazing! What a trip! How long is it going to take?
R Nine months to a year – we think.

T 11.7 Describing a holiday

1 A Where are they going?
  B To the South of France.
2 A When are they going?
  B On May the 21st.
3 A How are they travelling?
  B By plane and hired car.
4 A How long are they staying?
  B For ten days.
5 A Where are they staying?
  B In a house in a village.
6 A What are they going to do?
  B They're going to swim, go shopping in the markets, read and relax, and eat in good restaurants.

T 11.8 Song: Ed, Will, and Ginger – *Oats and beans*

Oats and beans and barley grow
As you and I and everyone knows,
Oats and beans and barley grows
As you and I and everyone knows,
A-waiting for a partner.

First the farmer sows his seeds,
Then he stands and takes his ease,
Stamps his feet and claps his hands
And turns around to view his lands
A-waiting for a partner

Now you're married you must obey,
Must be true in all you say,
Must be kind and must be good
And help your wife to chop the wood,
A-waiting for a partner

Oats and beans and barley grow
As you and I and everyone knows,
Oats and beans and barley grows
As you and I and everyone knows,
A-waiting for a partner.

T 11.9 What's the weather like?

Presenter: Here's Fiona with the weather for Europe for the next 24 hours.
Fiona: Hello there.
Here's the forecast for Europe today. At the moment there's some wet and windy weather over the UK and Scandinavia, and this is going to move south and east over Poland and Germany. Temperatures in Berlin and Warsaw are now about 20°C but it's cooler in London, 19°C, and cooler still in Oslo, 17°C. To the south it's a bit warmer, in Budapest, 23°C, but to the east, cool and cloudy in Moscow, where the temperature is a welcome 15°C after all that extreme summer heat. Moving south it's getting warmer, 24°C in Rome, but it's going to be cloudy and showery across much of Italy and also over northern Turkey, with heavy rain in Istanbul and a temperature of 21°C. Most other Mediterranean countries are going to be warm and dry. Greece will be hot and sunny with a lot of late summer sunshine, 28°C in Athens and warmer still in Portugal and Spain with temperatures up to 32°C. France is going to be cool and cloudy in the north, 20°C in Paris, and hot and stormy in the south with a high of 29°C in Nice.
And that's your European weather for today. I'll be back at lunchtime with an update.
Presenter: Thank you Fiona, and now …

T 11.10 see p92

T 11.11

A What's the weather like today?
B It's cool and cloudy.
A What was it like yesterday?
B Oh, it was wet and windy.
A And what's it going to be like tomorrow?
B I think it's going to be warm and sunny.

T 11.12 Making suggestions

1 A What a lovely day!
  B Yeah! It's really warm and sunny. What shall we do?
  A Let's go for a walk!
2 A What an awful day! It's raining again.
  B I know. It's so cold and wet! What shall we do?
  A Let's stay in and watch a DVD.

T 11.13 What shall we do?

1 A What a lovely day!
  B Yeah! It's really warm and sunny. What shall we do?
  A Let's go for a walk!
  B Oh no! It's too hot to walk.
  A OK, let's go to the beach.
  B Good idea! Why don't we take a picnic?
2 A What an awful day! It's raining again.
  B I know. It's so cold and wet! What shall we do?
  A Let's stay in and watch a DVD.
  B Oh no, that's boring! We did that last night.
  A OK then, shall we go out for a coffee?
  B Great! I'll get my coat and an umbrella!

UNIT 12

T 12.1 Been there! Done that!
K = Kyle   L = Lara

K Hi Lara! Are you and Mel ready for your trip?
L Yeah, nearly, we leave next Monday for Rome.
K Ah, Rome, I've been to Rome many times.
L Well, I've never been there. It's my first time in Europe.
K Really? What about your friend, Mel?
L She's been to London and Paris, but she hasn't been to Rome.
K Ah, London and Paris. I've been there, too. I studied in Paris for a year before I went to work in New York. Have you ever been to the US?
L No, I haven't, I haven't travelled much at all, so I'm really excited.
K Oh, I've been to North *and* South America so many times, and I've …
L I'm sure you have, Kyle. Oh dear, look at the time! Mel's waiting for me. We've got so much to do. Bye Kyle, we'll send you a postcard.

T 12.2 see p94

T 12.3
A Have you ever been to Greece?
B No, I haven't.
A Have you ever been to Italy?
B Yes, I have.
A When did you go?
B Two years ago.
A Where did you go?
B Rome, Florence, and Venice.
A Fantastic! Did you have a good time?
B Yes, I did. It was great!

T 12.4 Getting ready to go!
L = Lara   M = Mel

L Where's the list?
M I've got it. OK, let's check through. Er– we've bought new backpacks, we did that a while ago.
L They look quite big. I hope we can carry them.
M No worries. I haven't finished packing mine yet. Have you?
L Not yet, just one or two more things to go in. Oh, have you collected the euros from the bank?
M Yup. I've just collected five hundred for you and five hundred for me.
L All our savings. I hope it's enough!
M No worries. We can stay with my aunt in London.
L Have you emailed her yet?
M Yeah, she's just emailed back. She's going to meet us at the airport when we fly in to London from Rome.
L Fantastic. Hey, look, I've just found out the weather in Rome for next week. Hot and sunny!
M Yeah, it's going to be so good. We're going to leave winter here, and arrive in the middle of summer in Europe.
L What about the tickets?
M I think we only need passports, but I've printed e-tickets just in case, but I haven't checked in online yet. You can only do that 24 hours before the flight.
L Oh Mel! I am so excited. I can't wait.

T 12.5 Tense revision
Lara I'm really excited about my trip to Europe. I haven't travelled much outside Australia before. Just once, two years ago, I went on holiday to Bali with my family, but I've never been to Europe or the US. I often travel inside Australia. Last year I flew to Perth to visit my cousin, who lives there. It's a five-hour flight from Sydney, where I live. Australia's a big country! Also, I've been up to Cairns in the north three times. I learned to scuba dive there on the Great Barrier Reef.
   We've just finished packing, and now we're waiting for the taxi to take us to the airport. I've never flown on a 747 before. It's a very long flight. It takes 20 hours to get to Rome. I'm going to watch films all the way. I can't wait!

T 12.6 No, not yet!
1 A Have you checked your emails yet?
   B Yes, I've just checked them but there wasn't one from you.
2 A Have you done the shopping?
   B No, I haven't. I'm too tired to go out.
3 A Have you washed your hair?
   B Yes, I've just washed it.
4 A Have you cleaned the car yet?
   B Yes, I've just cleaned your car and mine!
5 A Mum, have you made the dinner yet?
   B Yes, dinner's ready. Go and wash your hands.
6 A Have you done the washing-up yet?
   B No. I did it last night. It's your turn!
7 A Have you met the new student yet?
   B Yes, I have. I met her on the way to school this morning.
8 A Have you finished the exercise?
   B Yes, I've just finished it. Thank goodness!

T 12.7 Song: Turin Brakes – *They can't buy the sunshine*

T 12.8
1 Elsa from Birmingham, England
OK, I've been to Glastonbury five times now. My highlights this year were: pear cider to drink, and the American diner van with the best sausages and chips ever. However, I was very disappointed with the music on Saturday night. DJs played House music all night. I love House but this was rubbish. I got really bored, so I went back to my tent to finish a bottle of pear cider with friends!

2 Daniel Evans from Wales
Last Wednesday at 2.30 in the afternoon, I decided that I wanted to go to Glastonbury. I was lucky! I found a ticket on the Glastonbury message boards. I'm so glad I went. The music was brilliant. Sometimes it took a long time to get to the stages. The queues were long but always friendly. In the busy "real world" it's difficult to have good conversations with people. At Glastonbury you can do this. It's a great festival, with a great crowd of people. What more could you want? 100,000 friendly people. I wish the rest of life was the same! Four days out of 365 is a good start!

T 12.9 Take and get
1 A Ugh! It's really hot in here.
   B Why don't you take off your jumper?
2 A Is your office near where you live?
   B No, it takes a long time to get to work.
3 A What are your work colleagues like?
   B Great! We all get on really well.
4 A How often are there exhibitions in the museum?
   B They take place regularly, every two months.
5 A Do you like learning English?
   B It's OK, but sometimes I get really bored!

T 12.10
1 The best way to get to the airport is to take a taxi.
2 How long does it take if you go by train?
3 I haven't got a camera. I take photos with my iPhone.
4 Sue has taken her driving test three times, and she's failed every time.
5 Are you still getting ready? We're going to be so late!
6 The doctor told me to take it easy if I want to get better soon.
7 It rained on the day we got married. We got very wet, but still had a great day.
8 You can't get on the bus with that big dog. Please, get off!

T 12.11 Travel announcements
1 The 11.55 for Newcastle stopping at Peterborough, York, and Darlington is now ready to board on Platform 10. There is a buffet car on this train. Please check that you have all your luggage with you.
2 This is the number 22 for Piccadilly Circus. Next stop Green Park. Stand back from the doors, please.
3 Flight BA1536 to New York is now ready for boarding at Gate 58. Will passengers in rows 12 to 20 please board first. Passengers are reminded to keep their hand luggage with them at all times.

T 12.12
Conversation 1
A Next, please!
B A day return to Oxford, please.
A That's £12.70.
B Thank you. What time does the next train leave?
A At 9.55. The platform number has just gone up on the departures board.
B Oh, yes. I can see. Thank you very much.
A Have a good journey!

Conversation 2

A Excuse me, does the number 24 go to the Natural History Museum?
B No, it doesn't. You need the 360.
A Where can I get it?
B From that bus stop over there.
A Oh, thanks for your help.
B Don't mention it.

T 12.13

A = Assistant   L = Lara   M = Mel

A Have you checked in online?
M Yes, we have.
A Fine. How many suitcases have you got?
L We haven't got suitcases, just backpacks.
A Oh, yes. Can you put them on the scales?
M Here you are …
A They're fine. And how many pieces of hand luggage?
L Just these bags.
A They're fine, too. You board from Gate 9 at 10.20.
L Where do we go now?
A To the departure gate and security check. They're over there. Have a nice flight!
M Thanks very much. Goodbye.

T 12.14 see p117

Grammar Reference

UNIT 1

1.1 Verb *to be*

Positive

I	'm		I'm = I am
He / She / It	's	from Bristol.	He's = He is / She's = She is / It's = It is
We / You / They	're		We're = We are / You're = You are / They're = They are

Negative

I	'm not	from Italy.	I'm not = I am not NOT ~~I amn't~~
He / She / It	isn't	married?	He isn't = He is not / She isn't = She is not / It isn't = It is not
We / You / They	aren't		We aren't = We are not / You aren't = You are not / They aren't = They are not

Questions with question words   **Answers**

What	's your name? / 's her surname? / 's his phone number?	Alicia. Johnson. 07773 321456	What's = What is
Where	are you from? / 's she from?	London.	Where's = Where is
Who	's Lara? / 's she?	She's my sister.	Who's = Who is
How / How old	are you?	Fine, thanks. I'm 22.	NOT ~~I have 22 years.~~

Yes/No questions   **Short answers**

Is	he / she / it	nice?	Yes, he is. NOT ~~Yes, he's.~~ / No, she isn't. / Yes, it is. NOT ~~Yes, it's.~~
Are	you / they	married?	Yes, I am./No, I'm not. / Yes, we are./No, we aren't. / Yes, they are./No, they aren't.

1.2 Possessive adjectives

What's	my / your / his / her / its	name?
This is	our / your / their	house.

1.3 Possessive 's

my wife's name = her name = the name of my wife
Andy's dictionary = his dictionary
my parents' house = their house

Prepositions

Where are you **from**?

I live **with** my parents.
My brother's **at** work/school.
We live **in** London.

I go **to** school **by** bus.
My school is **near** the shops.

Here are some photos **of** me.
There are a lot **of** coffee bars.

UNIT 2

2.1 Present Simple he/she/it

1. The Present Simple expresses a fact which is always true, or true for a long time.
   He **comes** from New Zealand.   She **works** with her husband.
2. The Present Simple also expresses a habit or a routine.
   He often **goes** to the gym.   She **walks** her dog every day.

Positive

He She It	lives	in Hungary.

Negative

He She It	doesn't live	in Belgium.	doesn't = does not

Question

Where	does	he she it	live?

Yes/No questions

Does	he she it	live	in America? in France?

Short answers

Yes, he does.
No, she doesn't.
Yes, it does.

2.2 Spelling of the third person singular

1. Most verbs add *-s* in the third person singular.
   wear → wear**s**   speak → speak**s**   live → live**s**
   But *go* and *do* are different. They add *-es*.
   go → go**es**   do → do**es**
2. If the verb ends in *-s*, *-sh*, or *-ch*, add *-es*.
   finish → finish**es**   watch → watch**es**
3. If the verb ends in a consonant + *-y*, the *-y* changes to *-ies*.
   fly → fl**ies**   study → stud**ies**
   But if the verb ends in a vowel + *-y*, the *-y* does not change.
   play → play**s**
4. *Have* is irregular.
   have → has

2.3 Pronouns

1. Subject pronouns come before the verb.
   He likes them.   **I** love him.   **She** wants it.
2. Object pronouns come after the verb.
   He likes **them**.   I love **him**.   She wants **it**.

Prepositions

He works **for** a big company.
He works **on** an oil rig.
She earns **about** $60,000 a year.

He works all **over** the world.
He plays music **for** his friends.
He writes a blog **on** the Internet.

It's just **after** six o'clock.

UNIT 3

3.1 Present Simple

Positive

I We You They	live	in New York.
He She It	lives	

Negative

I We You They	don't	live	in New York.
He She It	doesn't		

Question

Where	do	I you we they	live?
	does	he she it	

Yes/No questions

Do	you	like	playing cards?
	they		
Does	he she	go	out on Sunday?

Short answers

Yes, I do./No, I don't.
Yes, we do./No, we don't.
Yes, they do./No, they don't.
Yes, he does./No, he doesn't.
Yes, she does./No, she doesn't.

Grammar Reference 2.1–3.1   135

3.2 Adverbs of frequency

0%		50%		100%
never	sometimes	often	usually	always

1 These adverbs usually come before the main verb.
   She **never** goes out on Sundays.
   I **sometimes** work late.
   I **often** eat in a restaurant.
   I **usually** go to bed at about 11.00.
   We **always** stop work at 6.00.

   They come after the verb *to be*.
   She's **always** late.
   I'm **never** hungry in the morning.

2 *Sometimes* and *usually* can also come at the beginning or the end of a sentence.
   Sometimes we go out.   We go out **sometimes**.
   Usually I walk to school.   I walk to school **usually**.

3 *Never* and *always* don't come at the beginning or the end of a sentence.
   NOT ~~Never I go to the theatre.~~
           ~~Always I have tea in the morning.~~

3.3 like/love + verb + -ing

When *like* and *love* are followed by another verb, it is usually the *-ing* form.

   I **like** cook**ing**.
   She **loves** listen**ing** to music.
   I don't **like** study**ing**.

▶▶ See Verb patterns on p158

Prepositions

From Monday **to** Friday I work **in** a bookstore.
On Saturdays I have another job.

I'm a singer **with** a band.
I start work **at** 6.00.
I work **until** 10.00 **at** night.
I'm **at** home **on** Saturdays.
I stay late **at** work.

On Saturday evenings I sing **in** clubs.
I don't go to bed **until** 4 o'clock **in** the morning.
Do you relax **at** weekends?
We go **to** Spain or France.
I go skiing **in** winter.
I listen **to** music.
My garden is full **of** flowers.

UNIT 4

4.1 There is/are ...

Positive

There	is	a sofa.	(singular)
	are	two bedrooms.	(plural)

Negative

There	isn't	a shower.	(singular)
	aren't	any pictures.	(plural)

Yes/No questions   **Short answers**

Is	there	a table?
Are		any photos?

Yes, there is.
No, there isn't.
Yes, there are.
No, there aren't.

4.2 How many ...?

How many bathrooms are there?

4.3 some/any

Positive
There are **some** pictures.   *some* + plural noun

Negative
There aren't **any** glasses.   *any* + plural noun

Question
Are there **any** books?   *any* + plural noun

4.4 a lot of

She has **a lot of** clothes.

4.5 this/that/these/those

1 We use *this/these* to talk about people/things that are near to us.
   I like **this** picture.   How much are **these** mugs?
2 We use *that/those* to talk about people/things that aren't near to us.
   Can you see **that** man?   Who are **those** children outside?
3 We can use *this/that/these/those* without a noun.
   This is lovely.   **That**'s horrible.
   Can I have **this**?   **These** are my favourite.
   I don't like **that**.   I don't want **those**.

Prepositions

The flat is **in** Queen's Road.
It's **on** the third floor.
The chemist's is **next to** a café.
There's a shop **below** the flat.
There's a bus stop **outside** the post office.
It's **opposite** the park.
My flat is **near** the town centre.
The bench is **under** the tree.

What's **in** your bag?
There's a window **behind** the desk.
There's a fire **at** the other end.
This is a picture **of** my sister.

UNIT 5

5.1 can/can't

Can and can't have the same form in all persons.
There is no do or does.
Can is followed by the infinitive (without to).

Positive

I He/She/It We/You/They	can	swim.

Negative

I He/She/It We/You/They	can't	dance.

NOT *He doesn't can dance.*

Question

What	can	I he/she/it we/you/they	do?

Yes/No questions

Can	you/she/they/etc.	drive? cook?

Short answers

Yes, she can.
Yes, they can.
No, I can't.

5.2 was/were

Was/Were is the past of am/is/are.

Positive

I He/She/It	was	in Paris yesterday.
We/You/They	were	in England last year.

Negative

I He/She/It	wasn't	at school yesterday.
We/You/They	weren't	at the party last night.

Question

Where	was	I? he/she/it?
	were	we/you/they?

Yes/No questions

Was	he/she	at work?
Were	you/they	at home?

Short answers

Yes, she was.
No, he wasn't.

Yes, I was./Yes, we were.
No, they weren't.

was born

I was born in 1980.   NOT *I am born …*
She was born in Manchester.

Questions

Where	was	he/she	born?
When	were	we/you/they	

5.3 could/couldn't

Could is the past of can.
Could and couldn't have the same form in all persons.
Could is followed by the infinitive (without to).

Positive

I He/She/It We/You/They	could	swim.

Negative

I He/She/It We/You/They	couldn't	dance.

NOT *He didn't could dance.*

Question

What	could	I he/she/it we/you/they	do?

Yes/No questions

Could	you/she/they/etc.	drive? cook?

Short answers

Yes, she could.
Yes, they could.
No, we couldn't.

NOT *Do you can drive?*

Prepositions

I was **at** school.
They're **on** holiday.
I was **at** an exhibition.
She's **in** bed.

He was born **in** January.
He was born **on** January 14.

He's a professor **of** art.
He's good **at** drawing.
What's the Spanish **for** pencil?

She's married **to** Mike.
What's **on** TV tonight?
What do you want **for** your birthday?
Can I speak **to** Dave?
Can I pay **by** credit card?

UNIT 6

6.1 Past Simple – spelling of regular verbs

1 The normal rule is to add -*ed*.
   work → work**ed**
   start → start**ed**
   If the verb ends in -*e*, add -*d*.
   live → live**d**
   love → love**d**

2 If the verb has only one syllable and one vowel and one consonant, double the consonant, and add -*ed*.
   stop → stop**ped**
   plan → plan**ned**

3 Verbs that end in a consonant + -*y*, change to -*ied*.
   study → stud**ied**
   carry → carr**ied**

6.2 Past Simple

The Past Simple expresses a past action that is finished.
   I **lived** in Rome when I was six.
   She **started** school when she was four.
The form of the Past Simple is the same in all persons.

Positive

I He/She/It You/We/They	lived	in London in 1985.

Negative
We use *didn't* + infinitive (without *to*) in all persons.

I He/She/It You/We/They	didn't	live	in Madrid.

Question
We use *did* + subject + infinitive (without *to*) in all persons.

When Where	did	I he/she/it we/you/they	go?

Yes/No questions

Did	you she they etc.	like enjoy	the film? the party?

Short answers

No, I didn't.
No, we didn't.
Yes, she did.
No, they didn't.

6.3 Irregular verbs

To be is irregular and has two forms in the past.
   be → was/were
Other irregular verbs have only one form in the past.
   go → went
   can → could

▶▶ See Irregular verbs p158

6.4 Time expressions

last	night month week year Saturday

yesterday	morning afternoon evening

Prepositions

She talks **to** a lot **of** people.
She helps people all **over** the world.
He talks to friends **on** his phone.
I play **with** my children.
I'm very interested **in** art.
It's the third **of** April.

UNIT 7

7.1 Past Simple

For the forms of the Past Simple, see Unit 6 on p138.
He **published** his theory of relativity in 1905.
Man **landed** on the moon in 1969.
The Berlin Wall **came down** in 1989.

Questions
When **did** it **happen**?
How long ago **did** it **sell**?
How much pocket money **did** you **get**?

But:
How many people **died** in the war?
How many programmes **were** there?

7.2 Time expressions

in/at/on

in	the twentieth century / 1924 / the 1990s winter / summer / the evening / the morning / September
on	10 October / Christmas Day / Saturday / Sunday evening
at	seven o'clock / weekends / night

ago

I went there	ten years / two weeks / a month	ago.

7.3 Adverbs

Adjectives describe nouns.
   a **big** dog   a **careful** driver
Adverbs describe verbs.
   She ran **quickly**. He drives too **fast**.
To form regular adverbs, add -*ly* to the adjective. Words ending in -*y* change to -*ily*.

Adjective	Adverb
quick	quickly
slow	slowly
bad	badly
careful	carefully
real	really
immediate	immediately
easy	easily

Some adverbs are irregular.

Adjective	Adverb
good	well
hard	hard
early	early
fast	fast

Prepositions

It happened **about** 60 years ago.
How many people died **in** the Second World War?
We didn't have computers **in** those days.

He stepped **onto** the moon.
He flew **from** Calais **to** Dover.
He couldn't walk because **of** an injury **to** his leg.
The plane flew **at** 40mph.
I wasn't worried **about** the machine.

UNIT 8

8.1 Count and uncount nouns

There are countable nouns. These can be singular or plural.
   a book → **two** books   **an** egg → **six** eggs
There are uncountable nouns.
   bread   rice
❗ Some nouns are both.
   We'd like three **ice-creams**, please.   Do you like **ice-cream**?

8.2 *some/any*

We use *some* in positive sentences with uncount nouns and plural nouns.

There is	some	bread	on the table.
There are		oranges	

We use *some* in questions when we ask for things and offer things.

Can I have	some	coffee, please?
Would you like		grapes?

We use *any* in questions and negative sentences with uncount nouns and plural nouns.

Is there	any	water?	I don't know if there is any water.
Does she have		children?	I don't know if she has any children.
We haven't got		rice.	
There aren't		people.	

8.3 *would like*

Would is the same in all persons.
We use *would like* in offers and requests.

Positive

I/He/She We/You/They	'd like	a cup of coffee.	'd = would

Yes/No questions

Would	you/he/she/they	like a biscuit?

Short answers
Yes, please.
No, thank you.

8.4 *How much...?/How many...?*

We use *How much...?* with uncount nouns.
   How much rice is there?   There isn't **much** rice.
We use *How many...?* with plural count nouns.
   How many apples are there?   There aren't **many** apples.

Prepositions

'Pasta **for** me.' 'Same **for** me.'
This book is **by** Patricia Cornwell.
I like Apple Macs more **than** PCs.
This is a recipe **for** cottage pie.
Put potatoes **on** the list.

He ate it **with** his fingers.
Put the ham **between** two slices of bread.

A packet **of** four batteries, please.

UNIT 9

 ## 9.1 Comparative and superlative adjectives

London is **bigger than** Paris.
Paris is **more romantic**.
It's **the most exciting** place!
This is **the best** restaurant in the world.

Form

	Adjective	Comparative	Superlative
One-syllable adjectives	old safe big hot	old**er** saf**er** big**ger*** hot**ter***	the old**est** the saf**est** the big**gest*** the hot**test***
Adjectives ending in -y	noisy dirty	nois**ier** dirt**ier**	the nois**iest** the dirt**iest**
Two or more syllable adjectives	boring beautiful	**more** boring** **more** beautiful	the **most** boring** the **most** beautiful
Irregular adjectives	good bad far	**better** **worse** **further**	the **best** the **worst** the **furthest**

* Adjectives which end in one vowel and one consonant double the consonant.
     fit → fit**ter**   thin → thin**ner**

** Most two-syllable adjectives use *more and most*, but some two syllable adjectives use -er/-est.
     modern → **more** modern → **most** modern
     polite → **more** polite → **most** polite
     quiet → quiet**er**/quiet**est**
     clever → clever**er**/clever**est**

1. We can make a comparison stronger using *much* and *a lot*.
   London is **much more beautiful** than Paris.
   Dave's **a lot more handsome** than Pete.

2. Adverbs also have comparatives.
   He works **harder than** you.
   Can you come **earlier than** 8.30?

 ## 9.2 have got and have

Have got means the same as *have* to talk about possession, but the form is different. We often use *have got* in spoken English.

have got

Positive

I/You/We/They	have	got	a garden. a cat.
He/She/It	has		

Negative

I/You/We/They	haven't	got	a car. a garage.
He/She/It	hasn't		

Questions   **Short answers**

Have	I/we/you/they	got	any money?
Has	he/she/it		a sister?

Yes, I have.
No, I haven't.
Yes, she has.
No, she hasn't.

have

Positive

I/You/We/They	have	a garden. a cat.
He/She/It	has	

Negative

I/You/We/They	don't	have	a car. a garage.
He/She	doesn't		

Questions   **Short answers**

Do	I/you/we/they	have	any money?
Does	he/she/it		a sister?

Yes, I do.
No, I don't.
Yes, she does.
No, she doesn't.

Past
The past of both *have* and *have got* is *had/didn't have*.
   We **had** a lovely holiday.
   I **didn't have** a happy childhood.
   What did you **have** for lunch?
   When I was young I **had** a bike.
   I **didn't have** any money.

Prepositions

The city is **in** the north.
It's **on** the River Seine.
It's about 200 km **from** the sea.

London's a lot bigger **than** Paris.
Tokyo is **on** the east coast.
It is surrounded **by** mountains.

Go **over** the bridge.
Go **along** the path.
Go **past** the hotel.
Go **round** the bend.
Go **up** the hill and **down** the hill.
Go **through** the wood.
Go **under** the bridge.

UNIT 10

10.1 Present Continuous

1 The Present Continuous describes an activity that is happening now.
She's **wearing** jeans.
I'm **studying** English.

Positive and negative

I	am / 'm not	watching TV.
He/She/It	is / isn't	
We/You/They	are / aren't	

Question

What	am	I	thinking?
	is	he/she/it	
	are	we/you/they	

Yes/No questions
Are you having a good time?
Is my English getting better?
Are they having a party?

Short answers
Yes, we are.
Yes, it is.
No, they aren't.

Spelling of verb + -ing
1 Most verbs add -ing.
wear → wear**ing**
go → go**ing**
cook → cook**ing**

2 If the infinitive ends in -e, drop the -e and add -ing.
write → writ**ing**
smile → smil**ing**

3 When a one-syllable verb has one vowel and ends in a consonant, double the consonant and add -ing.
sit → si**tt**ing
get → ge**tt**ing
run → ru**nn**ing

10.2 Present Simple and Present Continuous

1 The Present Simple describes things that are always true, or true for a long time.
I **come** from Switzerland.
He **works** in a bank.
He **wears** a suit to work.
Do you **watch** much TV?

2 The Present Continuous describes activities happening now, and temporary activities.
Dave**'s coming** to see us now.
I**'m working** very hard this week.
Why **are** you **wearing** yellow trousers?
Shh! I'm **watching** TV!

10.3 something/nothing...

Form

THING	some**thing**/any**thing**/every**thing**/no**thing**
BODY	some**body**/any**body**/every**body**/no**body**
WHERE	some**where**/any**where**/every**where**/no**where**

something/anything...

The rules are the same as for *some* and *any*.

Positive
I'd like **something** to eat.
Somebody phoned you.

Negative
I didn't go **anywhere**.
I don't know **anybody**.

Question
Does **anybody** know the answer?
Would you like **something** to drink? (= an offer)

nobody/nothing/nowhere

1 The forms *nobody/nothing/nowhere* can be stronger than *not anybody/anything/anywhere*.
I didn't buy **anything**.
I bought **nothing**. (= stronger, more emphatic)

2 We use these forms as the subject of a sentence.
Nobody loves me.
Nothing is cheap these days.

3 We use them in one word answers.
'Where did you go?' '**Nowhere**.'

4 We don't use two negatives.
I **didn't** see **anybody**.   NOT ~~I didn't see nobody.~~
Nothing is easy.   NOT ~~Nothing isn't easy.~~

Prepositions

I'm **on** my way home.
She's working **on** her laptop.

He works **for** an international bank.
Who are you talking **to**?
They're looking **at** a photo.
There's someone **on** the phone **for** you.

We are learning **about** history.
Astronauts work **during** the week.
They like to look out **of** the window.

UNIT 11

11.1 going to

1 *Going to* expresses a person's plans and intentions.
   She's **going to be** a ballet dancer when she grows up.
   We're **going to stay** in a villa in France this summer.

2 We also use *going to* when we can see now that something is sure to happen in the future.
   Look at those clouds. It's **going to rain**. (= I'm sure.)

Positive and negative

I	'm		have a break.
He/She/It	's	(not) going to	stay at home.
We/You/They	're		be late.

Questions

When	am	I		have a break?
	is	he/she/it	going to	stay at home?
	are	we/you/they		

11.2 going to and Present Continuous

1 The Present Continuous can also describe a future intention.
   I'm **playing** tennis this afternoon.
   Jane's **seeing** her boyfriend tonight.

2 Often there is little difference between *going to* and the Present Continuous to refer to future time.
   I'm **seeing** Peter tonight.
   I'm **going to see** Peter tonight.

3 With the verbs *to go* and *to come*, we usually use the Present Continuous.
   We're **going to** Paris next week.
   Joe and Tim **are coming** for lunch tomorrow.
   NOT ~~We're going to go ….~~
   ~~They're going to come …~~

11.3 Infinitive of purpose

The infinitive can express why a person does something.
   I'm saving my money **to buy** a CD player.
   (= I want to buy a CD player.)

   We're going to Paris **to have** a holiday.
   (= We want to have a holiday.)

   NOT ~~I'm saving my money for to buy a CD player.~~
   ~~I'm saving my money for buy a CD player.~~

Prepositions

I'm going **on** holiday in ten days' time.
I spend my money **on** CDs.
I often go **on** the Internet.

He's **on** top of the wall.

I'm going **on** safari.
I'm happy **with** my life.

What's the weather **like**?

UNIT 12

12.1 Present Perfect

1 The Present Perfect is formed with *have/has* + past participle.
▶▶ See Irregular past participles p158

2 The Present Perfect refers to an action or experience that happened at some time before now.
   She's **travelled** to most parts of the world.
   Have you ever **been** in a car accident?

Positive and negative

I/We/You/They	have		
He/She/It	has	(not) been	to the Czech Republic.

I've been = I have been
We've been = We have been
They've been = They have been

Question

Where	have	I/you/we/they	been?
	has	she/he/it	

Yes/No questions
Have you been to Russia?

Short answers
Yes, I have./No, I haven't.

been and gone
She's **gone** to Portugal. (= she's there now)
She's **been** to Portugal. (= now she has returned)

12.2 Past Simple and Present Perfect

1 If we want to say **when** an action happened, we use the Past Simple not the Present Perfect.
   She **went** to Russia **two years ago**.   I **was** in a crash **when I was 10**.

2 Notice the time expressions used with the Past Simple.

   last night / yesterday / in 1990 / at three o'clock / on Monday

12.3 Indefinite time

Ever, never, yet, and *just* refer to indefinite time.

ever and never
We use *ever* in questions.
   Have you **ever** been to Russia?
We use *never* in negative sentences.
   I've **never** been to Russia.

yet and just
We use *just* in positive sentences.
   I have **just** done it. (= a short time before now)
We use *yet* in negative sentences and questions.
   Have you done your homework **yet**?
   I haven't done it **yet**. (= but I'm going to)

Prepositions

She's excited **about** her trip.
I haven't travelled **outside** Australia.
I travel **inside** my country.
We're waiting **for** the taxi.

I've never heard **of** that band.

Word list

Here is a list of most of the new words in the units of *New Headway Elementary, Fourth edition* Student's Book.

adj = adjective
adv = adverb
conj = conjunction
pl = plural
prep = preposition
pron = pronoun
pp = past participle
n = noun
v = verb
infml = informal
US = American English

UNIT 1

age *n* /eɪdʒ/
all right *adj* /ɔːl raɪt/
American *adj* /əˈmerɪkən/
aunt *n* /ɑːnt/
bad *adj* /bæd/
beautiful *adj* /ˈbjuːtɪfl/
big *adj* /bɪɡ/
blog *n* /blɒɡ/
boyfriend *n* /ˈbɔɪfrend/
brother *n* /ˈbrʌðə(r)/
bye /baɪ/
café *n* /ˈkæfeɪ/
car *n* /kɑː(r)/
centre *n* /ˈsentə(r)/
cheap *adj* /tʃiːp/
children *pl n* /ˈtʃɪldrən/
city *n* /ˈsɪti/
class *n* /klɑːs/
coffee bars *pl n* /ˈkɒfi bɑːz/
cold *adj* /kəʊld/
cousin *n* /ˈkʌzn/
darling *n* /ˈdɑːlɪŋ/
difficult *adj* /ˈdɪfɪkəlt/
doctor *n* /ˈdɒktə(r)/
easy *adj* /ˈiːzi/
Egypt *n* /ˈiːdʒɪpt/
email address *n* /ˈiːmeɪl əˈdres/
English *adj* /ˈɪŋɡlɪʃ/
Europe *n* /ˈjʊərəp/
expensive *adj* /ɪkˈspensɪv/
family *n* /ˈfæməli/
fast *adj* /fɑːst/
father *n* /ˈfɑːðə(r)/
first name *n* /ˈfɜːst neɪm/
free *adj* /friː/
French *adj* /frentʃ/
Friday /ˈfraɪdeɪ/
friendly *adj* /ˈfrendli/
from *prep* /frɒm/
gallery *n* /ˈɡæləri/
Germany *n* /ˈdʒɜːməni/
girl *n* /ɡɜːl/
girlfriend *n* /ˈɡɜːlfrend/
good *adj* /ɡʊd/
good afternoon /ɡʊd ˌɑːftəˈnuːn/
good morning /ɡʊd ˈmɔːnɪŋ/
good night /ˌɡʊdˈnaɪt/
goodbye /ˌɡʊdˈbaɪ/
grandfather *n* /ˈɡrænfɑːðə(r)/
grandmother *n* /ˈɡrænmʌðə(r)/
great *adj* /ɡreɪt/
hello /həˈləʊ/
her *pron* /hɜː(r)/
hi *pron* /haɪ/
his *pron* /hɪz/
home *n* /həʊm/
homework *n* /ˈhəʊmwɜːk/

horrible *adj* /ˈhɒrəbl/
hot *adj* /hɒt/
house *n* /haʊs/
Hungary *n* /ˈhʌŋɡəri/
husband *n* /ˈhʌzbənd/
interesting *adj* /ˈɪntrestɪŋ/
international *adj* /ˌɪntəˈnæʃnəl/
Italian *adj* /ɪˈtæliən/
Japan *n* /dʒəˈpæn/
language *n* /ˈlæŋɡwɪdʒ/
like *v* /laɪk/
live *v* /lɪv/
look *v* /lʊk/
love *v* /lʌv/
lovely *adj* /ˈlʌvli/
married *adj* /ˈmærɪd/
meal *n* /miːl/
meet *v* /miːt/
Mexico *n* /ˈmeksɪkəʊ/
Monday /ˈmʌndeɪ/
mother *n* /ˈmʌðə(r)/
museum *n* /mjuˈziːəm/
name *n* /neɪm/
near *adj* /nɪə(r)/
nephew *n* /ˈnefjuː/
nice *adj* /naɪs/
niece *n* /niːs/
office *n* /ˈɒfɪs/
old *adj* /əʊld/
parents *pl n* /ˈpeərənts/
park *n* /pɑːk/
people *n* /ˈpiːpl/
phone number *n* /fəʊn ˈnʌmbə(r)/
places *pl n* /ˈpleɪsɪz/
please /pliːz/
really *adv* /ˈrɪəli/
Rome *n* /rəʊm/
salesman *n* /ˈseɪlzmən/
same *pron* /seɪm/
school *n* /skuːl/
shopping *n* /ˈʃɒpɪŋ/
shops *pl n* /ʃɒps/
sister *n* /ˈsɪstə(r)/
slow *adj* /sləʊ/
small *adj* /smɔːl/
son *n* /sʌn/
Spain *n* /speɪn/
speak *v* /spiːk/
spell *v* /spel/
student *n* /ˈstjuːdnt/
sunny *adj* /ˈsʌni/
surname *n* /ˈsɜːneɪm/
Switzerland *n* /ˈswɪtsələnd/
teacher *n* /ˈtiːtʃə(r)/
thank goodness /θæŋk ˈɡʊdnəs/
thanks /θæŋks/

them *pron* /ðem/
today *n* /təˈdeɪ/
uncle *n* /ˈʌŋkl/
Underground *n* /ˈʌndəɡraʊnd/
understand *v* /ˌʌndəˈstænd/
university *n* /ˌjuːnɪˈvɜːsəti/
very well *adj* /veri ˈwel/
weather *n* /ˈweðə(r)/
weekend *n* /ˌwiːkˈend/
welcome /ˈwelkəm/
west *n* /west/
what *pron* /wɒt/
where *adv* /weə(r)/
wife *n* /waɪf/
year *n* /jɪə(r)/
young *adj* /jʌŋ/

UNIT 2

accountant n /əˈkaʊntənt/
actress n /ˈæktrəs/
airport n /ˈeəpɔːt/
animal n /ˈænɪml/
architect n /ˈɑːkɪtekt/
ballet dancer n /ˈbæleɪ dɑːnsə(r)/
banker n /ˈbæŋkə(r)/
Belgium n /ˈbeldʒəm/
Bengali adj /beŋˈɡɔːli/
building n /ˈbɪldɪŋ/
busy adj /ˈbɪzi/
capital n /ˈkæpɪtl/
clock n /klɒk/
come v /kʌm/
cost v /kɒst/
country n /ˈkʌntri/
cut v /kʌt/
dentist n /ˈdentɪst/
desert n /ˈdezət/
design v /dɪˈzaɪn/
disc jockey n /ˈdɪsk dʒɒki/
earn v /ɜːn/
engineer n /endʒəˈnɪə(r)/
exactly adv /ɪɡˈzæktli/
exciting adj /ɪkˈsaɪtɪŋ/
famous adj /ˈfeɪməs/
France n /frɑːns/
free time n /friː taɪm/
go v /ɡəʊ/
gym n /dʒɪm/
hair n /heə(r)/
hairdresser n /ˈheədresə(r)/
have v /hæv/
history n /ˈhɪstri/
hotel n /həʊˈtel/
hour n /ˈaʊə(r)/
housework n /ˈhaʊswɜːk/
hurry v /ˈhʌri/
India n /ˈɪndɪə/
Internet n /ˈɪntənet/
interpreter n /ɪnˈtɜːprɪtə(r)/
job n /dʒɒb/
journalist n /ˈdʒɜːnəlɪst/
law firm n /lɔː fɜːm/
lawyer n /ˈlɔːjə(r)/
learn v /lɜːn/
lucky adj /ˈlʌki/
lunch n /lʌntʃ/
many pron /ˈmeni/
maths n /mæθs/
model n /ˈmɒdl/
money n /ˈmʌni/
natural adj /ˈnætrəl/
never adv /ˈnevə(r)/
New Zealand n /ˌnjuː ˈziːlənd/
news story n /njuːz ˈstɔːri/
newspaper n /ˈnjuːzpeɪpə(r)/
nurse n /nɜːs/
oil rig n /ˈɔɪl rɪɡ/
outdoors n /ˌaʊtˈdɔːz/
physics n /ˈfɪzɪks/
pilot n /ˈpaɪlət/
play v /pleɪ/
poor adj /pɔː(r)/
pop star n /pɒp stɑː(r)/
reading n /ˈriːdɪŋ/

receptionist n /rɪˈsepʃənɪst/
salary n /ˈsæləri/
Scotland n /ˈskɒtlənd/
snooker n /ˈsnuːkə(r)/
sometimes adv /ˈsʌmtaɪmz/
Spanish adj /ˈspænɪʃ/
street n /striːt/
study v /ˈstʌdi/
taxi driver n /ˈtæksi ˌdraɪvə(r)/
teeth n /tiːθ/
time n /taɪm/
tired adj /ˈtaɪəd/
town n /taʊn/
travel v /ˈtrævl/
TV n /ˌtiː ˈviː/
village n /ˈvɪlɪdʒ/
visit v /ˈvɪzɪt/
walk v /wɔːk/
watch v /wɒtʃ/
work v /wɜːk/
world n /wɜːld/
write v /raɪt/
zoologist n /zuˈɒlədʒɪst/

UNIT 3

always adv /ˈɔːlweɪz/
apartment n /əˈpɑːtmənt/
application form n /ˌæplɪˈkeɪʃn fɔːm/
badminton n /ˈbædmɪntən/
band n /bænd/
barefoot adj /ˈbeəfʊt/
bath n /bɑːθ/
bed n /bed/
bilingual adj /ˌbaɪˈlɪŋɡwəl/
books pl n /bʊks/
bookstore n US /ˈbʊkstɔː/
boutiques pl n /buːˈtiːks/
cards pl n /kɑːdz/
chicken n /ˈtʃɪkɪn/
cinema n /ˈsɪnəmə(r)/
computer n /kəmˈpjuːtə(r)/
cook v /kʊk/
countryside n /ˈkʌntrisaɪd/
cycling n /ˈsaɪklɪŋ/
dancing n /ˈdɑːnsɪŋ/
early adj /ˈɜːli/
enjoy v /ɪnˈdʒɔɪ/
evening n /ˈiːvnɪŋ/
excuse me /ɪkˈskjuːs mi/
exercise n /ˈeksəsaɪz/
finish v /ˈfɪnɪʃ/
flowers pl n /ˈflaʊəz/
football n /ˈfʊtbɔːl/
foreign adj /ˈfɒrən/
garden centre n /ˈɡɑːdn sentə(r)/
get up v /ɡet ˈʌp/
golf n /ɡɒlf/
grass n /ɡrɑːs/
happy adj /ˈhæpi/
holiday n /ˈhɒlədeɪ/
indoor adj /ˈɪndɔː(r)/
Indian adj /ˈɪndiən/
Japanese adj /ˌdʒæpəˈniːz/
listen v /ˈlɪsn/
little adj /ˈlɪtl/
massage n /ˈmæsɑːʒ/
mobile phone n /ˈməʊbaɪl fəʊn/
music n /ˈmjuːzɪk/
often adv /ˈɒftən/
outdoor adj /ˈaʊtdɔː(r)/
pardon /ˈpɑːdn/
personal adj /ˈpɜːsənl/
poker n /ˈpəʊkə(r)/
post code n /ˈpəʊst kəʊd/
postcard n /ˈpəʊstkɑːd/
problem n /ˈprɒbləm/
programme n /ˈprəʊɡræm/
pub n /pʌb/
pudding n /ˈpʊdɪŋ/
restaurant n /ˈrestrɒnt/
roast n /rəʊst/
running n /ˈrʌnɪŋ/
sailing n /ˈseɪlɪŋ/
Saturday /ˈsætədeɪ/
singer n /ˈsɪŋə(r)/
skiing n /ˈskiːɪŋ/
spa n /spɑː/
squash n /skwɒʃ/
sticky adj /ˈstɪki/
Sunday /ˈsʌndeɪ/

swimming n /ˈswɪmɪŋ/
takeaway n /ˈteɪkəweɪ/
tennis n /ˈtenɪs/
Thursday /ˈθɜːzdeɪ/
toffee n /ˈtɒfi/
traffic n /ˈtræfɪk/
Tuesday /ˈtjuːzdeɪ/
Turkey n /ˈtɜːki/
usually adv /ˈjuːʒəli/
warm adj /wɔːm/
Wednesday /ˈwenzdeɪ/
week n /wiːk/
windsurfing n /ˈwɪndsɜːfɪŋ/

UNIT 4

above *prep* /əˈbʌv/
address book *n* /əˈdres bʊk/
amazing *adj* /əˈmeɪzɪŋ/
armchair *n* /ˈɑːmtʃeə/
awful *adj* /ˈɔːfl/
balcony *n* /ˈbælkəni/
bathroom *n* /ˈbɑːθruːm/
bedroom *n* /ˈbedruːm/
bench *n* /bentʃ/
birthday *n* /ˈbɜːθdeɪ/
bookshelves *pl n* /ˈbʊkʃelvz/
boss *n* /bɒs/
bowling alley *n* /ˌbəʊlɪŋ ˈæli/
bus fare *n* /bʌs feə(r)/
bus stop *n* /ˈbʌs stɒp/
carpet *n* /ˈkɑːpɪt/
cathedral *n* /kəˈθiːdrəl/
chemist's *n* /ˈkemɪsts/
choose *v* /tʃuːz/
clothes *pl n* /kləʊðz/
coat *n* /kəʊt/
colour *n* /ˈkʌlə/
comfortable *adj* /ˈkʌmfətəbl/
cooker *n* /ˈkʊkə(r)/
cup *n* /kʌp/
curtains *pl n* /ˈkɜːtnz/
desk *n* /desk/
diary *n* /ˈdaɪəri/
dining room *n* /ˈdaɪnɪŋ ruːm/
dinner *n* /ˈdɪnə(r)/
DVD player *n* /ˌdiː viː ˈdiː ˈpleɪə(r)/
eat *v* /iːt/
elevator *n US* /ˈelɪveɪtə(r)/
excellent *adj* /ˈeksələnt/
fabulous *adj* /ˈfæbjələs/
fantastic *adj* /fænˈtæstɪk/
fireplace *n* /ˈfaɪəpleɪs/
first floor *n* /ˌfɜːst ˈflɔː(r)/
flat *n* /flæt/
fridge *n* /frɪdʒ/
fruit *n* /fruːt/
furniture *n* /ˈfɜːnɪtʃə(r)/
gardener *n* /ˈɡɑːdnə(r)/
gift *n* /ɡɪft/
glass *n* /ɡlɑːs/
government building *n* /ˈɡʌvənmənt ˈbɪldɪŋ/
grow *v* /ɡrəʊ/
guest *n* /ɡest/
in *prep* /ɪn/
jogging track *n* /ˈdʒɒɡɪŋ træk/
kettle *n* /ˈketl/
keys *pl n* /kiːz/
kitchen *n* /ˈkɪtʃɪn/
lamp *n* /læmp/
library *n* /ˈlaɪbri/
lipstick *n* /ˈlɪpstɪk/
living room *n* /ˈlɪvɪŋ ruːm/
mirror *n* /ˈmɪrə(r)/
movie theater *n US* /ˈmuːvi ˈθɪətə(r)/
mug *n* /mʌɡ/
next to *prep* /ˈnekst tuː/
on *prep* /ɒn/
opposite *prep* /ˈɒpəzɪt/

outside *prep* /ˌaʊtˈsaɪd/
oven *n* /ˈʌvn/
party *n* /ˈpɑːti/
pavement *n* /ˈpeɪvmənt/
pen *n* /pen/
phone *n* /fəʊn/
picture *n* /ˈpɪktʃə(r)/
plate *n* /pleɪt/
post office *n* /ˈpəʊst ˌɒfɪs/
president *n* /ˈprezɪdənt/
public *n* /ˈpʌblɪk/
purse *n* /pɜːs/
relax *v* /rɪˈlæks/
rent *v* /rent/
shoes *pl n* /ʃuːz/
shower *n* /ˈʃaʊə(r)/
sleep *v* /sliːp/
sofa *n* /ˈsəʊfə/
swimming pool *n* /ˈswɪmɪŋ puːl/
table *n* /ˈteɪbl/
tennis court *n* /ˈtenɪs kɔːt/
terrible *adj* /ˈterəbl/
third floor *n* /ˌθɜːd ˈflɔː(r)/
towel *n* /ˈtaʊəl/
tree *n* /triː/
under *prep* /ˈʌndə(r)/
unfortunately *adv* /ʌnˈfɔːtʃənətli/
vegetables *pl n* /ˈvedʒtəblz/
visitor *n* /ˈvɪzɪtə(r)/
wall *n* /wɔːl/
wallet *n* /ˈwɒlɪt/
washing machine *n* /ˈwɒʃɪŋ məʃiːn/
wedding *n* /ˈwedɪŋ/
window *n* /ˈwɪndəʊ/
wine *n* /waɪn/
wing *n* /wɪŋ/
wonderful *adj* /ˈwʌndəfl/
world-famous *adj* /ˌwɜːld ˈfeɪməs/

UNIT 5

advertisement *n* /ədˈvɜːtɪsmənt/
afford *v* /əˈfɔːd/
art *n* /ɑːt/
bag *n* /bæɡ/
bike *n* /baɪk/
borrow *v* /ˈbɒrəʊ/
business *n* /ˈbɪznəs/
cello *n* /ˈtʃeləʊ/
certainly *adv* /ˈsɜːtnli/
cheese *n* /tʃiːz/
child *n* /tʃaɪld/
Chinese *adj* /ˌtʃaɪˈniːz/
classical music *n* /ˈklæsɪkl ˈmjuːzɪk/
concert *n* /ˈkɒnsət/
country and western *n* /ˈkʌntri ənd ˈwestən/
credit card *n* /ˈkredɪt kɑːd/
cry *v* /kraɪ/
drive *v* /draɪv/
dry cleaning *n* /ˌdraɪ ˈkliːnɪŋ/
favour *n* /ˈfeɪvə(r)/
fly *v* /flaɪ/
foreign language *n* /ˈfɒrən ˈlæŋɡwɪdʒ/
glasses *pl n* /ˈɡlɑːsɪz/
guitar *n* /ɡɪˈtɑː(r)/
hard *adj* /hɑːd/
hard-working *adj* /ˌhɑːd ˈwɜːkɪŋ/
hero *n* /ˈhɪərəʊ/
housewife *n* /ˈhaʊswaɪf/
ice-cream *n* /ˈaɪs kriːm/
important *adj* /ɪmˈpɔːtnt/
independent *adj* /ˌɪndɪˈpendənt/
interested *adj* /ˈɪntrestɪd/
jeans *pl n* /dʒiːnz/
jump *v* /dʒʌmp/
lift *n* /lɪft/
light *n* /laɪt/
look after *v* /lʊk ˈɑːftə(r)/
menu *n* /ˈmenjuː/
metre *n* /ˈmiːtə(r)/
Mexican *n* /ˈmeksɪkən/
moment *n* /ˈməʊmənt/
motorbike *n* /ˈməʊtəbaɪk/
musical instrument *n* /ˌmjuːzɪkl ˈɪnstrəmənt/
occasion *n* /əˈkeɪʒn/
open *v* /ˈəʊpən/
painter *n* /ˈpeɪntə(r)/
painting *n* /ˈpeɪntɪŋ/
passionate *adj* /ˈpæʃənət/
pay *v* /peɪ/
petrol *n* /ˈpetrəl/
pianist *n* /ˈpɪənɪst/
post *v* /pəʊst/
prodigy *n* /ˈprɒdədʒi/
professionally *adv* /prəˈfeʃənəli/
proud *adj* /praʊd/
resort *n* /rɪˈzɔːt/
return *v* /rɪˈtɜːn/
rich *adj* /rɪtʃ/
ride *v* /raɪd/
sandwich *n* /ˈsænwɪdʒ/
see *v* /siː/
send *v* /send/

sentimental *adj* /ˌsentɪˈmentl/
shop *n* /ʃɒp/
sit *v* /sɪt/
skateboard *v* /ˈskeɪtbɔːd/
speed *n* /spiːd/
station *n* /ˈsteɪʃn/
stop *v* /stɒp/
succeed *v* /səkˈsiːd/
success *n* /səkˈses/
suit *n* /suːt/
sun *n* /sʌn/
talented *adj* /ˈtæləntɪd/
talk *v* /tɔːk/
television *n* /ˈtelɪvɪʒn/
text message *n* /tekst ˈmesɪdʒ/
ticket *n* /ˈtɪkɪt/
tie *n* /taɪ/
turn back *v* /tɜːn ˈbæk/
violin *n* /ˌvaɪəˈlɪn/
violinist *n* /ˌvaɪəˈlɪnɪst/
water *n* /ˈwɔːtə(r)/
wear *v* /weə(r)/

UNIT 6

advice n /əd'vaɪs/
again adv /ə'geɪn/
annoyed adj /ə'nɔɪd/
any more adv /eni 'mɔː/
arrive v /ə'raɪv/
artistic adj /ɑː'tɪstɪk/
ask v /ɑːsk/
award n /ə'wɔːd/
before prep /bɪ'fɔː(r)/
begin v /bɪ'gɪn/
behaviour n /bɪ'heɪvjə(r)/
best friend n /best frend/
billionaire n /ˌbɪljə'neə(r)/
boat n /bəʊt/
bored adj /bɔːd/
born v pp /bɔːn/
breakfast n /'brekfəst/
businessman n /'bɪznəsmən/
catch v /kætʃ/
century n /'sentʃəri/
charity n /'tʃærəti/
childhood n /'tʃaɪldhʊd/
Christmas n /'krɪsməs/
clean v /kliːn/
clever adj /'klevə(r)/
coal mine n /'kəʊl maɪn/
company n /'kʌmpəni/
dad n /dæd/
date n /deɪt/
daughters pl n /'dɔːtəz/
designer n /dɪ'zaɪnə(r)/
die v /daɪ/
dollars pl n /'dɒləz/
drama n /'drɑːmə/
dyslexic adj /dɪs'leksɪk/
emails pl n /'iːmeɪlz/
enough adv /ɪ'nʌf/
entrepreneur n /ˌɒntrəprə'nɜː(r)/
everything pron /'evriθɪŋ/
everywhere adv /'evriweə(r)/
exam n /ɪg'zæm/
excited adj /ɪk'saɪtɪd/
exclaim v /ɪk'skleɪm/
export v /ek'spɔːt/
fashion show n /'fæʃn ʃəʊ/
film n /fɪlm/
first /fɜːst/
fish n /fɪʃ/
fisherman n /'fɪʃəmən/
football team n /'fʊtbɔːl tiːm/
friend n /frend/
full adj /fʊl/
funny adj /'fʌni/
gentleman n /'dʒentlmən/
give v /gɪv/
great-grandparents pl n /greɪt 'grænpeərənts/
help v /help/
interview v /'ɪntəvjuː/
last night /lɑːst naɪt/
last year /lɑːst jɜː(r)/
late adj /leɪt/
laugh v /lɑːf/
leave v /liːv/
lecture n /'lektʃə(r)/
local adj /'ləʊkl/

longer adj /'lɒŋgə(r)/
lose v /luːz/
lottery n /'lɒtəri/
lots (of sth) pl n /lɒts/
make v /meɪk/
marathon n /'mærəθən/
match n /mætʃ/
matter v /'mætə(r)/
millionaire n /ˌmɪljə'neə(r)/
minutes pl n /'mɪnɪts/
month n /mʌnθ/
move v /muːv/
much det /mʌtʃ/
nationality n /ˌnæʃə'næləti/
news n /njuːz/
nothing pron /'nʌθɪŋ/
present n /'preznt/
problems pl n /'prɒbləmz/
radio station n /'reɪdiəʊ ˌsteɪʃn/
receive v /rɪ'siːv/
richest adj /'rɪtʃɪst/
run a company /rʌn ə kʌmpəni/
scholarship n /'skɒləʃɪp/
siesta n /si'estə/
software n /'sɒftweə(r)/
start v /stɑːt/
stay in touch /steɪ ɪn tʌtʃ/
successful adj /sək'sesfl/
talk show n /'tɔːk ʃəʊ/
toast n /təʊst/
tomorrow n /tə'mɒrəʊ/
TV star n /ˌtiː 'viː stɑː(r)/
Valentine's Day n /'væləntaɪnz deɪ/
watch v /wɒtʃ/
win v /wɪn/
women pl n /'wɪmɪn/
word n /wɜːd/
worried adj /'wʌrid/
yesterday /'jestədeɪ/

UNIT 7

accident n /'æksɪdənt/
air n /eə(r)/
altitude n /'æltɪtjuːd/
arthritis n /ɑː'θraɪtɪs/
astronaut n /'æstrənɔːt/
at prep /æt/
aviation n /ˌeɪvi'eɪʃn/
badly adv /'bædli/
because conj /bɪ'kɒz/
cake n /keɪk/
carefully adv /'keəfəli/
channels pl n /'tʃænlz/
collect v /kə'lekt/
college n /'kɒlɪdʒ/
comics pl n /'kɒmɪks/
compass n /'kʌmpəs/
complete v /kəm'pliːt/
congratulations pl n /kənˌgrætʃu'leɪʃnz/
crash v /kræʃ/
crossing n /'krɒsɪŋ/
dangerous adj /'deɪndʒərəs/
deeply adv /'diːpli/
dishwasher n /'dɪʃwɒʃə/
education n /ˌedʒu'keɪʃn/
enormous adj /ɪ'nɔːməs/
equipment n /ɪ'kwɪpmənt/
events pl n /ɪ'vents/
exploration n /ˌeksplə'reɪʃn/
fast food n /ˌfɑːst 'fuːd/
finally adv /'faɪnəli/
fireworks pl n /'faɪəwɜːks/
flag n /flæg/
flight n /flaɪt/
fluently adv /'fluːəntli/
fog n /fɒg/
fortunately adv /'fɔːtʃənətli/
giant adj /'dʒaɪənt/
habit n /'hæbɪt/
high school n /'haɪ skuːl/
hits pl n /hɪts/
hospital n /'hɒspɪtl/
ill adj /ɪl/
immediately adv /ɪ'miːdiətli/
impossible adj /ɪm'pɒsəbl/
injury n /'ɪndʒəri/
inscription n /ɪn'skrɪpʃn/
invitation n /ˌɪnvɪ'teɪʃn/
invite v /ɪn'vaɪt/
It sounds great! /ɪt saʊndz greɪt/
join v /dʒɔɪn/
journey n /'dʒɜːni/
know v /nəʊ/
land v /lænd/
leap v /liːp/
life n /laɪf/
lift off v /'lɪft ɒf/
lunar module n /'luːnə(r) ˌmɒdjuːl/
man n /mæn/
mankind n /mæn'kaɪnd/
midnight n /'mɪdnaɪt/
modern adj /'mɒdn/
moon n /muːn/
movie n /'muːvi/
no idea /nəʊ aɪ'dɪə/

non-stop adj /ˌnɒn 'stɒp/
on prep /ɒn/
passport n /'pɑːspɔːt/
peace n /piːs/
philosophy n /fə'lɒsəfi/
pioneer n /ˌpaɪə'nɪə(r)/
planes pl n /pleɪnz/
pocket money n /'pɒkɪt mʌni/
prepare v /prɪ'peə(r)/
professor n /prə'fesə(r)/
psychology n /saɪ'kɒlədʒi/
publish v /'pʌblɪʃ/
put up v /pʊt 'ʌp/
quickly adv /'kwɪkli/
quietly adv /'kwaɪətli/
relativity n /ˌrelə'tɪvəti/
remember v /rɪ'membə(r)/
reporters pl n /rɪ'pɔːtəz/
rocket n /'rɒkɪt/
rocks pl n /rɒks/
roses pl n /'rəʊzɪz/
sailor n /'seɪlə(r)/
samples pl n /'sɑːmplz/
sell v /sel/
shirt n /ʃɜːt/
slowly adv /'sləʊli/
space n /speɪs/
spend (time) v /spend/
step v /step/
suddenly adv /'sʌdənli/
summer n /'sʌmə(r)/
surface n /'sɜːfɪs/
sweets pl n /swiːts/
term n /tɜːm/
theme parks pl n /'θiːm pɑːks/
theory n /'θɪəri/
umbrella n /ʌm'brelə/
voyage n /'vɔɪɪdʒ/
wake up v /weɪk 'ʌp/
wave v /weɪv/
whole adj /həʊl/
wool n /wʊl/

UNIT 8

adaptor n /ə'dæptə(r)/
add v /æd/
any det /'eni/
apple n /'æpl/
apple juice n /'æpl dʒuːs/
aspirin n /'æsprɪn/
bacon n /'beɪkən/
banana n /bə'nɑːnə/
basil n /'bæzl/
batteries pl n /'bætəriz/
beef n /biːf/
biscuits pl n /'bɪskɪts/
boil v /bɔɪl/
boring adj /'bɔːrɪŋ/
bottle n /'bɒtl/
boy n /bɔɪ/
bread n /bred/
broccoli n /'brɒkəli/
butter n /'bʌtə(r)/
carrots pl n /'kærəts/
cartoon characters pl n /kɑː'tuːn 'kærəktəz/
cats pl n /kæts/
chef n /ʃef/
chips pl n /tʃɪps/
chocolate n /'tʃɒklət/
chop v /tʃɒp/
club n /klʌb/
coach n /kəʊtʃ/
cold drink n /kəʊld drɪŋk/
cookbook n /'kʊkbʊk/
cooking n /'kʊkɪŋ/
cottage pie n /ˌkɒtɪdʒ 'paɪ/
crisps pl n /krɪsps/
croissant n /'krwæsɒ̃/
daily adj /'deɪli/
delicious adj /dɪ'lɪʃəs/
disgusting adj /dɪs'gʌstɪŋ/
dry adj /draɪ/
eggs pl n /egz/
envelopes pl n /'envələʊps/
especially adv /ɪ'speʃəli/
fashionable adj /'fæʃnəbl/
favourite adj /'feɪvərɪt/
fish fingers pl n /ˌfɪʃ 'fɪŋgəz/
forget v /fə'get/
fry v /fraɪ/
fussy adj /'fʌsi/
gamble v /'gæmbl/
grams pl n /græmz/
ham n /hæm/
hardware shop n /'hɑːdweə(r) ʃɒp/
herbs pl n /hɜːbz/
honey n /'hʌni/
how much /haʊ mʌtʃ/
hungry adj /'hʌŋgri/
I'm afraid /aɪm ə'freɪd/
ingredient n /ɪn'griːdiənt/
kid n /kɪd/
large adj /lɑːdʒ/
layer n /'leɪə(r)/
list n /lɪst/
magazine n /ˌmægə'ziːn/
meat n /miːt/
medium adj /'miːdiəm/
milk n /mɪlk/
minced adj /mɪnst/
miss v /mɪs/
mix v /mɪks/
mustard n /'mʌstəd/
need v /niːd/
newsagent's n /'njuːzeɪdʒənts/
no problem /nəʊ 'prɒbləm/
notebook n /'nəʊtbʊk/
nuts pl n /nʌts/
oil n /ɔɪl/
olives pl n /'ɒlɪvz/
onions pl n /'ʌnjənz/
order v /'ɔːdə(r)/
out prep /aʊt/
packet n /'pækɪt/
pasta n /'pæstə/
peanut butter n /ˌpiːnʌt 'bʌtə(r)/
peas pl n /piːz/
pepper n /'pepə(r)/
plasters pl n /'plɑːstəz/
pocket n /'pɒkɪt/
popular adj /'pɒpjələ(r)/
potatoes pl n /pə'teɪtəʊz/
raspberry n /'rɑːzbəri/
recipe n /'resəpi/
record v /rɪ'kɔːd/
salad n /'sæləd/
salt n /sɒlt/
scissors pl n /'sɪzəz/
screwdriver n /'skruːdraɪvə(r)/
sellotape n /'seləteɪp/
shampoo n /ʃæm'puː/
size n /saɪz/
slice n /slaɪs/
smoothie n /'smuːði/
some det /sʌm/
sorry /'sɒri/
spaghetti n /spə'geti/
spend v /spend/
spices pl n /spaɪsɪz/
sports pl n /spɔːts/
stamp n /stæmp/
starving adj /stɑːvɪŋ/
stationer's n /'steɪʃnəz/
steak n /steɪk/
still adv /stɪl/
strawberries pl n /'strɔːbəriz/
sugar n /'ʃʊgə(r)/
survey n /'sɜːveɪ/
tap water n /'tæp wɔːtə(r)/
tea n /tiː/
thyme n /taɪm/
tomatoes pl n /tə'mɑːtəʊz/
toothpaste n /'tuːθpeɪst/
try v /traɪ/
until prep /ən'tɪl/
waitress n /'weɪtrəs/
worldwide adv /'wɜːldwaɪd/
worry v /'wʌri/
yoghurt n /'jɒgət/

UNIT 9

accent n /'æksent/
air n /eə(r)/
architecture n /'ɑːkɪtektʃə(r)/
area n /'eəriə/
artists pl n /'ɑːtɪsts/
banks pl n /bæŋks/
blossom n /'blɒsəm/
capital city n /'kæpɪtl 'sɪti/
careful adj /'keəfl/
celebrities pl n /sə'lebrətiz/
central adj /'sentrəl/
change v /tʃeɪndʒ/
cherry n /'tʃeri/
climate n /'klaɪmət/
clubs pl n /klʌbz/
church n /tʃɜːtʃ/
coast n /kəʊst/
colonial adj /kə'ləʊniəl/
commercial centres pl n /kə'mɜːʃl 'sentəz/
commuter n /kə'mjuːtə(r)/
cool adj /kuːl/
crowded adj /'kraʊdɪd/
culture n /'kʌltʃə(r)/
earthquake n /'ɜːθkweɪk/
east n /iːst/
electricity n /ɪˌlek'trɪsəti/
elegant adj /'elɪgənt/
emperor n /'empərə(r)/
empire n /'empaɪə(r)/
Englishman n /'ɪŋglɪʃmən/
experience n /ɪk'spɪəriəns/
extreme adj /ɪk'striːm/
fashion n /'fæʃn/
fishing n /'fɪʃɪŋ/
food n /fuːd/
foreigners pl n /'fɒrənəz/
generally adv /'dʒenrəli/
gold n /gəʊld/
goods pl n /gʊdz/
handicrafts pl n /'hændikrɑːfts/
headquarters n /ˌhed'kwɔːtəz/
high-class adj /ˌhaɪ 'klɑːs/
hill n /hɪl/
historic adj /hɪ'stɒrɪk/
huge adj /hjuːdʒ/
humid adj /'hjuːmɪd/
hundreds pl n /'hʌndrədz/
independence n /ˌɪndɪ'pendəns/
industry n /'ɪndəstri/
invade v /ɪn'veɪd/
jewellery n /'dʒuːəlri/
kilometre n /kɪ'lɒmɪtə(r)/
latest adj /'leɪtɪst/
loud adj /laʊd/
market n /'mɑːkɪt/
megacity n /'megəˌsɪti/
Metro n /'metrəʊ/
mountains pl n /'maʊntənz/
multicultural adj /ˌmʌlti'kʌltʃərəl/
mysterious adj /mɪ'stɪəriəs/
nightclub n /'naɪtklʌb/
north n /nɔːθ/
of course /ɒv kɔːs/
orange adj /'ɒrɪndʒ/
originally adv /ə'rɪdʒənəli/
palace n /'pæləs/
pedestrian crossing n /pə'destriən krɒsɪŋ/
pink adj /pɪŋk/
polite adj /pə'laɪt/
pollution n /pə'luːʃn/
population n /ˌpɒpju'leɪʃn/
poverty n /'pɒvəti/
prefer v /prɪ'fɜː(r)/
produce v /prə'djuːs/
public bath n /pʌblɪk 'bɑːθ/
public transport n /pʌblɪk 'trænspɔːt/
quality n /'kwɒləti/
quieter adj /'kwaɪətə(r)/
railway system n /'reɪlweɪ 'sɪstəm/
rainy adj /'reɪni/
river n /'rɪvə(r)/
romantic adj /rəʊ'mæntɪk/
roundabout n /'raʊndəbaʊt/
safe adj /seɪf/
sanitation n /ˌsænɪ'teɪʃn/
season n /'siːzn/
shrine n /ʃraɪn/
skyscrapers pl n /'skaɪskreɪpəz/
slums pl n /slʌmz/
snacks pl n /snæks/
somewhere adv /'sʌmweə(r)/
south n /saʊθ/
spring n /sprɪŋ/
square n /skweə(r)/
stone adj /stəʊn/
subway system n /'sʌbweɪ sɪstəm/
sunrise n /'sʌnraɪz/
sunset n /'sʌnset/
surrounded adj /sə'raʊndɪd/
take place v /teɪk pleɪs/
tall adj /tɔːl/
tattoo n /tə'tuː/
temple n /'templ/
theatre n /'θɪətə(r)/
tourist attraction n /'tɔːrɪst ə'trækʃn/
toy shop n /tɔɪ ʃɒp/
traditional adj /trə'dɪʃənl/
traffic lights pl n /'træfɪk laɪts/
traffic sign n /'træfɪk saɪn/
transport n /'trænspɔːt/
true adj /truː/
unique adj /ju'niːk/
up-to-date adj /ˌʌp tə 'deɪt/
valley n /'væli/
variety n /və'raɪəti/
wet adj /wet/
wood n /wʊd/

UNIT 10

actor *n* /ˈæktə(r)/
affect *v* /əˈfekt/
alike *adj* /əˈlaɪk/
attached *adj* /əˈtætʃt/
bank holiday *n* /ˌbæŋk ˈhɒlədeɪ/
below *prep* /bɪˈləʊ/
blond *adj* /blɒnd/
blue *n* /bluː/
bone *n* /bəʊn/
boots *pl n* /buːts/
brown *n* /braʊn/
build *v* /bɪld/
coat *n* /kəʊt/
compartment *n* /kəmˈpɑːtmənt/
compete *v* /kəmˈpiːt/
conditions *pl n* /kənˈdɪʃnz/
couple *n* /ˈkʌpl/
dark *adj* /dɑːk/
decide *v* /dɪˈsaɪd/
detective *n* /dɪˈtektɪv/
develop *v* /dɪˈveləp/
dress *n* /dres/
earth *n* /ɜːθ/
effects *pl n* /ɪˈfekts/
experiment *n* /ɪkˈsperɪmənt/
fair *adj* /feə/
fight *v* /faɪt/
float *v* /fləʊt/
glasses *pl n* /ˈɡlɑːsɪz/
good-looking *adj* /ˌɡʊd ˈlʊkɪŋ/
gravity *n* /ˈɡrævəti/
handsome *adj* /ˈhænsəm/
happen *v* /ˈhæpən/
hat *n* /hæt/
identical *adj* /aɪˈdentɪkl/
incredible *adj* /ɪnˈkredəbl/
instruments *pl n* /ˈɪnstrəmənts/
jeans *n* /dʒiːnz/
laboratory *n* /ləˈbɒrətri/
laptop *n* /ˈlæptɒp/
long *adj* /lɒŋ/
message *n* /ˈmesɪdʒ/
muscle *n* /ˈmʌsl/
never mind /ˈnevə(r) maɪnd/
noise *n* /nɔɪz/
orbit *v* /ˈɔːbɪt/
origin *n* /ˈɒrɪdʒɪn/
oxygen *n* /ˈɒksɪdʒən/
planet *n* /ˈplænɪt/
preparation *n* /ˌprepəˈreɪʃn/
pretty *adj* /ˈprɪti/
purple *n* /ˈpɜːpl/
research *n* /ˈriːsɜːtʃ/
romance *n* /ˈrəʊmæns/
sauce *n* /sɔːs/
scarf *n* /skɑːf/
shoes *pl n* /ʃuːz/
short *adj* /ʃɔːt/
shorts *pl n* /ʃɔːts/
skirt *n* /skɜːt/
spicey *adj* /ˈspaɪsi/
spoon *n* /spuːn/
star *n* /stɑː(r)/
suit *n* /suːt/
supplies *pl n* /səˈplaɪz/
switch on *v* /swɪtʃ ˈɒn/

T-shirt *n* /ˈtiː ʃɜːt/
tall *adj* /tɔːl/
tasty *adj* /ˈteɪsti/
tin *n* /tɪn/
trainers *pl n* /ˈtreɪnəz/
truth *n* /truːθ/
twins *pl n* /twɪnz/
universe *n* /ˈjuːnɪvɜːs/
unusual *adj* /ʌnˈjuːʒuəl/
washing-up *n* /ˌwɒʃɪŋ ˈʌp/

UNIT 11

backpack *n* /ˈbækpæk/
carry *v* /ˈkæri/
climb *v* /klaɪm/
colourful *adj* /ˈkʌləfl/
cruise *n* /kruːz/
do the washing *v* /duː ðə ˈwɒʃɪŋ/
drop *v* /drɒp/
due *adj* /djuː/
fall *v* /fɔːl/
fields *pl n* /fiːldz/
folk song *n* /ˈfəʊk sɒŋ/
freedom *n* /ˈfriːdəm/
frightened *adj* /ˈfraɪtnd/
future *n* /ˈfjuːtʃə(r)/
grow up *v* /ɡrəʊ ˈʌp/
harmony *n* /ˈhɑːməni/
hat *n* /hæt/
hire *v* /ˈhaɪə(r)/
hospitality *n* /ˌhɒspɪˈtæləti/
human *adj* /ˈhjuːmən/
jacket *n* /ˈdʒækɪt/
kiss *v* /kɪs/
passers-by *pl n* /ˌpɑːsəz ˈbaɪ/
pay rise *n* /ˈpeɪ raɪz/
peaceful *adj* /ˈpiːsfl/
perfect *adj* /ˈpɜːfɪkt/
picnic *n* /ˈpɪknɪk/
plan *v* /plæn/
podcasts *pl n* /ˈpɒdkɑːsts/
pyramids *pl n* /ˈpɪrəmɪdz/
retire *v* /rɪˈtaɪə(r)/
safari *n* /səˈfɑːri/
sign *n* /saɪn/
simple *adj* /ˈsɪmpl/
smile *v* /smaɪl/
sneeze *v* /sniːz/
soon *adv* /suːn/
storm *n* /stɔːm/
stressful *adj* /ˈstresfl/
suitcase *n* /ˈsuːtkeɪs/
supper *n* /ˈsʌpə(r)/
thunder *n* /ˈθʌndə(r)/
Wales *n* /weɪlz/
walking stick *n* /ˈwɔːkɪŋ stɪk/
website *n* /ˈwebsaɪt/
woods *pl n* /wʊdz/

UNIT 12

acres *pl n* /ˈeɪkəz/
acts *pl n* /ækts/
atmosphere *n* /ˈætməsfɪə(r)/
attend *v* /əˈtend/
Australia *n* /ɒˈstreɪliə/
Brazil *n* /brəˈzɪl/
brilliant *adj* /ˈbrɪliənt/
cancel *v* /ˈkænsl/
check in *v* /tʃek ˈɪn/
China *n* /ˈtʃaɪnə/
cider *n* /ˈsaɪdə(r)/
colleague *n* /ˈkɒliːɡ/
continual *adj* /kənˈtɪnjuəl/
crowd *n* /kraʊd/
death *n* /deθ/
definite *adj* /ˈdefɪnət/
departures board *n* /dɪˈpɑːtʃəz bɔːd/
disappointed *adj* /ˌdɪsəˈpɔɪntɪd/
Egypt *n* /ˈiːdʒɪpt/
ever *adv* /ˈevə(r)/
express *v* /ɪkˈspres/
fail *v* /feɪl/
festival *n* /ˈfestɪvl/
festival goers *pl n* /ˈfestɪvl ˈɡəʊəz/
get on *v* /ˈɡet ɒn/
Great Britain *n* /ˌɡreɪt ˈbrɪtn/
Greece *n* /ɡriːs/
hand luggage *n* /ˈhænd lʌɡɪdʒ/
Italy *n* /ˈɪtəli/
Japan *n* /dʒəˈpæn/
jumbo jet *n* /ˌdʒʌmbəʊ ˈdʒet/
just *adv* /dʒʌst/
knees *pl n* /niːz/
luggage *n* /ˈlʌɡɪdʒ/
memories *pl n* /ˈmeməriz/
mud *n* /mʌd/
noisy *adj* /ˈnɔɪzi/
open-air *adj* /ˌəʊpən ˈeə(r)/
packing *n* /ˈpækɪŋ/
performer *n* /pəˈfɔːmə(r)/
piece *n* /piːs/
platform *n* /ˈplætfɔːm/
poem *n* /ˈpəʊɪm/
print *v* /prɪnt/
queue *n* /kjuː/
refer to *v* /rɪˈfɜː tə/
rise *v* /raɪz/
rock concert *n* /rɒk ˈkɒnsət/
rubbish *adj* /ˈrʌbɪʃ/
savings *pl n* /ˈseɪvɪŋz/
scuba dive *v* /ˈskuːbə daɪv/
security *n* /sɪˈkjʊərəti/
slogan *n* /ˈsləʊɡən/
stage *n* /steɪdʒ/
sunshine *n* /ˈsʌnʃaɪn/
taxi *n* /ˈtæksi/
tent *n* /tent/
the US *n* /ðə juː ˈes/
trip *n* /trɪp/
van *n* /væn/
yet *adv* /jet/

Pairwork Student A

 **UNIT 4** *p31*

PRACTICE

Location, location, location

1. You want a flat to rent. You and your partner have two different adverts.

   Read the information in your advert. Ask and answer questions to find out details about your partner's advert. Make notes in the chart.

Street:
Price:
Rooms:
Location:
Shops and transport:

Which flat do you want to rent? Why?

HEADLAND PROPERTIES

Flat to rent: Hill Street

£300 per week

- 3 bedrooms
- 1 bathroom
- Lovely living room with views over the town
- Small kitchen

A beautiful flat on the third floor only ten minutes from the town centre.

Local shops (chemist's, café, newsagent's) just five minutes away. With a park across the road. On major bus routes.

 **UNIT 7** *p56*

PRACTICE

Bill's life

2 You and your partner have different information about Bill Cole's life. Take turns to ask and answer questions to find out the missing information to complete the text.

Bill Cole was born in London in (1) __1951__ (When …?). He had two brothers and a sister. His father was a (3) _____ (What … his father do?) and his mother was a cleaner. They lived in (5) _____ (Where …?), a poor area of London. They had an old house with two bedrooms and no bathroom.

Bill went to school in (7) _____ (Where …?). He didn't pass any exams, and he left school when he was sixteen. He worked in a shop until he was 18, and then he (9) _____ (What … do?).

He met his wife in Germany, and they got married in (11) _____ (When …?). They had two children. After he left the army, Bill studied (13) _____ (What …?) at university, and worked as a teacher for the rest of his life.

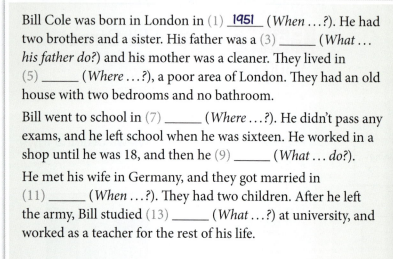

Close your books. Work with your partner. What can you remember about Bill?

 UNIT 9 *p72*

PRACTICE

I've got a bigger house than you!

4 Work with a partner. Imagine you are both millionaires. Tell each other about your house. Who has the best house?

Your house has:
- ten bedrooms
- 7 bathrooms
- 2 kitchens and staff accommodation
- private parking
- a ballroom
- a garden with an orchard
- a tennis court
- a swimming pool
- a private golf course
- a private road

150   Pairwork   Student A

UNIT 11 p92

VOCABULARY AND LISTENING
What's the weather like?

6 Work with a new partner. Ask and answer questions to complete the information about world weather tomorrow.

> What's the weather going to be like in Berlin?
>
> Rainy and cold. 7 degrees.

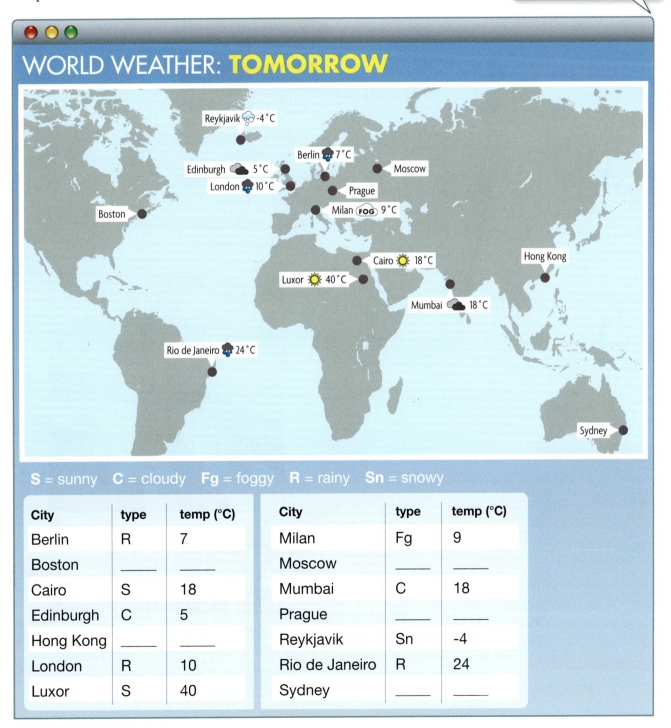

S = sunny   C = cloudy   Fg = foggy   R = rainy   Sn = snowy

City	type	temp (°C)	City	type	temp (°C)
Berlin	R	7	Milan	Fg	9
Boston	___	___	Moscow	___	___
Cairo	S	18	Mumbai	C	18
Edinburgh	C	5	Prague	___	___
Hong Kong	___	___	Reykjavik	Sn	-4
London	R	10	Rio de Janeiro	R	24
Luxor	S	40	Sydney	___	___

Which city is going to be the hottest? Which city is going to be the coldest? Which month do you think it is?

Pairwork Student A

Pairwork Student B

 **UNIT 4** *p31*

PRACTICE

Location, location, location

1 You want a flat to rent. You and your partner have two different adverts.

Read the information in your advert. Ask and answer questions to find out details about your partner's advert. Make notes in the chart.

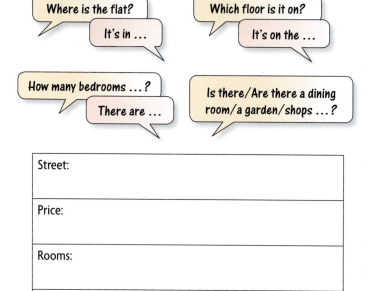

Street:
Price:
Rooms:
Location:
Shops and transport:

Which flat do you want to rent? Why?

HEADLAND PROPERTIES

Flat to rent: Craven Road

£375 per week

- 2 bedrooms
- 2 bathrooms
- Large living room
- Dining room
- Beautiful kitchen with washing machine and dishwasher

A beautiful flat on the first floor in the centre of town, above a newsagent's.

High Street shops and railway station only five minutes away.

UNIT 7 p56

PRACTICE

Bill's life

2 You and your partner have different information about Bill Cole's life. Take turns to ask and answer questions to find out the missing information to complete the text.

> How many brothers and sisters did he have?

> He had two brothers and a sister.

Bill Cole was born in London in 1951. He had (2) __two__ brothers and a sister (*How many …?*). His father was a butcher, and his mother was a (4) _____ (*What … his mother do?*). They lived in Deptford, a poor area of London. They had an (6) _____ house (*What sort of house … have?*).

Bill went to school in New Cross. He didn't pass any exams, and he left school when he was (8) _____ (*How old … when he left school?*). He worked (10) _____ (*Where?*) until he was 18, and then he joined the army.

He met his wife in (12) _____ (*Where …?*), and they got married in 1964. They had (14) _____ children (*How many children … have?*). After he left the army, Bill studied maths at university, and worked as a teacher for the rest of his life.

Close your books. Work with your partner. What can you remember about Bill?

UNIT 9 p72

PRACTICE

I've got a bigger house than you!

4 Work with a partner. Imagine you are both millionaires. Tell each other about your house. Who has the best house?

Your house has:
- eight bedrooms on the first floor
- five bedrooms on the second floor
- 10 bathrooms
- a dining hall
- an enormous garden
- a cinema
- a bowling alley
- six garages
- an indoor and an outdoor swimming pool
- stables for the horses, and a field
- electric gates and CCTV

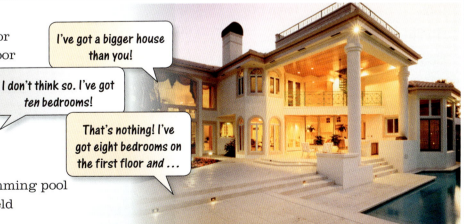

> I've got a bigger house than you!

> I don't think so. I've got ten bedrooms!

> That's nothing! I've got eight bedrooms on the first floor and …

Pairwork Student B 153

UNIT 11 *p92*

VOCABULARY AND LISTENING
What's the weather like?

6 Work with a new partner. Ask and answer questions to complete the information about world weather tomorrow.

> What's the weather going to be like in Boston?
>
> Foggy. 6 degrees.

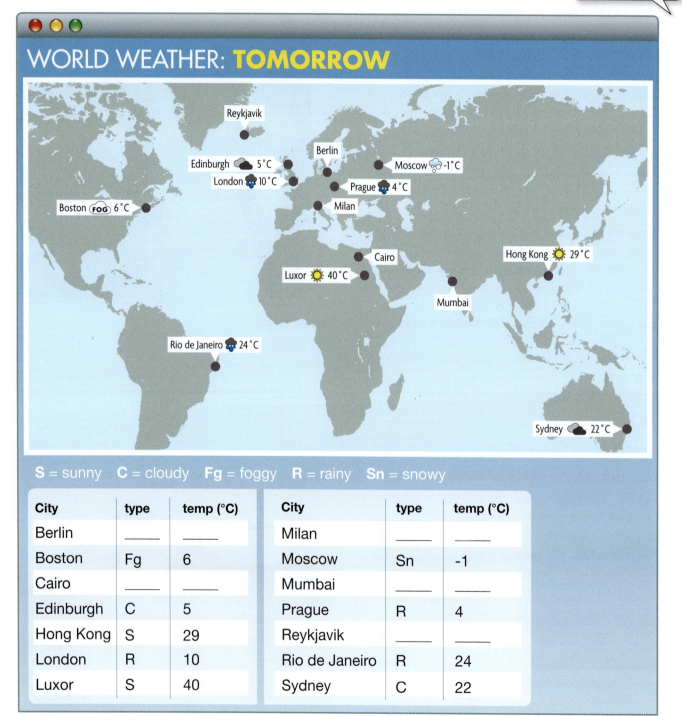

S = sunny   C = cloudy   Fg = foggy   R = rainy   Sn = snowy

City	type	temp (°C)	City	type	temp (°C)
Berlin	___	___	Milan	___	___
Boston	Fg	6	Moscow	Sn	-1
Cairo	___	___	Mumbai	___	___
Edinburgh	C	5	Prague	R	4
Hong Kong	S	29	Reykjavik	___	___
London	R	10	Rio de Janeiro	R	24
Luxor	S	40	Sydney	C	22

Which city is going to be the hottest? Which city is going to be the coldest? Which month do you think it is?

154   Pairwork   Student B

Extra materials

UNIT 8 *p65*

STARTERS   SOUPS   **MAIN COURSES**   SIDES & SALADS   20 MINUTE MEALS   DESSERTS

Cottage pie

preparation: 45 mins
cooking: 30 mins
serves four

Ingredients:

2 medium onions, chopped
500g minced beef
10ml oil
2 medium carrots, chopped
400g tomatoes
1 tbsp thyme
Salt and black pepper

Method:

Preheat the oven to 190C/375F/Gas mark 5.

1. Chop the onions and carrots.
2. Heat the oil in a large pan. Add the onion and carrot and cook over a medium heat for 5 minutes until soft.
3. Add the minced beef and cook for 3 minutes to brown.
4. Add the tomatoes and thyme.
5. Season with salt and pepper. (You can also use a stock cube.)
6. Cover and cook for 30 minutes.

Topping:

4 large potatoes
50g butter
15ml milk
100g Cheddar cheese

Make the topping:

7. Boil the potatoes in water until soft.
8. Mix the potatoes with the butter and milk until smooth.
9. Add the grated cheese. Mix again.
10. Season with salt and pepper.
11. Spoon the meat into an ovenproof dish.
12. Top with the potato and cheese mixture.
13. Bake in the oven for 30 minutes until golden brown.

g = gram
ml = millilitre
tbsp = tablespoon

Notes

Notes

Irregular verbs

Base form	Past Simple	Past participle
be	was/were	been
become	became	become
begin	began	begun
break	broke	broken
bring	brought	brought
build	built	built
buy	bought	bought
can	could	been able
catch	caught	caught
choose	chose	chosen
come	came	come
cost	cost	cost
cut	cut	cut
do	did	done
draw	drew	drawn
drink	drank	drunk
drive	drove	driven
eat	ate	eaten
fall	fell	fallen
feel	felt	felt
find	found	found
fly	flew	flown
forget	forgot	forgotten
get	got	got
give	gave	given
go	went	gone/been
grow	grew	grown
have	had	had
hear	heard	heard
keep	kept	kept
know	knew	known
learn	learnt/learned	learnt/learned
leave	left	left
lose	lost	lost
make	made	made
meet	met	met
pay	paid	paid
put	put	put
read /ri:d/	read /red/	read /red/
ride	rode	ridden
run	ran	run
say	said	said
see	saw	seen
sell	sold	sold
send	sent	sent
sing	sang	sung
sit	sat	sat
sleep	slept	slept
speak	spoke	spoken
spend	spent	spent
stand	stood	stood
swim	swam	swum
take	took	taken
teach	taught	taught
tell	told	told
think	thought	thought
try	tried	tried
understand	understood	understood
wake	woke	woken
wear	wore	worn
win	won	won
write	wrote	written

Verb patterns

Verb + -ing	
like	
love	swimming
enjoy	
hate	cooking
finish	
stop	

Verb + to + infinitive	
choose	
decide	
forget	
promise	to go
need	
help	
hope	
try	to work
want	
would like	
would love	

Verb + -ing or to + infinitive	
begin	raining/to rain
start	

Modal auxiliary verbs	
can	
could	go
shall	
will	arrive
would	

Phonetic symbols

Consonants

1	/p/	as in	**pen** /pen/
2	/b/	as in	**big** /bɪg/
3	/t/	as in	**tea** /tiː/
4	/d/	as in	**do** /duː/
5	/k/	as in	**cat** /kæt/
6	/g/	as in	**go** /gəʊ/
7	/f/	as in	**four** /fɔː/
8	/v/	as in	**very** /ˈveri/
9	/s/	as in	**son** /sʌn/
10	/z/	as in	**zoo** /zuː/
11	/l/	as in	**live** /lɪv/
12	/m/	as in	**my** /maɪ/
13	/n/	as in	**now** /naʊ/
14	/h/	as in	**happy** /ˈhæpi/
15	/r/	as in	**red** /red/
16	/j/	as in	**yes** /jes/
17	/w/	as in	**want** /wɒnt/
18	/θ/	as in	**thanks** /θæŋks/
19	/ð/	as in	**the** /ðə/
20	/ʃ/	as in	**she** /ʃiː/
21	/ʒ/	as in	**television** /ˈtelɪvɪʒn/
22	/tʃ/	as in	**child** /tʃaɪld/
23	/dʒ/	as in	**German** /ˈdʒɜːmən/
24	/ŋ/	as in	**English** /ˈɪŋglɪʃ/

Vowels

25	/iː/	as in	**see** /siː/
26	/ɪ/	as in	**his** /hɪz/
27	/i/	as in	**twenty** /ˈtwenti/
28	/e/	as in	**ten** /ten/
29	/æ/	as in	**bag** /bæg/
30	/ɑː/	as in	**father** /ˈfɑːðə/
31	/ɒ/	as in	**hot** /hɒt/
32	/ɔː/	as in	**morning** /ˈmɔːnɪŋ/
33	/ʊ/	as in	**football** /ˈfʊtbɔːl/
34	/uː/	as in	**you** /juː/
35	/ʌ/	as in	**sun** /sʌn/
36	/ɜː/	as in	**learn** /lɜːn/
37	/ə/	as in	**letter** /ˈletə/

Diphthongs (two vowels together)

38	/eɪ/	as in	**name** /neɪm/
39	/əʊ/	as in	**no** /nəʊ/
40	/aɪ/	as in	**my** /maɪ/
41	/aʊ/	as in	**how** /haʊ/
42	/ɔɪ/	as in	**boy** /bɔɪ/
43	/ɪə/	as in	**hear** /hɪə/
44	/eə/	as in	**where** /weə/
45	/ʊə/	as in	**tour** /tʊə/

OXFORD
UNIVERSITY PRESS

Great Clarendon Street, Oxford OX2 6DP

Oxford University Press is a department of the University of Oxford. It furthers the University's objective of excellence in research, scholarship, and education by publishing worldwide in

Oxford New York

Auckland Cape Town Dar es Salaam
Hong Kong Karachi Kuala Lumpur Madrid
Melbourne Mexico-City Nairobi New Delhi
Shanghai Taipei Toronto

With offices in

Argentina Austria Brazil Chile Czech Republic
France Greece Guatemala Hungary Italy Japan
Poland Portugal Singapore South Korea
Switzerland Thailand Turkey Ukraine Vietnam

OXFORD and OXFORD ENGLISH are registered trade marks of Oxford University Press in the UK and in certain other countries

© Oxford University Press 2011

The moral rights of the author have been asserted

Database right Oxford University Press (maker)

First published 2011

2018 2017 2016
11

No unauthorized photocopying

All rights reserved. No part of this publication may be reproduced, stored in a retrieval system, or transmitted, in any form or by any means, without the prior permission in writing of Oxford University Press, or as expressly permitted by law, or under terms agreed with the appropriate reprographics rights organization. Enquiries concerning reproduction outside the scope of the above should be sent to the ELT Rights Department, Oxford University Press, at the address above

You must not circulate this book in any other binding or cover and you must impose this same condition on any acquirer

Any websites referred to in this publication are in the public domain and their addresses are provided by Oxford University Press for information only. Oxford University Press disclaims any responsibility for the content.

ISBN: 978 0 19 476898 6

Printed in China

This book is printed on paper from certified and well-managed sources.

ACKNOWLEDGEMENTS

The authors and publisher are grateful to those who have given permission to reproduce the following extracts and adaptations of copyright material: p.15 information about Claudia Luke reproduced by permission of Claudia Luke; p.26 adapted from 'My perfect weekend: Jamie Cullum' by Sylvia Roger, Telegraph.co.uk, 29 April 2006. © Telegraph Media Group Limited 2006. Reproduced by permission; p.26 audio extract of *Twenty Something* by Jamie Cullum is reproduced by kind permission of Universal Music Operations Limited; p.27 adapted from 'My perfect weekend: Shilpa Shetty' by Lorraine McBride, 19 June 2009, Telegraph.co.uk. © Telegraph Media Group Limited 2009. Reproduced by permission; p.43 adapted from 'Relative Values: Nicola Benedetti and her father, Gio' by Beverly D'Silva, *The Sunday Times Magazine*, 30 September 2007. © Beverley D'Silva/The Sunday Times Magazine/nisyndication.com. Reproduced by permission; p.91 adapted from 'Singing for their supper' by Paul Kingsnorth, 16 April 2009. © Telegraph Media Group Limited 2009. Reproduced by permission; p.90 audio recording of *Oats And Beans* used by kind permission of Walk Around Britain Ltd. www.awalkaroundbritain.com.

Additional information: p.19 Babur Ali The direct quotations in this story have been adapted to assist understanding; p.48 This interview with Ben Way is fictitious and is based on factual information from a number of sources; p.58 *1909 – the first air journey* The direct quotations in this story have been adapted to assist understanding.

Illustrations by: Jonathan Burton, p.60; Gill Button p.6, p.9, p.36, p.44, p.79, p.88, p.96, p.100; Jonathan Keegan p.52, p.62; Claire Littlejohn pp.76/77; Debbie Powell p.93; Gavin Reece p.20, p.31, p.50/51, p.68/69, p.80, p.110, p.149, p.152.

Commissioned photography by: Gareth Boden pp.6 (Bill & receptionist); 7 (Bill); 8 (Rick, Rick with Mum & Dad, Edward, Rick & Lily); 10 (house, Rick's Mum & Dad, family, Rick, Edward & Annalisa, school, male students, Annalisa & teacher, Annalisa); 11 (Annalisa), 21 (clock on sky, clock on grass, clock on pebbles); 22/23 (Lisa); 29 (all); 30 (Josie & Emily); 32/33 (Josie & Emily shopping); 62 (various food items); 63/64 (Duncan & Nick); 67 (sandwich); 68 (various items); 78 (Tony & Nina, Fiona & Pete); 85 (boy & drinks machine); 94 (Lara & Kyle); 96 (Lara & Mel); 97 (Lara); 101 (Lara & Mel); 112 (Duncan in kitchen). Models supplied by Elliott Brown Agency

The publisher would like to thank the following for their help with locations: Barcelo Hotel; Blacks Leisure Group plc.; Branca; David Lloyd Leisure Ltd.; First Great Western; James C. Penny Estate Agents; The Oxford Boot Store; Portabello Restaurant; Quod Brasserie; Radmila Novakovic; Ruth Crofton-Briggs; The Albion Beatnik Bookshop; The Oxford English Centre; The Regal; University of Oxford Botanic Garden & Harcourt Arboretum

We would also like to thank the following for permission to reproduce the following photographs: Alamy pp.10 (Big Ben/Andy Myatt), 10 (Trafalgar Square/Peter Barritt, Tower Bridge/Jon Arnold Images Ltd), 11 (Hyde Park/Eric Nathan), 12 (sister/Catchlight Visual Services), 14 (oil rig/Ace Stock Limited), 24 (jogging/Ace Stock Limited), 25 (shopping/Image Source, cinema/Kuttig – People, golf/Amana Images inc.,reading/Chris Stock Photography, sailing/Stephen Dorey), 35 (drawing/North Wind Picture Archives), 41 (*Guernica*/© Succession Picasso/DACS, London 2011/Ingolf Pompe 85), 55 (beach/Mary Evans Picture Library, car/Colin Bowling), 58/59 (sky/Paul Paladin), 61 (valentine/totalphoto), 66 (Earl of Sandwich/Classic Image), 67 (Ulla/Tony French, Angus/Image Source, child/Design Pics Inc.), 71 (rain/Choice), 72/73 (Camden/LH Images), 74 (Tokyo/Patrick Batchelder, Lourdes/Image Source, Vimahl/dbimages), 75 (Mumbai/Dinodia Images, Mexico City/Peter Adams Photography Ltd, taxi/Robert Harding Picture Library Ltd), 85 (party/Christoph & Friends/Das Fotoarchiv.), 86 (home/Larry Lilac, pay rise/ImageState, arrive/Image Source), 98 (mud/Apex News and Pictures Agency), 99 (tents/Steve Speller), 101 (plane/Chris Pancewicz); Allsorts Licensing p.67 (Dagwood/Reproduced with the kind permission of King Features, a division of Hearst Holdings, inc.); Anant Media Private Limited pp.18/19 (blackboard/Samrat Chakrabarti), 19 (Babar Ali/Samrat Chakrabarti, children studying/Samrat Chakrabarti); Pearl Bevan p.85 (shopping); Big Pictures (UK) Ltd p.27 (Sophie and Jamie/Eliot); Car Photo Library p.43 (Jaguar); Cat Music p.41 (Cleopatra Stratan); Claudia Luke, Sonoma State University p.15 (Claudia); Corbis UK Ltd. pp.6 (handshake/Eric Audras/Photoalto), 7 (Sabine/Tony Alan Anderson/Superstock), 13 (kiss/Odilon Dimier/Photoalto), 25 (windsurfing/Henry Georgi, watching TV/Image Source, skiing/Owen Robson/Beneluxpress), 27 (nightclub/Dosfotos/Lebrecht Music & Arts), 37 (one/Randy Faris), 47 (school/Kim Ludbrook/Epa), 58 (plane/Bettmann), 59 (Louis Bleriot/Bettmann), 81 (eating/Glowimages), 85 (married/Redlink, bye/Roy Mcmahon), 88 (tent/Paul Souders, steam/Momatiuk - Eastcott, temple/Jose Fuste Raga, River/Louis-Marie Preau/Hemis, Uluru/Tim Wimborne/Reuters, snow/Yann Arthus-Bertrand), 89 (tiger/Theo Allofs, Machu Pichu/Bob Krist, pyramids/Jacques Sierpinski/Hemis), 99 (girls/Luke Macgregor/Reuters); Getty Images pp.7 (Switzerland/Art Wolfe), 12 (wife/Dougal Waters, daughter/Fuse, baby/Jim Esposito Photography L.L.C., grandmother/REB Images), 13 (shopping/Henrik Sorensen, handshake/Blend Images/Hill Street Studios, computer/Caroline von Tuempling/Iconica), 14 (Andrew/Digital Vision), 15 (desert/David Kiene/Flickr), 16 (David Guetta/Pascal Le Segretain), 17 (notice board/Chris Windsor/Stone), 24 (cooking/Carlos Spottorno/Taxi), 26 (Jamie Cullum/Marco Prosch), 27 (field/Michael McQueen/The Image Bank, Shilpa Shetty/Stuart Wilson, Shilpa and Raj/Yogen Shah/India Today Group), 28 (commuters/Brian Lawrence/Photographer's Choice), 31 (kitchen/Johnny Bouchier/Red Cover, bedroom/Sasfi Hope-Ross/Red Cover, livingroom/Roger T. Schmidt/Photographer's Choice), 32 (boxes/David Lees/Photodisc), 32/33 (sale/Jack Hollingsworth/Photodisc), 33 (Christina/Dex Image), 34/35 (Oval Office/Dirck Halstead/Time Life Pictures), 34 (White House/Dave Etheridge-Barnes), 35 (crowd/Dave Etheridge-Barnes), 37 (94/Diane Collins and Jordan Hollender, 21/Tooga, 45/Brian Cruickshank, 215/Jason Edwards/National Geographic), 38 (boy/Oksana Struk/Photodisc), 38/39 (street/Panoramic Images), 39 (girl/Bob Carey/Photodisc), 40 (woman/David Clifford/Aurora, child/Don Mason/Blend Images), 41 (Picasso/Apic/Hulton Archive, Marc Yu/Tiziana Fabi/AFP), 43 (violin/Howard Kingsnorth/Stone), 45 (barrista/ColorBlind Images, crutches/Andersen Ross, beckoning/Jupiterimages, waiting/Antonello Turchetti), 46/47 (Oprah Winfrey/Frazer Harrison), 54 (Beatles/David Redfern/Redferns), 55 (Tommy and Bill/Camille Tokerud, Bilko/CBS Photo Archive), 56 (football/Hulton Archive/Bill Brandt), 57 (classroom/Blend Images, toast/Bounce/UpperCut Images), 61 (Easter/Tooga/Digital Vision, Easter eggs/Creative Crop/Digital Vision, mother's day/Jim Cummins, halloween/Peter Dazeley, bride/Jupiterimages, christmas/Grove Pashley, presents/Oppenheim Bernhard/Digital Vision, new year/Reggie Casagrande/Workbook Stock), 67 (Marianne/Zia Soleil/Iconica), 70 (Gherkin/Michael Blann), 70 (Eiffel Tower/Bavaria), 71 (Rob/Image Source, Metro/Loic Venance/AFP, cafe/Bruno De Hogues/Photographer's Choice), 72 (Chantal/Karan Kapoor/Cultura), 74 (temple/Akira Kaede, Makiko/Kazuhiro Tanda, texture/Doable/A.collection), 81 (shopping/Asia Images, bath/Elyse Lewin/Brand X Pictures), 84 (Cheryl/Mary Ellen McQuay, Tanya/Lane Oatey, Matt and Simon/Image Source, Stephanie/Jupiterimages, Amy/Hiep Vu/Radius Images, Ruby/Tony Garcia/Digital Vision, Giles/Jupiterimages), 85 (cinema/PhotoAlto/Alix Minde, phone/Image Source, 86 (kids/Design Pics/Ron Nickel), 87 (grow up/Chris Tobin, lesson/ColorBlind Images), 89 (map/Jamie Grill), 95 (Italy/Satellite Aerial Images/Universal Images Group), 98 (singer/Ian Gavan, Glastonbury at night/Matt Cardy), 106 (woman/Urs Kuester, woman/Urs Kuester), 107 (woman/Anna Emilia Lundgren), 108 (Carl/Echo, Bath/Digital Vision), 109 (Gabriella/Leonard Mc Lane), 112/113 (writing/Thomas Barwick), 114 (Big Ben/Grant Faint), 115 (brothers/Alexa Miller), 117 (man/Philip Haynes/Flickr), 150 (house/Oleksandr Ivanchenko/Photographer's Choice, teacher/SuperStock), 153 (wedding/Archive Holdings Inc., house/Tom Knibbs/The Image Bank); iStockphoto pp.6 (background/Viktoriya Yatskina), 12 (mother/Sheryl Griffin, silhouette/A-Digit), 13 (bye/Sean Locke), 16 (ballet shoes/Diane Diederich, headphones/aldra), 21 (wall clock/Carlos Alvarez), 22 (skyline/Ceren Evin Erkan), 25 (trees/Kudryashka), 27 (cards/tomograf), 53 (dates/Kutay Tanir), 55 (television/Ina Peters), 75 (texture/Heidi Kalyani), 83 (starburst/Sergii Tsololo), 86 (India/Jeremy Mayes), 94 (Brazil/Matt Trommer, Egypt/Yuriy Kirsanov, Italy/visual7, Japan/visual7, Spain/Björn Kindler, Switzerland/Yuriy Kirsanov, Greece/Yuriy Kirsanov), 95 (globe/geopaul), 104 (blog/Franck Boston), 105 (dancers/Tatiana Georgieva), 109 (texture/Retrovizor, threads/Floortje), 112 (dancing/Dmitriy Shironosov); John Lawrence Photographer pp.91 (singing), 91 (walking); Mary Evans Picture Library pp.54 (Ford, Einstein/Scherl/SZ Photo, soldiers/(c)Imperial War Museum/Robert Hunt Library); NASA pp.58 (astronaut/Kennedy Space Center), 58 (rocket), 59 (astronauts/Kennedy Space Center, stars/ESA/Hubble Heritage Team/STScI/AURA), 82/83 (ISS), 82 (astronaut), 83 (space walk, chess, group); News International Syndication p.42 (Nicola & Gio Benedetti/Wattie Cheung/Sunday Times Magazine); Oxford University Press p.7 (Chicago/Photodisc), 12 (father/Digital Vision, Joseph/John-Patrick Morarescu/Westend61), 13 (ordering/Digital Vision), 17 (Charlotte/Blend Images/Rolf Bruderer), 21 (clouds/Photodisc), 24 (cycling/Photodisc), 25 (cards/Onoky/Alain Chederros, tennis/Creatas), 28 (Dr Hill/Fancy/Klaus Tiedge), 67 (John/Cultura, Tom/Tanya Constantine), 81 (computer/Radius Images), 92 (weather girl/Stockbyte), 94 (Australia/EyeWire, China/EyeWire, UK/EyeWire, Hungary/EyeWire, USA/Photodisc), 98 (Dave/Red Chopsticks, Marina/Stockbyte, Izzy, Len/photolibrary.com); Photolibrary Group pp.15 (snake/Jack Goldfarb/Design Pics Inc), 25 (video game/Benoit Regent), 27 (pool/Age fotostock, chicken/Fresh Food Images, pizza/FoodCollection), 61 (birthday/Stockdisc/White), 71 (doorman/Simon Winnall/Britain on View), 79 (girls/PureStock), 85 (garage/Radius Images), 86 (retire/Dorian Weber/age fotostock); Press Association Images p.43 (daughters/David Cheskin); Reproduced with kind permission of the Dan Dare Corporation limited p.55 (comic/Mary Evans Picture Library); Reuters Media p.47 (interview/Sam Emerson); Rex Features pp.16 (Darcey Bussell/Reg Wilson), 25 (swimming/Sipa Press), 38 (Superman/c. Warner Br/Everett), 43 (parents/Ross McDairmant), 46 (child), 105 (David Guetta/Unimedia Images), 18 (Cathy & David Guetta/Action Press); Shutterstock pp.25 (dancing/Dmitriy Shironosov), 25 (gym/Andresr), 57 (Moscow/Losevsky Pavel), 64, 155 (cottage pie/Joe Gough), 84 (Mark/Yuri Arcurs), 116 (France/Paul Atkinson), superstock ltd. pp.12 (brother/Prisma), 37 (36/age fotostock, 19/age fotostock, 117/George Ostertag), 37 (ninety one/GlowImages Cuisine); Toast PR pp.48 (Ben Way), 49 (Ben Way); Universal Music p.27 (album); Vecteezy p.92 (map/MacDaddy); www.awalkaroundbritain.com p.90 (doorway/Copyright Branching Arts).